# HIS LAST WORDS. OUR FIRST PRIORITY.

## JOSHUA WAGNER

WAGNER PUBLISHING

© 2017 by Joshua Wagner

Published by Wagner Publishing
8521 N. 156th E. Ave, Owasso, OK 74055
www.wagnerministries.org

Printed in the United States of America

ISBN: 978-0-9844259-6-9

One dollar from the sale of each book will go toward a missions organization who is actively fulfilling the Great Commission by working in God's harvest fields.

*Dedicated to my father and mother,*

*Kevin & Nicole Wagner*

*Dad, you taught me to love Jesus and to
reach people, and that there is no greater work
in this world than to do those two things.
Mom, you taught me to read and write,
to laugh and love, and that I could do
anything with Christ's help.
I am forever thankful to God for giving
me the best parents in the world.
I love you.*

# TABLE OF CONTENTS

Preface.................................................................................I
Section 1: Motivations for Evangelism
    Chapter 1: Follow the Leader.............................................1
    Chapter 2: Labor Pains.....................................................13
    Chapter 3: How Do You Say, "I Love You?"....................29
    Chapter 4: The Power of One...........................................45
    Chapter 5: From Theory to Reality.................................55
Section 2: Obstructions to Evangelism
    Chapter 6: Conscious Excuses.........................................75
    Chapter 7: Subconscious Excuses...................................101
    Chapter 8: Incorrect Evangelism....................................115
Section 3: Theological Implications
    Chapter 9: The Foundation..............................................135
    Chapter 10: Romans 1.....................................................143
    Chapter 11: Romans 2.....................................................161
    Chapter 12: Heresies.......................................................177
Section 4: Practical Implications
    Chapter 13: What Do I Believe?.....................................205
    Chapter 14: What Can I Do?...........................................221
Conclusion.......................................................................235
Endnotes..........................................................................239

# PREFACE

It was hot. And it wasn't that dry heat either. It was humid. The kind of humid where after five minutes outside people think you accidentally fell into a pool. The only relief we had was when we had the A/C on in our hotel room…until the power went out and in its place came the humidity. And we were thirsty. It seemed like it didn't matter how much water we drank, it was never enough. We could never drink enough water to offset the amount of water that we were losing by sweating. This was life in Kampong Thom City, Cambodia.

I was leading a mission trip of 27 people and for months we had been preparing. We had been raising funds for the trip. We had been practicing dramas for the trip, but we couldn't really prepare for the humidity. It was worth it, though. Months of preparation and we had finally arrived. Now practice was finally over and the game had begun.

We had had a successful week of ministry in Kampong Thom City and the surrounding villages. Each morning we would wake up early and travel to another village. As our vans arrived so too would the kids. As our vans kicked up dust on the dirt roads, the kids would run out to meet us, running alongside our vehicles like they were our own personal bodyguards. As we would reach the center of the village we would hop out of our vans to the laughter and cheering of the kids. With all of the commotion the women would begin to file out of their "houses." Upon noticing that they had guests, they would send some of the kids out into the rice fields to go get the men. In only a few minutes it seemed as though the whole village had surrounded us. Now we had an opportunity to do ministry.

Using a translator, we would tell the people that we were from America and how we would love to be able to talk to them for just a few minutes. We would start out with a few funny skits to get their attention and make them laugh. Then we would ask if we could tell them a story. Everywhere we went the people were so kind and we would proceed to do a drama that demonstrated the love of Jesus. Following the drama one of our team members would share their testimony and dozens of people would give their hearts to Jesus. These ministry experiences were so rewarding. I loved being able to share the love of Jesus with these people and see them receive salvation, healing, deliverance and the love of Christ.

All week our contact had been working to try to get our team to travel to one specific village. He and I had been talking about our desire to visit this village ever since he told me about it. He told me, "Joshua, there is a village a few miles from here on the banks of the Stung Sen River. This is a secluded village and is only accessible by boat. The Kampong Thom province is an unreached place but even so, many of the villages we have gone to thus far have heard the Gospel at least once before. But this village has not. To my knowledge, no white man has even ever visited this village and they have certainly never heard about Jesus." Of course, when I heard about this village, I told our contact, "We need to go to this village. If there is any way to get there, please take us."

Our entire week God was doing great things in all of the villages we were visiting, and I was incredibly grateful for all of the opportunities we had to minister, but I desperately wanted to go this river village. Then I got the news—we had gained access to a boat and would be visiting this village. I excitedly told my team and we began to prepare for our trip down the river the next day.

We started out early the next morning, loading our equipment onto our rented boat. This boat wasn't exactly a cruise ship. It was a little crowded and with each member of our team that stepped onto the boat we collectively held our breath, hoping we wouldn't be too heavy. We weren't, but it was close. We then began our trip down the Stung Sen River. It was a beautiful trip. The Cambodian countryside was covered in green—it felt like what you would expect to see floating down the Amazon River. The only thing that wasn't green was the water below us, which had more of a brown hue. The trip was roughly two hours from Kampong Thom City to the village.

The "bathroom" was simply a three-foot high square structure with a curtain for a door. Thus, only the bottom half of your body was covered in case you wanted to carry on conversation while using the bathroom. And watch your step, because there was no toilet, you simply stood on two pieces of wood with the rushing river flowing beneath you. As I said before, it wasn't exactly a cruise ship.

Finally, we arrived. When we did, the people didn't know what to expect. "Who were these white people? Why were they visiting our remote village?" So at first, the people were quite shy. As our translators told the people who we were and that we would like to do some dramas for them, they warmed up to the idea a little bit more and began to gather around us. We began with a few funny skits to lighten the mood and show them that we were there because we loved them. Then our team did a drama depicting the sacrifice of Christ and one of the girls on our team shared her testimony. By the end of our service our team was able to pray with dozens of individuals to give their hearts to Jesus. The pastor traveling with us made a connection with the people there and assured them that he would be back regularly to help them grow in their relationship with the Lord.

As we got onto the boat to leave, almost the entire village stood on the bank and waved to us. As our boat started to motor away, the kids ran on the shore shouting "Goodbye" to us. As we traveled back we started by thanking Jesus for giving us the opportunity to minister to this unreached village. Then we began discussing why this was such a special experience to us. Was it because we got to travel on a boat? I mean, yes, that was fun, but that wasn't why we were excited. Was it because we got to see more of the Cambodian countryside? Again, that was enjoyable, but you don't go on a mission trip to sightsee. Why were we so excited? It was the people. It was the opportunity to go where no missionary had gone before. It was the ability to tell these people about Jesus for the first time. It was the realization that if we didn't go, then these people wouldn't know. Ultimately, our joy was tied to the fact that we were able to lead people to Jesus.

Writing this book has been one of the biggest projects of my life. I have spent much time and effort into making this dream a reality. Yet, the purpose of this book has never been for my own self-promotion or personal pride. My prayer has, and continues to be, that this book will ignite a passion on the inside of people to reach this world for Jesus. I pray that as you read this book, you will be filled with a motivation and an inspiration to bring the message of the Gospel to the uttermost bounds of the earth. But most of all I pray that this book would cause you to fall more in love with Jesus. He is the Creator of all that is good. He is the Lamb slain before the foundations of the earth. He is the Word who became flesh. He is the suffering servant. He is the conquering King. He is the Beginning and the End. He was and is and is to come. And He is the desire of the nations who has entrusted us with the message of the Gospel. May His Great Commission become our great ambition.

For the King,

Joshua

# MOTIVATIONS FOR EVANGELISM

# CHAPTER 1

# FOLLOW THE LEADER

Have you ever wondered what it would have been like to be one of Jesus' disciples? You are one of only 12 men on the whole planet who have virtually unlimited access to Jesus. Every day you wake up and have your quiet time with Jesus…in the flesh. I wonder what it must have been like to be a disciple of Jesus? When having lunch, did they pray over the meal or just tell Jesus, "Thank you?" Anywhere they went they went with Jesus. When I think about being one of Jesus' disciples I think about what I would have been like and how I would have interacted with Him. Can you imagine the conversations the disciples must have heard? The Gospels provide us with only the tiniest glimpse of what life would have been like for the disciples. Think about it. John ends his Gospel by saying, "Jesus did many other things as well. If every one of them were written down, I suppose that even the whole world would not have room for the books that would be written"[1] (John 21:25).

I love the Gospels and have read them over and over again, but how exciting it would be to read some of those other unwritten books that John talked about! And so I think about the privilege that those 12 men had to spend three years of ministry with Jesus. That would be the ultimate university degree. Imagine Bartholomew at his 10-year high school reunion. "Hey Jude, how are you? What have you done since graduating?" "Well I went to the *University of Bethany* and played soccer for the fighting scapegoats. I did four years there and got my degree in Public Relations. How about you?" "Well, I actually spent the last three years at *Son of God University* with Jesus!"

I know I'm having some fun with the idea of being Jesus' disciple but the reality is that it truly would have been incredible. And when I think about being a part of Jesus' inner circle, surely I would have hung on his every word. I've got to think I would have taken notes every time He opened His mouth, right? I would have never forgotten a thing that He said. Jesus never would have had to repeat Himself, and yet, the disciples didn't exactly demonstrate that sort of perspective. I'm not saying that they were ungrateful or entitled but they didn't always "get it." In Mark chapter six Mark recounts how thousands of people had listened to Jesus teach the entire day until finally the sound of their stomachs was louder than Jesus' words. They were desperate for food and begged the disciples to help them. The disciples came to Jesus with a very compassionate response, "They want food. So tell them all to leave and get some themselves." Jesus responds very differently and ends up performing a miracle to feed thousands of men, women and children. There were even 12 basketfuls of leftovers for each disciple to take home and put in the fridge. Now, if I were one of those disciples that is a pretty transformational event. That miracle is not the type of thing I would soon forget, right? Wrong! Only two chapters later a similar event occurs:

*During those days another large crowd gathered. Since they had nothing to eat, Jesus called his disciples to him and said, "I have compassion for these people; they have already been with me three days and have nothing to eat. If I send them home hungry, they will collapse on the way, because some of them have come a long distance." His disciples answered, "But where in this remote place can anyone get enough bread to feed them?"* – Mark 8:1-4

Two chapters earlier the disciples had just seen Jesus perform an amazing miracle where He took five loaves of bread and two fish and fed 5,000 men! If there are 5,000 men, I'm going to guess that there were also somewhere around 5,000 women because in my experience, men like to hang out around women. And let's just say that there is one child for each adult represented. Then we can conservatively say that there were perhaps 20,000 people that Jesus fed with five loaves of bread and two fish. So, just two chapters later a similar event is taking place, only this time the crowd is smaller (4,000 men compared to 5,000 men). Jesus astutely remarks that the people are hungry and the disciples respond, "But where in this remote place can anyone get enough bread to feed them?" They had literally just seen Jesus do the same miracle for a larger number of people. You would think that they would remember, and yet they have the audacity to ask how to feed the people.

When I read this in Scripture it is really easy for me to think, "Why were the disciples so dumb? Why didn't they remember?" And yet, I really don't know if I would have been any different. The disciples were a group of young men, most of them probably teenagers.[2] I have worked with teenage boys. I have preached to teenage boys. I have been a teenage boy, and I can testify that the mind of a teenage boy is easily distracted and often forgetful. These were young men with lots of growing up to do. Even more than that, though, it is easy to criticize the disciples from this side of the resurrection. The disciples didn't have the Gospels to read to see how the story ends. Yes, they were aware that they were with someone special and they were a privileged group, but the gravity of what they were a part of was not realized until later. Despite Jesus' many teachings and allusions to His death and resurrection, John honestly remarks that even after Jesus' death, "They still did not understand from Scripture that Jesus had to rise from the dead" (John 20:9). It is easy for us to point at the disciples and say that we would have done better, but we don't know that for sure.

## *REPEAT AFTER ME*

It is for this reason that when you read the Gospels you find that Jesus will often repeat Himself or He will state the same truth in a variety of ways. For example, when communicating the Father's desire to find that which has been lost, Jesus tells three parables to demonstrate this point: the Lost Sheep, the Lost Coin and the Lost Son (Luke 15). Jesus knew that His audience needed things to be repeated in order for it to really sink in. And not only did His disciples need that, and not only did the first-century Jews need that, but 2,000 years later, we still need that. And that is one of the many reasons that we have four different Gospels. God wanted to communicate the story of Jesus not just once but multiple times. He wanted to provide us with "four different portraits of the Messiah"[3] so that we would be constantly reminded of what Jesus said.

Now, if Jesus says something once, it's important. Each of Jesus' commands are super important regardless of how many times He or Scripture repeats it. But there is added weight and importance to when Jesus repeats Himself or when Scripture reemphasizes it. This teaching tactic is not unique to Scripture either. Have you ever read or heard Martin Luther King, Jr.'s "I Have a Dream" speech? Here is an excerpt:

"I have a dream that one day this nation will rise up and live out the true meaning of its creed: 'We hold these truths to be self-evident, that all men are created equal.'

I have a dream that one day on the red hills of Georgia, the sons of former slaves and the sons of former slave owners will be able to sit down together at the table of brotherhood

I have a dream that one day even the state of Mississippi, a state sweltering with the heat of injustice, sweltering with the heat of oppression, will be transformed into an oasis of freedom and justice.

I have a dream that my four little children will one day live in a nation where they will not be judged by the color of their skin but by the content of their character.

I have a dream today!"[4]

Doctor King was employing an effective teaching method to communicate his point: repetition. All I have to say is "I Have a Dream" and you immediately know what I'm talking about. But if I simply say, "I am not unmindful that some of you have come here out of great trials and tribulations," or "We refuse to believe that the bank of justice is bankrupt," most people would not recognize the context or the speech. Why? Repetition. We know the heartbeat of Dr. King's speech because he demonstrated the focus of his speech through repetition.

The Bible does the same thing in many other forms of repetition, particularly in the Old Testament. To emphasize something in the Hebrew language an author would not underline or embolden or put an exclamation mark, instead the author would repeat himself. He would restate a word or phrase to emphasize its importance. In fact, one of the common tools used in hermeneutics is to evaluate how many words or phrases are repeated within a given verse or passage and this will inform the reader as to what the author was emphasizing. For example, in both Isaiah 6:3 and Revelation 4:8, the angels in Heaven do not simply call God "holy" but rather, "holy, holy, holy." The reason why "holy" is repeated is not because God is hard of hearing. It's because the angels are emphasizing God's holiness by making it stand out through repetition.

## THE GREAT COMMISSION

When it comes to the words and commands of Jesus, repetition becomes an important part of good Bible study. There are certain things that Jesus said or did that are repeated more than others in Scripture, and the Great Commission is at the top of that list. Knowing the tendency of humanity, God makes sure to repeat the Great Commission so that the command is loud and clear to the Church:

*Then Jesus came to them and said, "All authority in heaven and on earth has been given to me. Therefore go and make disciples of all nations, baptizing them in the name of the Father and of the Son and of the Holy Spirit, and teaching them to obey everything I have commanded you. And surely I am with you always, to the very end of the age." –* Matthew 28:18-20

*He said to them, "Go into all the world and preach the gospel to all creation. Whoever believes and is baptized will be saved, but whoever does not believe will be condemned. And these signs will accompany those who believe: In my name they will drive out demons; they will speak in new tongues; they will pick up snakes with their hands; and when they drink deadly poison, it will not hurt them at all; they will place their hands on sick people, and they will get well." –* Mark 16:15-18

*He told them, "This is what is written: The Messiah will suffer and rise from the dead on the third day, and repentance for the forgiveness of sins will be preached in his name to all nations, beginning at Jerusalem. You are witnesses of these things." –* Luke 24:46-48

*Again Jesus said, "Peace be with you! As the Father has sent me, I am sending you." –* John 20:21

*"But you will receive power when the Holy Spirit comes on you; and you will be my witnesses in Jerusalem, and in all Judea and Samaria, and to the ends of the earth."* – Acts 1:8

Five times the clear command to go into the world and preach the Gospel is given. Again, if Jesus says something once, or if Scripture records something once, that is more than enough to motivate us to listen and obey. But when the Bible records something five different times in five different books in five different ways, God is emphasizing the priority that this command has, and the necessity for it to be carried out.

### A LOAF OF BREAD

Imagine if one morning my wife, Michelle, came up to me and said, "Josh, tomorrow night we are having some friends coming over for dinner and I need you to stop by the grocery store and pick up some bread for dinner before tomorrow night. Can you please do that?" "Absolutely, Michelle. No problem." I go on with my day and don't have a chance to get to the store, but I still have plenty of time. We're having dinner that night, which sparks Michelle to ask, "Josh, did you pick up that bread yet?" "No, I didn't get a chance to do that today." She replies, "Ok, well just remember to do it before dinner tomorrow night." Fast forward to that night. Michelle and I are in bed. I am just on the verge of sleep; REM is within reach! And then I hear a voice, "Joshua, just wanted to remind you that I'm going to need that bread for dinner tomorrow night." "Yes, Michelle, thank you for that reminder just as I was about to start dreaming." I wake up the next morning (most likely having dreamed about bread), and just before Michelle leaves the house for work she slips in a reminder, "Hey babe, don't forget the bread."

That afternoon I head to the store. As I'm walking down the aisle my phone begins to vibrate. Want to take a guess as to who is calling? Yep, Michelle. "Hey Michelle, can't imagine what you're calling about..." "Yeah, just wanted to once again remind you to grab some bread." "Yes, thank you. Got it." Five times, Michelle has now asked me to get a loaf of bread. As I continue my way through the store I grab some toilet paper (we're almost out), I buy some

Chocolate Chip Cookie Dough Ice Cream (for obvious reasons), I get some Salt & Vinegar chips (because you have to balance the sweet snacks with some salty snacks), and I even get some flowers for Michelle. I head home and put out the flowers. I then proceed to clean. I vacuum the whole house. I clean the bathrooms. I make the bed. I wash the dishes. I dust (even underneath the furniture). I mow the lawn. I spend the entire afternoon making the house spotless. Michelle comes home from work and I'm excited for her to see everything I did to make the house perfect for our guests that night.

She walks into the house and I say, "Michelle, look, I cleaned, like really cleaned." I proceed to show her everything I did. She's happy, but eventually when I stop talking she asks the question, "Josh, this is wonderful! But I'm looking around in the kitchen and I can't seem to find the bread." After a long pause I respond, "Ok so here's the thing, I forgot the bread, but look at all these other things I did. Why can't you just appreciate all of these things that I did? Why do you have to focus on the bread?" "Josh, I really do appreciate all of the stuff that you did. It's great. But to be honest, I didn't ask you to do any of those things. In fact, I only asked you to do one thing. I asked you to please get me some bread. We can have a great night with our friends without the house being dusted. We don't need the lawn mowed in order for tonight to happen. But I do need bread for tonight. That was the *one* thing I asked you to do, and I asked you five separate times to demonstrate the importance of it. For me to come home and find that you did all of these other things yet failed to do the one thing I requested for you to do is really disappointing."

## *A LESSON FROM THE PHARISEES*

Now, thankfully that story isn't a true story for our marriage. However, sadly that story is true for many Christians when it comes to the Great Commission. The command to share the Gospel with the world was given by Christ five separate times in Scripture. If mentioned only once, that should be good enough, but for it to be mentioned five times, this is a command to be heeded. And yet, there are more non-Christians on the planet today than there ever have been in history. As a church, we have done a very poor job of fulfilling Christ's Great Commission. And how do you think Christ feels about that? How do you expect Jesus to respond when He comes to earth to find that while a lot of work has been done, the Great Commission has often been neglected? "Jesus, look at all of the work that we've done! We've built an orphanage. We renovated our church building. We have state of the art sound equipment. We wrote a book. Aren't you happy with what we've done?" And I have to imagine that His response would be something like this: "That's great! I'm happy to see all of the things you've accomplished, but I'm looking around and I'm wondering, what about the Great Commission?" "Well Jesus, you see, we've been so busy doing all of these other things that we had to put the Great Commission on the backburner. But why are you focusing on the one thing we didn't do instead of all of these other wonderful things that we did do?" Jesus would reply, "Listen, I'm happy you did these other things, but to be honest, I didn't ask you to do those things. What I asked you to do was very specific and I repeated it five times so that there would be no confusion about what my first desire was for you to accomplish; the Great Commission is my priority and I asked for it to be yours too. And yet, that is the one thing you have failed to do."

Now, please do not misunderstand me. I am not bashing the building of orphanages or ridiculing new church buildings or criticizing writing a book (that would be a bit contradictory, wouldn't it?). My point is that while those things are good, they are not the end goal. We shouldn't build an orphanage so that we can simply say, "We built an orphanage." We shouldn't renovate a church so that others can gawk and gaze. We shouldn't write a book so that we have a digital footprint on Amazon. The only reason why we should do any of those things is because Jesus commands us to do them. And the reason why He would command us to do them is because those things are tools to help us fulfill the ultimate goal of fulfilling the Great Commission. Why build an orphanage? To demonstrate the love of God to the least of these that they might be adopted into God's family. Why renovate your church building? So that it may attract people to come and join God's family. Why write a book? Ultimately, to help people come to know Jesus. Those things are the means to the end, not the end themselves, but all too often we have made them the end, forgetting the words of Jesus.

The Bible goes to great lengths to try to communicate the importance of the Great Commission. Each of the Gospel writers made it a priority to include the Great Commission. God made sure that the command to win this world was repeated time and again, and yet we live in a world today where we have all too often thrown the command of the Great Commission to the wayside in favor of something else. And many times, that "something else" is even a good thing, but when we substitute a good thing for the main thing, we have missed the mark. Serving at my local soup kitchen is a good thing, but if it inhibits me from spending time with my wife and developing our marriage, then it has become a bad thing. When our priorities get out of order, our mission becomes skewed. When we focus on the tools of evangelism rather than evangelism itself, our mission gets out of focus.

The remedy for this does not necessarily mean that you give up all of the outreaches and ministries that you're currently involved in; it just means that you reorganize your priorities to meet Christ's. Jesus' response to us is probably not that different than it was to the Pharisees when He said, "Woe to you, teachers of the law and Pharisees, you hypocrites! You give a tenth of your spices—mint, dill and cumin. But you have neglected the more important matters of the law—justice, mercy and faithfulness. You should have practiced the latter, without neglecting the former" (Matthew 23:23). Jesus was not upset with the Pharisees because they were tithing. He was upset because they had made the minor things major and the major things minor. Their focus was so much on tithing spices that they neglected showing justice, loving mercy and walking faithfully. I believe the words of Jesus to us today are not so dissimilar, "I'm not against you doing many good things in the Kingdom, I want you to continue, but do not neglect the Great Commission in the process."

## THE EPITAPH

Have you ever visited a cemetery? If so, I'm sure you've found yourself reading tombstones. Whenever I visit a cemetery I find myself reading people's tombstones. Sometimes a tombstone will have a picture on it. Usually a tombstone will have the date of birth and the date of death. And then one thing that almost every tombstone has is an epitaph. An epitaph is the phrase or statement written about the deceased person. It is the final way that that person wants to be remembered. It is the one sentence that defines a person. Of all the things that the deceased person wants to say or leave with those left behind, the epitaph is the final word.

What is written on Jesus' tombstone? What is his epitaph? Well, of course, we know that Jesus has no tombstone. You can travel to Israel today and you will find what the disciples found 2,000 years ago: "the stone rolled away from the tomb, and when they entered they did not find the body of the Lord Jesus...(for) He is not here; He has risen!" (Luke 24:2, 6). Jesus has no epitaph inscribed on a tombstone, for the tomb is empty. That being said, we need not wonder how Jesus would like for us to remember Him. We don't have to wonder what His final words would be, because the Bible has preserved those for us.

After Jesus rose from the dead the Bible records that He spent forty days with His disciples (Acts 1:3) and would have shared many things with them. Yet, after three years of ministry with His disciples, and after another forty days spent with them after the resurrection, He chose to leave His disciples with one final command. Of all the things that Jesus could have said to His disciples before ascending to Heaven, He gave the Great Commission. His final command was not to build churches or to write books or to even live a good life. His command was to go and make disciples. In other words, Jesus' epitaph is the Great Commission. How did He want to be remembered? What did He want to leave with those who would come after Him? The Great Commission.

Why was Jesus so concerned with leaving us with the Great Commission? Why did He choose to leave us with that command rather than any others? It is because Jesus puts a priority on eternity. He knows that while building schools and writing music and serving food are all good and important, buildings and music and food will not come with us to Heaven. The only thing that lasts forever is people. If you were to lean up against the chest of God and hear His heartbeat I believe you would hear the cadence of that heartbeat beat "people, people, people." People matter to Jesus. When He walked the earth Jesus was not concerned with owning a home or having good transportation. He was focused on people.

## COMIC BOOK CHRISTIANITY

The clear message of Scripture demonstrates the importance of the Great Commission. The teachings and commands of Christ demonstrate the importance of the Great Commission. But as the saying goes, many times actions speak louder than words, and Jesus' actions demonstrated a life devoted to fulfilling the Great Commission. Jesus didn't just talk about it; He showed us how to do it. Jesus didn't tell us to do something He wasn't already doing Himself. Jesus' entire life was a life dedicated to the Great Commission.

Did you read comic books growing up? I was never a big comic book fan but my youngest brother Luke was/is. Comic books were something that bonded Luke and my dad together. My dad collected comic books as a kid and when Luke started showing an interest in comic books, my dad went back to his parents' home and found all of his old comic books and gave them to Luke. Dad and Luke started collecting more and reading them. They loved the spectacular stories of superheroes found in the pages of those comic books. They were entertained. They were impressed. But not once did my dad or Luke ever read those comic books and think that they could do the same things as those superheroes. My dad and Luke never tried to fly or to punch through a brick wall. They were fully aware that the stories in the comic books were fictional.

One of the great tragedies of the past 100 years is that as "knowledge" has increased, so too has the criticism of the Bible. There are many who nowadays who consider the Bible a book of fairy tales or myths. Now, my guess is that many of you reading this book would not share the same feelings. However, functionally, I think that even Christians who believe the Bible treat it as though it is a comic book. It is impressive. It is entertaining. But we don't really believe that God could use us to do the same miraculous things that Moses or Elijah or Peter did. Perhaps we do this, most of all, though, with Jesus. I find that if I am not careful, I read the stories of Jesus teaching and healing and working miracles as though they happened for Jesus because He was a superhero. Now, Jesus is a superhero, the greatest superhero of all, but the things Jesus did when He walked the earth He did as fully man. In fact, Jesus makes one of the most outrageous statements in Scripture when He says, "Very truly I tell you, whoever believes in me will do the works I have been doing, and they will do even greater things than these, because I am going to the Father" (John 14:12). Jesus, who has never lied, tells us that each of us can be the sort of superhero that He is through the power of the Spirit.

Jesus demonstrated to us the type of Great Commission life that He expects each of His disciples to have. His encounters with Zacchaeus and Bartimaeus and Jairus' daughter did not happen because He was God, they happened because He chose to live a life dedicated to Great Commission work. Not only that, but He has empowered us to do the same. If we truly want to call ourselves disciples of Jesus Christ, then we must learn to follow His example. And the clear example of Christ in the Gospels is that He was about His Father's business of fulfilling the Great Commission. Let us now be about our Father's business and follow our leader.

# CHAPTER 2

# LABOR PAINS

### *COWBOYS, FIREMEN AND HOCKEY PLAYERS*

"What do you want to be when you grow up?" I can't remember how many times I heard that question growing up. I was a pastor's kid and so every person in the church felt compelled to talk with me, but when you're six years old, you don't care about talking with 60-year old Margaret, you're on the lookout for 6-year old Patrick. You want to play! However, 60-year old Margaret, and many others like her, would often corner me, and one of her default questions was, "What do you want to be when you grow up?" My answer evolved over the years. At one time I wanted to be a cowboy just like Little Joe from *Bonanza*. At another time I wanted to be a fireman (we had a fire truck come to our neighborhood as a kid and me and my brothers and our friends had a water fight with the firemen and their hoses…I'll let you guess who won). But since I grew up in Canada where hockey is bigger than life itself and I most definitely wanted to be a hockey player at one point. So, depending on when you asked me, I would give one of any number of answers. But, regardless of my answer, 60-year old Margaret's reply to me was always the same, "Honey, you can be whatever you want to be as long as you put your mind to it."

Now, I know that it is always good to build the dreams of young people. And I absolutely believe in the power of confession and faith to finish the race, but let's be honest, there are certain things that I could never, ever accomplish no matter how hard I tried. I could work my entire life but I'm never going to play Defensive Tackle (DT) in the NFL. The average height of a DT in the NFL is well over six feet. I'm 5'8." The average weight of a DT in the NFL is well over 300 pounds. I weigh 180 pounds. There is no way

I would have ever become a Defensive Tackle in the NFL. But, you know what, there's also no way that the DT is ever going to become a horse jockey! The average height of a horse jockey is 5'2." The average weight of a horse jockey is 120 pounds. No matter how hard he tried, no DT is going to become a horse jockey. And I am perfectly fine with that. It's not a negative confession. It's not a lack of faith. It's life.

So often we hear phrases like "You can be whatever you want to be as long as you put your mind to it" and because we hear them, we repeat them to others. I am all about building the dreams of others, but just because a phrase or a line sounds good, that doesn't make it true. Even more so, just because a phrase sounds good, that doesn't make it biblical.

## *THE BIBLE SAYS...OR DOES IT?*

One of the things that my family and I find funny (and, I guess, somewhat sad too) is how people misquote the Bible all the time. People say things like, "You know the Bible says that cleanliness is next to godliness" or "I love that verse, 'God works in mysterious ways.'" Sometimes when I'm preaching I'll test a congregation's biblical knowledge by asking them to turn to Hezekiah chapter one and see how long it takes for someone to call me out. It's cruel, I know, but Jesus and me have a good laugh over it.

One of my favorite instances like this was in the summer of 2010 in Dar es Salaam, Tanzania, Africa. I was leading an amazing team of eleven missionaries from Oral Roberts University. It was the summer in between my freshman and sophomore year and our team of eleven was spending a month ministering in Tanzania. We did a whole bunch of different ministry while we were there but at one point we spent a few days teaching at a Bible college. I had grown up preaching, and some of my teammates had some experience also, but for some this was going to be their first time to teach...and it was in Tanzania at a Bible college. While some were pretty nervous, all of them did a great job. But one of my teammates, a friend of mine named Matt did something I have remembered to this day.

Matt grew up in a Pentecostal church and had preached before. He was familiar with the Word and he preached a great message that morning. There was, however, one rather funny moment during his sermon. He was preaching and he was really getting on a roll when he shouted, "The Bible says, 'When the praises go up, the blessings come down!'" I heard him say this and sort of gave him an inquisitive look and shook my head at him, indicating that that wasn't in the Bible. Matt looked at me and after a pause he said, "Actually, the Bible doesn't say that but it's still a good principle to live by." Our entire team erupted in laughter, as did the Bible school students. It was hilarious and Matt was a good sport to let us laugh, in fact, I bet if Matt read this he would laugh once again. It was funny and certainly no harm was done. That being said, the story is a good reminder of how easily we can say something that sounds biblical but isn't.

One of the common phrases in the Church community is "See a need, fill a need." If you've spent any amount of time in church I'm sure you've heard this phrase before. The premise of the phrase is that when you see a needy area, a place where help is necessary, there is no one better to help fill that void than you. In fact, the fact that you recognized the need is probably an indicator that *you* are the one to fill it. For me, this phrase is similar to the "You can be whatever you want to be as long as you put your mind to it" phrase. It sounds good. It feels good. But is it true?

I want you to know that just because you see a need does not mean that you are the one to fill it. I was talking to a friend of mine recently who pastors a great church in rural Oklahoma. He was talking with me about his church and how he is desperately in need of a worship leader. His worship leader recently left and he told me, "Josh, we need help. We have some people stepping in but I've had people in my congregation come to me and tell me, 'Pastor, we are praying for a worship leader. Just wanted to let you know.'" People in his church can see the need, but that does not mean that every person who sees the need is the one who is supposed to fill it. In fact, the situation could get a lot worse if some of those people who saw the need, filled the need. If you can't sing, then you shouldn't be a worship leader. Seeing the need does not necessarily mean that the Lord has called you to fill it; it may mean that you are simply aware.

The phrase "See a need, fill a need" has become so commonplace that many people treat it as though it is found in

Scripture. Because of this, people meet needs that they were never intended to meet. Just because there is a need for Sunday school workers does not mean that you are supposed to fill it, particularly if you hate spending time with kids. Just because your church needs a women's ministry does not mean that you're supposed to start it, particularly if you are a man. In fact, sometimes the worst thing that you can do is fill an identified need out of turn, and there are two reasons for this.

1. When you fill a need that you were never meant to fill, you stop yourself from fulfilling the needs that God meant for you to fill. Each of us only has a certain amount of time and effort. Time cannot be created and effort has an end. When you fill up your schedule with one activity you are also saying "no" to another activity. One of the lessons I have had to learn the hard way is the art of saying "no." I'm a natural people pleaser and I hate saying "no" to people. But what I have had to learn is that when I say "yes" to everything, then I don't do any of those things to the standard that they need to be done. Additionally, I can think about times where I have committed to something that then inhibited me from doing something else that I really should have been doing instead.

In order to fulfill the call of God on your life, you are going to have to say "no" to the calls of other people. Jesus is a great example of this. Jesus didn't try to have a personal encounter with every person on earth while He was here. There were times when Jesus actually asked people to go away or leave the room (Mark 5:37). There were times when Jesus intentionally left the crowds (Matthew 13:36). There were times when Jesus even left His disciples to just be alone with His Father (Mark 1:35). Jesus understood that there were moments where He had to say "no." Jesus saw needs all around Him—poverty, sickness, corruption, hunger—but He didn't stop to meet every one of them. This was strategic. Jesus knew His mission. He said, "I was sent only to the lost sheep of Israel" (Matthew 15:24).

If Jesus knew the importance of saying "no" then we must learn it too. Jesus was not blind to the needs around Him, He was just focused on accomplishing His mission and He knew that if He spent His time meeting every need then He would never accomplish the need that the Father had destined for Him to accomplish. God has a unique plan for each of our lives but when we start filling needs out of our jurisdiction, we will leave this world having never finished the business God gave us to do.

2. When you fill a need that you were never meant to fill, you stop someone else from fulfilling the needs that God meant for him/her to fill. If there is a need, then it needs to be filled, but that doesn't mean that you are the one who is supposed to do it. When you meet a need never intended for you, you have taken over somebody else's calling and mission. This is precisely the point that Paul made when He wrote the following:

*Now if the foot should say, "Because I am not a hand, I do not belong to the body," it would not for that reason stop being part of the body. And if the ear should say, "Because I am not an eye, I do not belong to the body," it would not for that reason stop being part of the body. If the whole body were an eye, where would the sense of hearing be? If the whole body were an ear, where would the sense of smell be? But in fact God has placed the parts in the body, every one of them, just as he wanted them to be. If they were all one part, where would the body be? As it is, there are many parts, but one body. – 1 Corinthians 12:15-20*

Paul is making the point that there can only be so many eyes in the body because at the moment that the ear takes the place of the eye, now there is a gap where the ear should be and the eye's calling is no longer fulfilled. When you step into the destiny of someone else, you do a horrible disservice to your fellow brother or sister in Christ by inhibiting, or perhaps even eliminating his or her mission. One of the great examples of this is in the life of Jonathan.

Jonathan grew up as the son of Saul. He was in line to be the second king of Israel. Everything in the natural seemed to indicate that Jonathan was the next in command. And yet, God had a different plan. God anointed David to be the next king of Israel. This put Jonathan in a difficult position because David was his best friend. It would have been very easy for Jonathan to become jealous of David or to become entitled. In the natural, Jonathan was supposed to fill the need that Saul's death would one day create. But Jonathan knew that the Lord had spoken and instead of fulfilling a need that seemed his to fill, he kept that need open for his best friend David to fill.

If Jonathan had stepped into that opening as the next in line to the throne, think about how it would have negatively impacted David and the call of God on David's life.

None of us live in a vacuum. All of our decisions affect other people, and for this reason, we need to constantly be aware that our decision to fill a need simply because there is a vacancy may actually be stopping us from fulfilling our calling while at the same time stopping someone else from fulfilling his calling. This is why we must be Spirit-led believers.

Just because something looks good or sounds good does not make it true or good for you. In the natural, Jonathan was the man for the job. It made sense in the eyes of the world for him to step into that position, but that was never God's plan. And, in actuality, God often chooses to work this way. His ways are not our ways (Isaiah 55:8-9) and the sooner that we discover that, the better. God specializes in confounding what makes logical sense, as Paul states:

*But God chose the foolish things of the world to shame the wise; God chose the weak things of the world to shame the strong. God chose the lowly things of this world and the despised things—and the things that are not—to nullify the things that are, so that no one may boast before him.* – 1 Corinthians 1:25-27

This is the difference between Spirit-led ministry and need-based ministry. There are so many people who live their lives driven by need rather than by being led by the Spirit. There are so many in ministry who get burned out or discouraged or hurt because they have spent their lives meeting needs they were never meant to meet. They have spent their time being led by the needs around them, rather than being led by the Spirit. If we are to fulfill the call of God on our lives then we must learn to walk in step with the Spirit, as Paul says, "For those who are led by the Spirit of God are the children of God" (Romans 8:14). The children of God are not identified by how many tasks they accomplish or by how many projects they undertake. The children of God are those who are led by the Spirit of God.

My hope is that this revelation will be liberating for you. I have preached this before and seen the light bulb go on for people when they realize that they don't have to do it all. This is a book on evangelism and witnessing and missions and outreach and some of you may have been scared to read this book in fear that I'd tell each of you to drop what you're doing and move to Africa. Now, the Lord may speak that to some who do read this book, but that's the key— the Lord may speak that to you, not me. I did not write this book to force people into full-time evangelism. I did not write this book to guilt people into mission work. But perhaps most importantly, and germane to our conversation here, I did not write this book because there was a need to write it. I wrote this book because God said so, and I pray that it would accomplish everything that He had in mind for it do.

## *A LESSON IN FARMING*

I'm not a country boy. Let me be clear about that. I grew up in the city. I live in the city. And I plan on living in the city for the rest of my life. I'm not an animal lover. I don't know how to build a house. I'm a city boy. That being said, I have a number of family members who are. Many of those on my dad's side of the family are farmers. They have animals. They plant wheat. They own combines. They are farmers. So, while I am no country boy, I have been to farms, I have baled some hay, I have milked a cow and so I'm not completely unaware of what happens on a farm.

And one of the things that I learned by spending time around my farming family was the delicate nature of the seasons. There were years where it would get too cold too early and my uncles were concerned they would lose the crop. There were years where it would barely rain and they would pray for the rain to come or else they would lose the crop. The seasons fluctuated and you could never know for sure when it was going to be time to harvest, but what was always clear was that whenever the harvest was ready, they had to be ready too.[5]

When Jesus spoke about the state of the unreached, He often likened them to a harvest field. Jesus did this for a variety of reasons. First of all, this was a metaphor that his audience would understand. First-century Israel was a farming community. Much of Jesus' audience would have been farmers or at the very least familiar with farming. Secondarily, though, this metaphor works well because the unreached world is very much like a harvest field.

When you drive by a wheat field, for example, that field is representative of what could be. It is not a loaf of bread as it sits in the field, but it has the potential to be a loaf of bread. A wheat field is not the finished product. It is in the process of becoming the finished product, but it is not there yet. When referring to non-Christians my dad doesn't call them non-Christians or unsaved people, he typically calls them pre-Christians. He sees the potential for what they could be, just as Jesus does when He looks out at the harvest fields of people.

*Jesus went through all the towns and villages, teaching in their synagogues, proclaiming the good news of the kingdom and healing every disease and sickness. When he saw the crowds, he had compassion on them, because they were harassed and helpless, like sheep without a shepherd. Then he said to his disciples, "The harvest is plentiful but the workers are few. Ask the Lord of the harvest, therefore, to send out workers into his harvest field."* – Matthew 9:35-38

This passage explains that Jesus spent His time wandering from town to town. He rarely stayed in any one place for an extended period of time. He was constantly on the move looking for people, all kinds of people. Jesus looked for lost people, sick people, sad people, poor people and rich people. Jesus focused on people. And when He found them, His response was compassion. One of Jesus' primary motivations for evangelism was compassion. Jesus did what He did because He had compassion on people. In this story Matthew recounts how one day when Jesus was looking at the people with compassion, He spoke to His disciples in a sort of pre-Great Commission and said, "The harvest is plentiful..." There are a few things to mention about this small statement:

1. Context. There should be no doubt about whom Jesus is talking. The harvest is not some strange ethereal term for wisdom or understanding. Matthew is talking about Jesus' response to people. People are the focus of this conversation and so when Jesus describes the harvest He is talking about people.

2. Potential. By referring to people, specifically people that He has designated as "sheep without a Shepherd," it is clear that He is talking about a group of people that are not yet saved, but on the

20

precipice of salvation. All of the potential for salvation is there. The harvest waits, which says that much of the work has already been done, but it is certainly not finished. The most important job is yet to be completed—the bringing in of the harvest.

3. Present Tense. When Jesus speaks of the Harvest He does so in the present tense. This harvest is not something that might happen. It is not something that has happened. This harvest is happening right now. The harvest *is* plentiful (or as Jesus says elsewhere, "ripe"). As I said, I am not farmer, but you don't have to be a farmer to know that when the harvest is ready, it must be taken in. The moment that the harvest is ready the farmer must be ready and go out to reap the harvest.

4. Ripe. Jesus echoes the harvest metaphor once again in John 4:35 when He speaks to His disciples and says, "Don't you have a saying, 'It's still four months until harvest'? I tell you, open your eyes and look at the fields! They are ripe for harvest." When the harvest is ripe, we must not delay. If you wait too long, you may miss your opportunity. The harvest will not remain ready for forever. Jesus speaks of the harvest with urgency in His voice. The harvest isn't ripe in a month or in a year. This was his problem with the people around Him. Some were saying, "Four months more," but Jesus was saying, "Now! You have to get the harvest now!" The harvest is ripe right now and if you wait too long, it will no longer remain ripe and you will miss your opportunity.

Some people like to wait around until the environment is perfect in order to bring in the harvest. People like to take their sweet time and wait until the situation is perfect in order to reach the lost, but I'm telling you the same thing that Paul told the Corinthians, "Now is the time of God's favor, today is the day of salvation" (2 Corinthians 6:2). Stop putting off for tomorrow what needs to be done today! If today is the day of salvation, then let's do salvation work today!

It is so very easy to wait until everything is perfect before we start fulfilling the call of God. The reality is this, though, if you wait until you have everything figured out to start moving for the Lord, you will never move. If you wait for the perfect situation to start witnessing, you'll never lead a person to the Lord. My wife and I are new parents to our first child, Anna. She is an answer to prayer and far more amazing than I could have ever imagined. But I have a confession: Before she was born, I didn't have it all figured out. I didn't have everything perfectly prepared for my girl. I had not bought all of the diapers she would ever need. I had not saved up enough money to pay for her education. It would have been very easy for my wife and I to put off getting pregnant until the situation was perfect or until we had everything figured out. But if we had waited until we had every detail figured out and every expense already paid for, we would never have a child. If you wait until the situation is perfect, you will never start accomplishing the call of God for your life. No more excuses! Stop saying four months more and then the harvest. Start fulfilling the Great Commission today!

5. Plentiful. When Jesus describes the harvest fields He describes them as plentiful. Not only is the harvest ripe, it is plentiful, or as one translation says, it is "great." There is no time to delay in bringing in this harvest because the harvest will not remain ripe for forever, and there is much to bring in. Obviously this statement was true when Jesus said it 2,000 years ago, but if anything, it is even truer today. The world in which we live is incredibly ready for harvest, and the harvest is great. Two thousand years ago, when Jesus made this statement, there were only 300 million people living on the earth.[6] Today there are approximately 7.2 billion people on planet earth.[7] That's amazing, but what is brutally devastating is that of those 7.2 billion people, 40% (over three billion) of them are unreached, with the term "unreached" being defined as people groups where "no indigenous community with believing Christians with adequate numbers and resources to evangelize their own people"[8] exist. If the harvest was plentiful 2,000 years ago, how much more so is that true today? If you are looking for a motivation for evangelism, look no further than the fact that we live in a world that is full of people who need Jesus.

## *LET'S GET TO WORK*

Have you ever been presented with the question, "I've got good news and bad news; which do you want to hear first?" That question probably sends you, as it does me, on a roller coaster of emotions! We all love hearing good news and hate hearing bad news. For some people, they really struggle whether to hear the good news or the bad news first. For me, it has never been an issue. I *always* want to hear the bad news first because no matter how good the good news may be, if I hear it first, I won't be able to enjoy it whatsoever. I'll just be thinking about how the bad news affects this newly discovered good news.

Maybe the disciples were the opposite of me, though, because Jesus essentially comes to them and gives the same setup, "I've got some good news and bad news. The good news is that the harvest is ripe and plentiful." And this is good news. The fact that there is a harvest is always a good thing because it speaks to the opportunity for greatness! A farmer without a harvest won't be a farmer for much longer. Having a harvest is great news! Not only that, but having a ripe and plentiful harvest makes it even better. You won't just have a little harvest; you've got a great harvest. And the fact that it is ripe means that it has made it through the tough part and is now ready to be reaped. All of that is good news, and then comes the bad news, "…but the workers are few." A plentiful, ripe harvest is great news, unless you don't have the ability to bring in that harvest. That is the bad news Jesus presents to the disciples, but it is the same bad news that we deal with today.

I opened this chapter by talking about a common problem among Christians today, and that is the "see a need, fill a need" mentality. I believe everything I wrote, and yet, when it comes to the subject of evangelism, the Great Commission is the exception. When Jesus gave that commission it was given to all disciples, not just to those in the ministry, per se. So too, when Jesus mentions the fact that the laborers are few, He is essentially saying, "See the need." Jesus does not stop at simply identifying the problem, though. He continues on to state that the need must be filled. How can this happen? "Ask the Lord of the harvest, therefore, to send out workers into his harvest field."

The first thing that the Lord asks us to do is pray. How do we begin to bring in the harvest? Our first response must be prayer. Every missionary. Every evangelist. Every Christian who witnesses is an answer to this prayer. I believe that even the writing of this book is an answer to someone's prayer. And I want you who are reading this to know, you are an answer to my prayer. The privilege of witnessing to someone is even more amazing when you consider that it is an answer to someone's prayer. Prayer is the first step in meeting the greatest need of humanity: a life with Christ.

It does not stop at prayer, though. All of us are commanded to pray, but all of us are also commanded to fulfill that Great Commission. Now, this comes in all shapes and sizes. When some people hear that they are supposed to fulfill the Great Commission, they get concerned thinking that they now have to move to Mozambique as a full-time missionary. First of all, the call of God is not something to fear, it is something for which to look forward. God is a good God who gives good gifts to His children (Matthew 7:11). Furthermore, the promise of God is that if you delight yourself in Him, then He will give you the desires of *your* heart (Psalm 37:4). Walking with Christ will cause your desires to match His desires so that when He asks you to do something, you find that your desires are being fulfilled.

So, if the Lord calls you to be a missionary to Mozambique, then that is great news for you; that will be the fulfillment of a desire in your heart. But let me be clear, there are a whole lot of other ways to fulfill the Great Commission in addition to being a missionary in a far-away place. If the Lord has called you to be a businessman and make millions of dollars to help fund evangelistic work, then don't stoop to become a missionary. But if the Lord calls you to do missionary work in Asia, then don't stoop to become a millionaire businessman. All parts of the body are necessary for the health and success of the body.

The problem, though, has less to do with people fulfilling the wrong aspect of the Great Commission and more to do with people not even attempting to fulfill the Great Commission at all. Jesus asks us to pray for workers to be sent out into the harvest field. There are a few things to note about this command:

1. Workers. It is important to mention that Great Commission work is just that: work. In order for us to bring in the harvest it will demand that we put in effort. Sinners generally do not approach me asking for Jesus, I have to work to see people come to know Jesus. As workers, the job is not finished in a day. We must be diligent to

put in continuous work to fulfill this calling. Just as a large harvest is not reaped in a day, so too the harvest of souls will be a task that will take the rest of our lives; but there is no greater task.

2. Send. The Greek word that our English Bibles translate as "send out" is the word *ekballai*, which is the same word that is used to describe when a demon is "cast out" of a person. In other words, this word has forcefulness to it. Jesus is not saying to force people into evangelism, but He is saying to pray that people will be gripped with urgency to answer the call. Time is running out and we need people to respond immediately. When Jesus "cast out" a demon, it left immediately. My prayer is that as you read this book, the urgency of the harvest fields would grip you so much that you would rush to play your part in Great Commission work.

3. Activity. The prayer for workers to bring in the harvest is not just a prayer for new laborers but for current ones. The fact that Jesus is praying for laborers to be "cast out" into the fields could "even refer to workers already in the field,"[9] those who "need to have a fire lit under them to thrust them out of their comforts into the world of need."[10] There are many who already know the call of God, you may be one of them, but for any variety of reasons, you are not working in the harvest fields. Stop saying "four more months" and begin the work today.

The world in which we live has a massive need. There are literally billions of people who do not know Jesus, and many of them have never even heard of Him. Yes, the harvest is ripe and plentiful, that's the good news, but the bad news is that we are doing a very poor job of reaching them. That must change.

*PASTOR OLSEN*

I was really made aware of the power of prayer as it pertains to Great Commission work when I visited Madagascar in August of 2014. If I were being completely honest with you, before traveling to Madagascar I would say that the majority of what I knew about that country came from the cartoon movie by the same name. But this island nation was much more fantastic than any cartoon movie could have depicted. I went to the very northern tip of the country to the city of Antsiranana (or as the locals call it, Diego). This was a port city where there were very few Christians. Most of the people were either Muslim or animistic but we went to this city of 100,000 people and saw over 10,000 people attend our meetings there. Thousands were saved. Many were healed from sickness and disease. Hundreds of pastors and leaders were equipped. It was an amazing week of ministry.

My final day of ministry in Diego was Sunday and I went to minister in a church there. We had a great service. Many people came and the Lord touched so many of them. I got in the car to head back to the hotel to rest before the final night of the crusade… or so I thought. As I got in the car my translator told me, "Great message! Now we will head to another church! I have just been told that another church just started their service and they are now waiting for you to come and preach to them. Are you ready?"

Now, I know the token spiritual answer is, "Of course I'm ready—in season and out of season! The Lord has anointed me and appointed me to speak the oracles of God to the saints!" But that's not exactly how it came out. I was tired, like really tired. I was dealing with a nine-hour time change. I wasn't sleeping like I was used to. I wasn't eating my normal diet. I had been ministering all week and had just finished one service. I was ready to go back to my room and rest and prepare for the final night of the crusade. Yet, in the midst of all of those feelings was another one: humility. I was incredibly humbled by the fact that this church was waiting for me to come and preach. "Yes, I am ready. Let's go."

When I arrived I was greeted by the sound of worship and many smiling faces. I made my way up to the front of the church where Pastor Olsen greeted me. He couldn't have been more than 5 feet tall and weighed around 110 pounds soaking wet! He was such a happy man and kept smiling the entire time I was preaching. If I ever needed a vote of confidence during my sermon, I could just look at Pastor Olsen and there he would be smiling. We had a great service and the Lord touched many lives. After I sat down at the end of the service Pastor Olsen got up and began to speak. He didn't speak a word of English but as he spoke in Malagasy I could see the emotion. He looked at me and began to weep. My translator interpreted what he was saying. "Joshua, thank you for coming. Thank you for coming to my church. I have been a pastor for over 20 years at this church and not once has a missionary or an evangelist ever visited my church…until now. So thank you for coming. You have shown me that God has not forgotten about us; God has not forgotten about me."

Any thoughts or feelings I had about wanting to be back in my hotel room were immediately gone. I felt ashamed that I had even considered not coming to this church. I was completely overwhelmed with humility and gratitude that the Lord would choose to use me to provide encouragement to this pastor. After service he invited me to his home for snacks. His home was two rooms separated by a bed sheet. There was a kitchen the size of my closet, and then there was the main room, which doubled as their bedroom. It was the size of my master bathroom. In the midst of such poverty and difficulty, this pastor didn't stop grinning from ear to ear, thanking me for coming to his city and how my presence has transformed his church, his city, and himself.

As I left Pastor Olsen that day I had a number of thoughts but one of them was that I was very clearly made aware of truly how few laborers there are. Here was a man who had faithfully pastored for over 20 years and had never once had an evangelist or missionary come to his city or come to his church. And yet, I thank God that I was able to be the answer to Pastor Olsen's prayer. I was the laborer for which Pastor Olsen had prayed to the Lord of the harvest. Pastor Olsen's story is not unique, though. There are so many harvest fields that are ripe and ready for us to come, but there are not enough laborers. When you consider the motivations for evangelism and outreach, I hope that you remember Jesus' words that the harvest is plentiful, right now, but that we must pray and act to make sure that laborers are sent out into the harvest fields. May the story of Pastor Olsen, and the words of our Savior, be a motivation to work in the harvest fields today.

# CHAPTER 3

# HOW DO YOU SAY, "I LOVE YOU?"

*SEVEN PERCENT*

I love sports. I love playing sports. I love following sports. I love watching sports. I love what sports brings out in people. I love the competition. I love the childlike joy that a team has when it wins the championship. I love the raw emotion of a team that just won the championship. I love the determination of an athlete focused on winning. I love the family atmosphere of a team. I love how sports bring people together. And I love *my* teams. I love the Calgary Flames, the Oklahoma Sooners, the Oklahoma City Thunder, the St. Louis Cardinals and individual athletes like Phil Mickelson and Tim Tebow. I get so excited to watch my team play, and even though I have never met anyone from any of these teams, I feel like I know them. I love sports.

Now, I just spent an entire paragraph communicating how much I *love* sports, and while I mean that, I don't mean that I love them the same way that I love my wife, Michelle. We throw around the word "love" like it's a baseball. We use the same word to describe how we feel about a certain type of pizza as we do to describe our feelings towards our spouse. There's a disconnect there. Surely we don't feel the same way about pizza as we do about our spouse, and yet, we oftentimes use the same word. Part of this is because we only have one word for "love" while other languages, most notably the New Testament language of Greek, has multiple words.

In Greek, there are four different words that the English language translates as "love." They are *agape, eros, phileo* and *storge*. The one you have probably heard, if you've spent a considerable amount of time in the Church, is *agape*. This is the love of God. God loves us with an *agape* love and also asks us to love the world with an *agape* love. *Eros* describes a romantic or even sexual love and is the love that is to be demonstrated in a godly marriage. *Phileo* means "to have a special interest in someone or something, frequently with focus on close association; have affection for, like, or to consider someone a friend."[11] This is the love that you have with a brother or sister or close friend. The final word is *storge*, which is the "love and affection that naturally occurs between parents and children, can exist between siblings, and exists between husbands and wives in a good marriage."[12] So, in Greek if you wanted to tell your wife, "I love you," you would use a different word than you would to describe how much you love a certain sports team.

English, then, is at a disadvantage in communicating our true feelings. If I say that I love football but also say that I love my wife, how would you distinguish between the two kinds of love? For starters, my actions should prove it. I may love the Oklahoma Sooners, but I can promise you that I will never bring those football players a bouquet of flowers. I may love the Calgary Flames, but I'm not about to write the hockey team love letters or clean their bathrooms. But hopefully I will do those things for Michelle. For this reason, it is never enough to simply tell Michelle, "I love you," if my actions say otherwise.

Have you ever noticed that the words we speak communicate only a fraction of the actual message? Psychologists argue that the message we communicate is made up almost exclusively of nonverbal communication. The most widely held position is that our message is made up of the following three factors: 7% verbal + 38% tone of voice + 55% body language.[13] Seven percent! That is amazing! Those percentages seem staggering but think about it: if you went up to a brand new baby and said, "I love you. You are the smartest and cutest baby in the world," but did so with a scowl on your face as you shouted, that baby will cry; regardless of how kind your words may be, the baby will get a very different message. Conversely, let's say you go to a dog and say, "You are the stupidest dog in the whole world. You smell horrible and look ugly," but do so in a sweet voice while you rub his stomach, that dog will wag its tail and think you are quoting a love letter to him!

A man can tell me he loves his wife 100 times a day, but if he goes home every night and beats her, I don't believe him. A woman can tell me that she loves her husband on social media every single week, but if she's sleeping with a bunch of other men, I don't believe her. I can tell my wife that I love her every single day, but if I never take out the trash and never take her on a date and never turn off the football game to watch a romantic comedy with her, my words become empty very quickly because I'm trying to give a 100% statement but I'm topping off at 7%. You don't have to be a mathematician to know that if you score 7% on a test, you're failing. We live in a world that is constantly failing at loving God and loving people.

There are so many people in our world who, if you asked them, "Do you love Jesus?" would gladly respond, "Yes, I love Jesus." And yet, do they? It's really easy to *say* that we love Jesus, but do our actions reflect that? If we are to love God, then it is important to know how we are to love God because I fear that far too many people are scoring a 7% on that test. At this point, the logical question is, "How do I love Jesus?" Well, I'm glad you asked.

## *THE TOWER OF BABEL*

If you have never read Dr. Gary Chapman's book, *The 5 Love Languages*, then I highly recommend that you do so pronto. I didn't read this book until my first year of marriage and I wish I had read it earlier. This book was transformational for me as it made me aware of things in my relationships that I had never noticed before. The premise of the book is that people give and receive love in different ways. More specifically, this happens in one of these five ways: 1. Words of Affirmation. 2. Acts of Service. 3. Gifts. 4. Quality Time. 5. Physical Touch.[14] Now, while everybody gives and receives love in all of these five ways from time to time, each of us are "stronger" in one or two of these areas than we are in the others. In order to effectively communicate and receive love, we need to know our primary love languages or else we may labor in vain.

For example, my mom loves hearing my brothers and me tell her, "I love you." I am sure that every mom would love to hear that from her kids. But I have learned over the years that if I really want to show my mom that I love her, there is something that resonates a lot more than words: cleaning. For my mom, words of affirmation are not the primary way that she receives love. Instead, if I really want to show my mom that I love her, I will voluntarily begin to wash the dishes or vacuum the living room or clean the bathroom. I can say "I love you" all day long, and she will love that, but if I start to demonstrate my love to her through acts of service, she will really feel loved. That being said, I have had a conversation with a girl who questioned whether or not someone loved her because all he would do is work to help her and provide for her instead of spending quality time with her. It was not that he did not love her; it was that he was communicating his love in one language, and she was expecting to receive love in a different language. Many problems in relationships arise because people are speaking to each other in a different language.

In Genesis 11 there is an amazing story. At this point in history all of humanity spoke the same language. Communication was as easy as it has ever been. There was a group of people that lived in a place called Shinar and they devised a plan. They decided that they were going to build a tower that reached to the heavens. Now, a tall tower is not, in and of itself, sinful. The problem was that the people wanted to build this tower to exalt themselves in the eyes of the world. They were building their tower because of pride. The story tells us that God observed what these people were doing and He was not happy. And then comes one of the most shocking statements in Scripture:

*The Lord said, "If as one people speaking the same language they have begun to do this, then nothing they plan to do will be impossible for them. Come, let us go down and confuse their language so they will not understand each other." –* Genesis 11:6-7

We often quote verses like Luke 1:37 and Philippians 4:13 about how nothing is impossible with God. That seems like an audacious statement already, but this one is even more unbelievable. God said that if these people would continue to speak the same language that "nothing they plan to do will be impossible for them." These people were not pursuing a godly goal. They were not attempting some great feat for the Kingdom of God. They were building something to oppose God and elevate themselves in the eyes of the world, and yet if their language had not been confused, nothing would have been impossible for them. Do you see the power that unity has? Do you see the importance of speaking the same language?

If the power of speaking the same language was true for a proud, defiant group of people in Babel, then how much more so is it true for us today in our relationships? If we are going to change this world for Jesus, then we need to learn to walk in unity and start speaking the same language.

## GOD'S LOVE LANGUAGE

So, what is God's love language? If speaking the right love language is important with our friends and with our family and with our spouse, how much more is it important for our communication and relationship with God? There are many people who call themselves Christians and who say that they "love" Jesus but as you have seen in this chapter, talk can be cheap. Thankfully for us, we don't have to ask God to fill out a love language test in order to know what His love language is; Jesus already told us 2,000 years ago. Here are the words of Jesus:

*"If you love me, keep my commands... Whoever has my commands and keeps them is the one who loves me. The one who loves me will be loved by my Father, and I too will love them and show myself to them."* – John 14:15, 21

There it is. Jesus' love language is keeping His commands. You won't find a verse in the Bible where Jesus tells us to say, "I love you." Jesus isn't interested in people *saying* they love Him; He wants people to *show* that they love Him. You don't show Jesus that you love Him by checking off the box that says you read your Bible today. You don't show Jesus that you love Him by praying before you eat. You don't even show Jesus that you love Him by saying, "I love you." Are those things wrong? Not at all. They're all good things that He enjoys, but they are not the demonstration of your love, they are the overflow of your love. You love Jesus with your actions. You love Jesus when your life lines up with His commands. There are many who think they love Jesus but are speaking an entirely different language.

Jesus says that our love to Him is demonstrated when we keep His commands. Now, Jesus made a lot of commands, so a natural follow-up question would be, "Which commands?" Jesus gave many commands and the reality is that not all of them apply to us. For example, just because Jesus told the Rich Young Ruler to go and sell everything he had does not mean that each of us is to do the same. Thus, priority must be given to those commands that are given to all disciples, and specifically to those commands that appear most frequently and are emphasized most emphatically. As I outlined in the opening chapter, there are few commands that fit this description better than the Great Commission. In other words, if you really want to tell Jesus that you love Him, then show it by fulfilling the Great Commission. Jesus isn't interested in lip service; He is interested in life service. I believe there is no greater motivation for evangelism and outreach than this truth: if you love Jesus, then you will fulfill the Great Commission.

## *SHEEP AND GOATS*

Jesus loved to communicate the Gospel through parable and stories. He often used metaphors to get His point across, and He did so right until the very end. In fact, Matthew records that just two days before the Passover Jesus told the last parable recorded in our Bible. It wasn't the Good Samaritan or the Parable of the Prodigal Son. It was the parable of the Sheep and the Goats. With the cross steadily on His mind, Jesus chose to share this story.

The parable of the Sheep and the Goats is a story about the end. This story focuses on the day when all of humanity shall gather before Christ on the great Day of Judgment. At that time, Jesus will divide everyone into two groups: one group—the sheep—will be on His right, while the other group—the goats—will be on His left. After dividing them, Matthew records the parable this way:

*"Then the King will say to those on his right, 'Come, you who are blessed by my Father; take your inheritance, the kingdom prepared for you since the creation of the world. For I was hungry and you gave me something to eat, I was thirsty and you gave me something to drink, I was a stranger and you invited me*

*in, I needed clothes and you clothed me, I was sick and you looked after me, I was in prison and you came to visit me.'"*

*"Then the righteous will answer him, 'Lord, when did we see you hungry and feed you, or thirsty and give you something to drink? When did we see you a stranger and invite you in, or needing clothes and clothe you? When did we see you sick or in prison and go to visit you?' "The King will reply, 'Truly I tell you, whatever you did for one of the least of these brothers and sisters of mine, you did for me.'"*

*"Then he will say to those on his left, 'Depart from me, you who are cursed, into the eternal fire prepared for the devil and his angels. For I was hungry and you gave me nothing to eat, I was thirsty and you gave me nothing to drink, I was a stranger and you did not invite me in, I needed clothes and you did not clothe me, I was sick and in prison and you did not look after me.'"*

*"They also will answer, 'Lord, when did we see you hungry or thirsty or a stranger or needing clothes or sick or in prison, and did not help you?' "He will reply, 'Truly I tell you, whatever you did not do for one of the least of these, you did not do for me.' "Then they will go away to eternal punishment, but the righteous to eternal life."* – Matthew 25:34-46

This story is one of the most startling and powerful stories in Scripture. Jesus speaks to the sheep, the believers, and gives them the best news: they are part of the eternal Kingdom of God. Jesus doesn't just stop at the "what," though; He also gives the "why." He says that the reason why the sheep are part of His family is because of how they treated Jesus. They visited Him, clothed Him, fed Him and helped Him in a variety of ways. Thankful, but perplexed, the sheep wonder when they did any of those things to Jesus! They never met Jesus in the flesh, at least not that they could remember. Surely they would have remembered giving Jesus food or clothes. Then Jesus explains, "Truly I tell you, whatever you did for one of the least of these brothers and sisters of mine, you did for me." Jesus opens their eyes (and our eyes as well) by showing them that the way we treat people is the way we treat Jesus. To love Jesus, is to love people. Each time they helped someone in need, even the very least of society, they were not just serving that individual; they were serving Jesus.

The other side has a very different fate, but it is based on the same criteria and situations. Jesus explains that the goats do not have Heaven to look forward to, but Hell instead. The reason for this is the same as it was for the sheep. Jesus was sick and cold and hungry and imprisoned, but while the sheep helped Christ, the goats never did. Desperately the goats retort, "Jesus, when did we see you? When did we ever meet you? If you ever came to me in need of help I gladly would have helped." And Jesus' response is familiar, "Truly I tell you, whatever you did not do for one of the least of these, you did not do for me."

This story gives us a picture of what it means to be a Christian. To love Christ is to love people. It is not just enough to say that you love Christ; you must show Him. But it is also not enough to simply serve and love Christ; we must love people. There is no separation between loving God and loving people.

The reality is this: there are many people today who claim Christ but who hate people. What Jesus is saying is that it is impossible for someone to love Jesus and hate people, both cannot be true. There are many Christians, even Christian leaders, who think they are living for Jesus and loving Jesus but who are not. If they walk in hatred and discord with the people around them, they can't love Jesus. Jesus echoes this by declaring:

*"Not everyone who says to me, 'Lord, Lord,' will enter the kingdom of heaven, but only the one who does the will of my Father who is in heaven. Many will say to me on that day, 'Lord, Lord, did we not prophesy in your name and in your name drive out demons and in your name perform many miracles?' Then I will tell them plainly, 'I never knew you. Away from me, you evildoers!'"* – Matthew 7:21-23

Jesus isn't talking about those in the world. Jesus isn't talking about only those who call themselves Christians. Jesus is talking about people who are involved. Flippant or halfhearted Christians who only go to church on Christmas and Easter are usually not prophesying and driving out demons. Most people would look at a man performing miracles as a strong Christian, but Jesus has a different standard. Jesus is far less concerned with miracles than He is with obedience. That was the whole reason why Saul was removed as king. Saul was interested in putting on a show for God (sacrifice), but God was interested in Saul's obedience. For this reason, God speaks through Samuel and says, "To obey is better than sacrifice" (1 Samuel 15:22).

The Apostle John dealt with a similar problem in the Church at Ephesus. This was a church that he helped to oversee as its spiritual father. He had influence over this congregation and he cared for them deeply. While away, false teachers had infiltrated the church and started preaching heresy. A byproduct of that heresy was that the people were only focusing on their love towards God with a disregard for their love for one another. It is within this context that John writes,

*"Whoever claims to love God yet hates a brother or sister is a liar. For whoever does not love their brother and sister, whom they have seen, cannot love God, whom they have not seen. And he has given us this command: Anyone who loves God must also love their brother and sister."* – 1 John 4:20-21

John lays it out loud and clear. It is *impossible*—not unlikely or improbable—it is impossible to love God and hate people. And yet, there are many who call themselves Christians who act like an angel toward God but act like the devil towards people. You can't be in London while you are also in Beijing. It's impossible. You can't be a man and a woman (regardless of what our culture says). It's impossible. And you can't love God and hate people.

### *A GOOD QUESTION*

I love asking people questions. I intentionally try to ask as many questions as I can because asking questions is how you learn. My favorite questions are questions about people. And when you ask people about themselves, they light up. Whether we want to admit it or not, we love talking about ourselves. So, I ask questions. Some of my questions are serious. Some are funny. Some are theological. Some are natural. Some are general. Some are specific. I run the gamut of questions (so, if you don't like talking, I'd suggest not trying to become my best friend).

Now, when it comes to asking questions, parents or teachers will usually say, "There is no such thing as a stupid question" or

"The only bad question is the one you never ask." I know they mean well, but let's be honest, they're wrong. There are stupid questions. There are bad questions. We've all heard them. For example, unless you are 100% sure, never ask a woman if she is pregnant. That is a stupid question that can easily turn out horribly wrong. There are many stupid questions, which is probably why I appreciate good questions.

Much of the Gospels center around questions: Jesus is asking His disciples questions or people are asking Jesus questions. Now, all of Jesus' questions were good, but some of the questions that people asked Jesus were not. Think about the question that James and John asked Jesus in Mark 10, "When you become king, can one of us sit on your right and the other one on your left?" Or what about the story I referenced earlier in the book when the disciples asked Jesus how He was going to feed the four thousand when He had just fed the five thousand two chapters earlier? Then there is the Sadducee in Mark 12 who asks Jesus this ridiculous hypothetical question about a woman who marries seven brothers in consecutive order and whose wife she will be in Heaven. Jesus answers his question well, but you can see His frustration with the bad question by ending His answer exclaiming, "You are badly mistaken!"

Immediately after that question, a teacher of the Law asks Jesus a question, "Of all the commandments, which is the most important?" I can just imagine Jesus sitting there and saying, "Finally! A good question." And indeed it is. What is the most important commandment? The entire Old Testament is filled with commands that God gave His people. The New Testament is filled with commands from Jesus and the apostles. But if you had to choose one command, which one is the most important?

*"The most important one," answered Jesus, "is this: 'Hear, O Israel: The Lord our God, the Lord is one. Love the Lord your God with all your heart and with all your soul and with all your mind and with all your strength.' The second is this: 'Love your neighbor as yourself.' There is no commandment greater than these."* – Mark 12:29-31

If you didn't already know the answer, and you had to guess what was the most important commandment, you may very well have said "Love God." That part was predictable. But what happens next was not. Jesus was specifically asked for the *best* commandment. Not one of the best; not a few of the best; but the *best*. Now, the word "best" is a superlative. In English we use adjectives to describe things but also to compare things, and there are three types of comparing adjectives: absolute, comparative and superlative. For example, if I say, "Italian food is good food," that is an absolute adjective. If I want to use a comparative adjective I might say, "Italian food is better than Indian food (I mean, isn't that obvious?)." But if I am using a superlative I would say, "Italian food is the best food." A superlative is the highest and the greatest. Nothing beats it. It stands alone at the top.

When the teacher of the Law asked Jesus His question he asked for the greatest commandment, the most important one. This was a superlative question. He wasn't interested in a good commandment. He wasn't interested in one of the best commands. He wanted to know the greatest commandment. By definition, there can only be one commandment that is the greatest, but Jesus broke the rules. He said what all of us would expect, "Love God," but He didn't stop there. He went on to say "…and love your neighbor as yourself." Jesus was not asked for the top two commandments. He was asked for the top, the best. So why did He break the rules and give two commandments?

When Jesus was asked this question, He didn't give one answer because He couldn't give one answer. There is a two-way tie for the greatest commandment. Or perhaps said better, there are two sides to the coin. The greatest commandment is to love God, but if you don't love people then you have violated the commandment to love God. And when you love people, you are obeying the greatest commandment to love God. Jesus gave two answers because they are really two parts to the same answer. You cannot separate the love that you have for God and the love that you have for people. If you love God, then you will love people.

Our love for God is an amazing motivation to fulfill the Great Commission, but so too is our love for people. If we truly love people, then we will be motivated to fulfill the Great Commission. I have spent much of my life traveling with our ministry, Wagner Ministries International, to some of the most remote areas of the world preaching the Gospel and I am often asked, "Why do you go to the places that you do? Wouldn't it be easier to stay at home? Isn't it dangerous over there? Don't you find all of the travel and time changes and diet restrictions to be exhausting? Why do you go?" My answer is always the same: people. Whatever struggles or discomfort I experience in my going is far outweighed by the motivation to love people. The reality is this: if you really, truly love people, then you will fulfill the Great Commission; you will tell them about Jesus. There is no greater gift that you can give someone than to introduce him/her to Jesus. There is nothing more valuable that you can do for people than to save them from eternity in Hell and instead help them to spend eternity in Heaven. If we truly want to love God and love people, then fulfilling the Great Commission must become one of our chief priorities. Let me illustrate this truth in the following story.

## THE CURE

It all started in a small town in northern Norway. At first, no one knew what was happening. One man came home from his day of work with an awful cough. The next day, though, his cough had become much worse and the man began to black out and become virtually paralyzed. Within 48 hours this man had undergone a host of painful and devastating symptoms until he finally died. Unfortunately, before doing so, four other citizens in the town somehow contracted what he had, also succumbing to the same fatal sickness. The town's doctors had no idea what the sickness was or how to stop it. They sent for help from the best doctors in Oslo, but those doctors were also unsuccessful in identifying or treating the sickness. The blood work for these patients was sent to some of the best doctors and scientists in the world but no one was able to help. Unfortunately, Norway was only the beginning.

Only a week after the first man's sickness began, the same sickness showed up in Buenos Aires, Argentina, Vijayawada, India and Saskatoon, Canada. This time the reach of the disease was greater and just two weeks from the first case the death toll had reached nearly 100 individuals. All the major medical and scientific agencies in the world began to focus their attention on this unknown virus, which had been labeled "Strain #1 Norway" or "S1N" for short. Of course, along with the rest of the world, S1N became the focus for the Centers for Disease Control (CDC) in Atlanta, Georgia.

Chris Tucker had only been working at the CDC for three months. He was thrilled to have gotten this job right after graduating from West Virginia University. Chris had never been the smartest kid and many times had to work very hard just to pass his classes. There were many who doubted him and multiple times his family had tried to talk him out of his chemistry major, arguing that he would never make it. Chris was determined, though, and landing this job at the CDC, even just as a simple lab analyst, was a huge success. When he received the job, though, his superiors made it clear to him that in this competitive market, even one misstep could cost him his job, and that in order to keep his job he would do well to stay in the background and keep quiet, simply doing what he was told.

One late night as Chris was finishing up his work and putting vials back in the freezer he saw some vials containing the infamous S1N virus. Despite his bosses' constant warnings to not do anything beyond his simple job description, Chris decided to take a closer look at S1N himself. Yes, he was just a lowly lab analyst but Chris had been devastated by the symptoms and deaths that this virus had caused all over the world and he at least wanted to take a look at it himself. Chris spent the entire night looking at the virus and working on a way to create an antivirus. By the next morning Chris could hardly believe it; he believed that he had created a cure for S1N! His joy and excitement, though, soon turned to fear and uncertainty as one of his superiors walked in on him to find him using the blood work from S1N. His superior was livid and immediately ordered Chris to return the blood work. Chris, though, explained to his boss that he believed he had found a cure to S1N. His boss would hear none of it. "Tucker," he said, "the best minds in the world are working on this and haven't been able to find a cure. Do you really think that you have? No way! Listen, Tucker, you better keep this quiet or you'll be applying at the local Wal-Mart real soon. I promise you, if you tell anyone about your crazy-eyed theory, I will personally see to it that you are fired and never work in the scientific field again."

Chris was so torn. Here he was with what he thought was a legitimate cure, a chance to help prevent deaths. But at the same time, he didn't want to throw away his career on a hunch. He had worked so hard to get where he was. Was he really ready to throw it all away? This would ruin his career and all he had worked for, not to mention how it would fuel his family's skepticism of him as a chemist or even a success. Chris decided that instead of risking his job, his livelihood, his comfort and what others would think of him, he would keep his secret to himself.

Three days later, S1N broke out again in Mombasa, Kenya killing 34 more people. Chris could hold it in no longer and went to one of the top scientists at the CDC with his antivirus. The scientist immediately went to work to test the virus and found that Chris had indeed created a cure for S1N. The antivirus was immediately shipped to Mombasa and treatments were started. The strain would continue to pop up in different parts of the world but then so too would Chris Tucker's antivirus and never again did someone die from S1N thanks to the CHRIS-T antivirus. When asked why Chris didn't come forward with the antivirus earlier, he responded, "I was afraid. I was afraid that I would be throwing away my career and all I had worked for. I was afraid that I wouldn't be able to make the same money and enjoy the same comforts. I was afraid of how other people, especially my family, would perceive me. But I was most afraid about what would happen if I didn't do anything at all, and that nightmare came to life when 34 people died in Mombasa. I knew then that I had to do the right thing, for I had the cure, the CHRIS-T antivirus, and without me countless others would die from S1N." Doing the right thing may involve sacrificing comfort and money and people's perception, but if you have the cure to save someone's life, then there is no alternative. To help is a necessity. To not help is a tragedy, the greatest tragedy of all.

While this story is fictional, it is incredibly helpful in demonstrating the position of the Church. We live in a world surrounded by people living with the most fatal virus in the universe: sin. Every other virus can only damage in this life, but sin's effect reverberates in eternity. Every Christian holds the cure for this virus, the only cure for this virus. And yet, so many of us go through our entire lives and never once share that cure with those who need it.

# HOW DO YOU SAY, "I LOVE YOU?"

The message of the Great Commission is of utmost importance because it is the only cure for the world in which we live. This is why it was at the forefront of Jesus' mind. If we truly love God, then we will be motivated to speak His love language by keeping His commands, and that most definitely includes the Great Commission. Not only that, but if we say we love God, then we will also love people. And if we truly love people, then we will care enough about them to give them the cure that they so desperately need. Our love for God and our love for people are two of the strongest motivations to fulfill the Great Commission.

## SATISFACTION GUARANTEED

Do you remember when you were eight years old? I don't remember everything but there are a few stories that stand out to me. I remember my youngest brother Luke being born and how excited I was to a big brother once again. I remember my parents taking us to Disneyland! We drove all the way from Canada to California. I'm sure there were times my parents regretted that decision, but I never did—going to Disneyland was incredible! I remember going to my first hockey game in Calgary, Alberta to see my beloved Calgary Flames. The things I remember about being eight years old are landmark events, things that had a big impact on me and ones that I remember very fondly. There is another eight-year old story that I remember well.

I forget the boy's name. We weren't great friends, but he lived in my neighborhood and we used to play hockey and ride bikes together. He was my friend. I have no idea how the conversation started but we started talking about Jesus. I told him about how I read my Bible every day and I went to church and that I loved Jesus. He was intrigued and kept asking me questions about it. I remember feeling a lump in my throat and a little nervous, but as we were talking I asked him, "Do you know Jesus?" "No," he replied. With butterflies I asked him, "Do you want to pray and ask Jesus into your heart?" He paused for a while and said, "I don't know. I need to think about it. Maybe next time." I was sad, but I was also happy that I had asked.

A few days later we were playing again and took a break from whatever we were doing. We were sitting underneath my basketball net on my driveway when he once again asked me about Jesus. I told him some stories from the Bible and how it was so wonderful having Jesus in my heart. I was nervous, but once again I asked him, "Would you like to ask Jesus to come into your heart?" He paused again, even longer this time, and then nodded his head, "Yes, I want to do that. What do I do?" I had never led anyone to Jesus before but I had seen my dad do it and heard him lead others in prayer and so I told him, "Repeat after me…Dear Jesus, I'm sorry for my sins. Please forgive me. Come and live inside my heart and be my best friend. I love you, Jesus. Amen." I opened my eyes and looked at him smiling. He was smiling too. "Did I do it?" "Yes," I told him, "Great job!"

We probably played a little while after that but when he left I ran into the house and told my parents what I had just done: I just led someone to Jesus! I was ecstatic! To this day I remember eight-year old Josh's feelings and it was wonderful! Almost 20 years later I can tell you that I have those same feelings every time I have the honor of praying with someone to receive Jesus. If you have ever led someone to Jesus, then you know what it feels like. It is one of the greatest feelings in the world to know that you played a part in helping someone come into the family of God. I am motivated to lead people to Jesus if only to experience that feeling. If you will devote your life to winning people to Jesus and fulfilling His Great Commission, you will experience joy in your life, as you've never known before. With the Great Commission, satisfaction is guaranteed!

# CHAPTER 4

# THE POWER OF ONE

## *THE 1%*

In the 14<sup>th</sup> century a war between France and England began that would last for one hundred years. England was winning and the war had devastated France. In addition to the war, France's economy and population had been completely demoralized as a result of the Black Plague. After almost one hundred years of fighting, France was beginning to lose hope. But in 1428 a teenage girl named Joan of Arc approached the French army to offer her services. God had called her to action and she had to be obedient. It was unheard of for an uneducated peasant woman to join the army, particularly one only seventeen years old, but she was determined to bring liberty to her nation and to obey the call of God. She was given an opportunity to fight and quickly climbed the ranks until she was leading four thousand men into battle...and winning. She was captured by the English only two years later and was burned at the stake. As she was tied to the stake her one request was for a cross to be positioned in front of her, and history records that the last word she ever spoke was "Jesus." This seemed like a defeat but her life and death inspired the French people and twenty-two years later, France won the war, due in large part to the military tactics inspired by Joan of Arc. One woman's actions inspired a nation and brought victory in a war that had lasted a century.[15]

I was reading a book recently when a certain statement stopped me in my tracks. The book stated that the vast majority of our world's history has been determined by only 1% of humanity.[16] History tells "us that 1% of a group of people has been able to impact the other 99% over and over again."[17] Think about that: 1% of people have impacted the lives of the other 99%! We often limit ourselves by thinking that one person cannot affect change, and yet history has shown us the value that one person's life can have.

The pages of history books are filled with the stories of ordinary men and women who did extraordinary things. The greatest discoveries and exploits and moments of history are not achieved by superheroes; they are achieved when a regular person does something bigger than himself. In fact, many times it is not organizations or countries or kingdoms that shape history; it is individuals. The Greek empire controlled the whole known world only when Alexander the Great came into power. By the age of 30 he was literally the king of the world. But within only a few years of his death, the Greek empire had divided and started its decline. Alexander the Great was part of the 1%.

Nazi Germany was moving at what seemed to be an unstoppable pace, conquering one European country after another. For years Britain had done nothing, but when Winston Churchill stepped into office and stood up against the Nazis, so began the decline of the Third Reich and the end of World War II. Winston Churchill was part of the 1%.

Our world has been shaped by the lives of the 1% because individuals hold power. One person can set the course for an entire nation. One person can create the landscape for an entire environment. One person can shift the trajectory of an entire society. No one, of course, has done this more than Jesus Christ. Jesus is the principal character in the drama of history. When He came, He turned the world upside down. His life and death is the basis for our calendar. His life and death is the central story for the best-selling book in history. His followers outnumber any country or movement in human history. Joan of Arc and Alexander the Great and Winston Churchill may be part of the 1%, but Jesus is in His own demographic, not of 1% but of simply one!

Jesus was the most famous and popular man on the planet. Crowds would travel for days to hear Him speak. The Jewish people wanted to crown Him as King. Little did they know that He was already King, having come from Heaven as the Son of God. He had every reason and excuse to act better than everyone else. If anyone had justification to be proud and self-promoting, it would have been Jesus. Yet, what is so amazing about Jesus is that despite His position and His ontology, He was the humblest of all humanity. Jesus never took advantage of His deity; instead He emptied Himself to take the position of a servant (Philippians 2:5-8). In fact, Jesus explains quite clearly to His disciples that His role on earth, the reason why He came, was to serve humanity (Mark 10:45). And Jesus spent His entire life fulfilling that mission. Wherever He went, He improved the situation. Whenever He spoke, His words brought life. Whomever He encountered, He brought value to their lives. And Jesus, more than anyone else demonstrated the intrinsic value of each person. Jesus never underestimated the power of one person, because He knew the impact that one person could have, and He knew the value that one person was worth.

## CROSS THE LAKE

When you read the Gospels you quickly see what was important to Jesus. Jesus spent His time and effort reaching people. Apart from His solitary time in prayer with His Father, He was always with people. He taught His disciples. He ate with tax collectors and sinners. He redeemed prostitutes. He healed the sick. He raised the dead. He was always focused on people. And He would go to great lengths in order to reach people.

Mark tells a story about Jesus that so clearly demonstrates the value that Jesus placed on even one person's life. The story begins in the end of chapter 4 where Jesus says to His disciples, "Let's go over to the other side of the lake." Mark didn't mention why Jesus wanted to go, only that He did. So Jesus and disciples start out to cross the lake. On the way a huge storm arrives. This storm was so severe that the disciples, many of which were professional fishermen, came to Jesus terrified and asked, "Teacher, don't you care if we drown?" Jesus then rebukes the wind and the waves and they continue on their way across the lake.

When they reached the other side of the lake they were immediately met by a demon-possessed man. Mark explains that this man lived outside the city in the tombs because when he was chained in the city he would break the chains apart and cause terror in the town. Since no one could control him he was put outside the city where "night and day among the tombs and in the hills he would cry out and cut himself with stones" (Mark 5:5). This man was tormented.

He comes up to Jesus and introduces himself as Legion. The word "legion" was a title given to a large number in the Roman army at the time of Christ. It represented a group of Roman soldiers that numbered in the thousands.[18] In other words, this was a man who was possessed by many demons, perhaps thousands of demons (this is further demonstrated by the fact that when Jesus cast out the demons they went into a herd of 2,000 pigs that ran off the cliff and were drowned). Needless to say, this man was being terrorized by a large number of evil spirits, but Jesus changed that. With a word, He cast out the demons and the man was instantly freed!

Now, you would think that the people in the town would have been happy that this man had been set free but instead they were too selfish and only lamented the fact that they had lost their pigs. They cared more about animals than people (which, sadly happens a whole lot in our world today too). Mark tells us that the people came and begged Jesus to leave their region. In fact, the Greek word that Mark uses, *parakaleo*, means "to implore" or "to urge."[19] The people were basically forcing Jesus to leave them. They wanted nothing to do with Him.

As Jesus was stepping back into the same boat that He had just gotten out of only a few minutes earlier, Legion saw the way that the people were treating Jesus and asked if he could leave with Jesus too. It makes sense. These people wanted nothing to do with him before, and now they were urging his healer to leave the area. Why should he expect for them to treat him well now? So, he asked to join Jesus and travel across the lake with him. But the Bible says:

*Jesus did not let him, but said, "Go home to your own people and tell them how much the Lord has done for you, and how he has had mercy on you." So the man went away and began to tell in the Decapolis how much Jesus had done for him. And all the people were amazed. When Jesus had again crossed over by boat to the other side of the lake, a large crowd gathered around him while he was by the lake.* – Mark 5:19-21

Instead of allowing the man to go with him, Jesus sent him back to his family and his community to be an evangelist to them. The Bible says that he went around the Decapolis sharing his testimony. The Decapolis was a region of ten cities (*deca*-ten, *polis*-city) in Eastern Israel. This was a large area for the man to cover but Christ had commissioned him to the Decapolis, just as he has commissioned us to this world. This story ends with Mark stating, "When Jesus had again crossed over by boat to the other side of the lake..." I don't want you to miss the significance of this statement.

If you will think back to the beginning of this story, it started out with Jesus getting in the boat and traveling through a potentially fatal storm to cross the lake. He gets to the other side, reaches only one person, Legion, and then gets in the boat and travels back to where he was initially. Jesus risked his life, spent hours each way to cross the lake to only reach one person. For most of us, it is "too much" to cross the office to share Jesus with our coworker. For most of us, it is "too much" to cross the street and share Jesus with our neighbor. For most of us, it is "too much" to even cross the living room and share Jesus with our family members! But Jesus went through so very much just to reach one person. If Jesus put that much time and effort and priority into reaching one person, don't you think we should do the same? Will you begin to cross the lake to reach people?

## THE RIPPLE EFFECT

The story of Legion helps to demonstrate the *value* of reaching one person while the story of the woman at the well demonstrates the *effect* of reaching one person. We will revisit this story in more depth next chapter but I want you to see the effect that reaching even one person can have on a family, a community and, in fact, the world.

In John 4 Jesus meets a woman at the well. He engages her in conversation and He learns that she is living in immorality. More specifically, this woman has had five different husbands and is currently living with someone who is not her husband. Jesus offers her the chance to drink of the living water and in that moment at the well, she accepts Christ and is marked forever by her encounter with living water. The story is only half over there, though. John continues:

*Then, leaving her water jar, the woman went back to the town and said to the people, "Come, see a man who told me everything I ever did. Could this be the Messiah?" They came out of the town and made their way toward him...Many of the Samaritans from that town believed in him because of the woman's testimony, "He told me everything I ever did." So when the Samaritans came to him, they urged him to stay with them, and he stayed two days. And because of his words many more became believers. They said to the woman, "We no longer believe just because of what you said; now we have heard for ourselves, and we know that this man really is the Savior of the world." –* John 4:28-30, 39-42

Jesus reached one woman, but the effect of that encounter did not stop with the woman. John tells us that she returned to her town and started calling the town together, "Hey, everyone, listen! I have met someone who has told me everything I ever did. Let me tell you what happened." As the woman began to share her testimony, look at what the Bible says, "Many of the Samaritans from that town believed in him because of the <u>woman's testimony</u>" (emphasis added). Her life had a ripple effect. The people believed in Jesus initially without having ever heard or even met Jesus. Their belief was based solely on this new believer's witness. She then introduced them to Jesus and the ripple effect continued, for John says that Jesus' words caused many more to become believers. Do you see the impact? Jesus took the time to invest in one person, but that person was then responsible for helping many more come into the family of God! Jesus would cross the lake to reach just one person because one person is of infinite worth. But Jesus would also cross the lake to reach one person because He knows the ripple effect that it can create. None of us live in a vacuum and when someone has a true experience with Jesus, it should cause him to want to tell everyone he meets about Jesus. Do not underestimate the power of one.

## *THE GUNSMITH MISSIONARY*

Towards the beginning of the 20ᵗʰ century a man named Luis Graf was living in America. He had just retired from his lifelong profession as a gunsmith when he heard the call of God to travel to Germany as a missionary. Luis obeyed and arrived in Germany. He rented a car and was driving through the countryside when his car broke down in a small village called Trunz, definitely not his desired destination. As soon as he arrived in Trunz, though, the Lord spoke to Him and told him he had an opportunity to witness in this little village. He began to witness to the mechanic but the mechanic didn't want to listen. He stopped for a while but then the Holy Spirit directed him to ask the mechanic, "Is there anyone sick in the village?" "Why?" he asked, "are you a doctor?" "No," Luis replied, "but if I pray for a sick person and he is healed, will you listen to my message?" He laughed and said, "Oh yes, we will allow you," all the while thinking he wouldn't have to listen to this crazy preacher because he had a man named August in mind.

August was plagued with gout and rheumatism, a pain that had plagued him for years. He would often cry out so loudly during the night that the whole town could hear him. He had traveled to many of the best doctors and tried all types of medicine but nothing helped. But as Luis entered August's home, he laid his hands on August and he was immediately healed. This man who had been bedridden for years now stood up and hugged his wife who was crying tears of joy. He grabbed his children, who for the first time in as long as they could remember saw their father without pain. After the celebration Luis prayed with August and his family to receive Jesus and his whole family was saved.

Eventually Luis' car was fixed and he continued on his way. The Lord used him at different points throughout his time in Germany but nothing incredibly fantastic. He returned home to America, not having had much success but always grateful for the opportunity to lead August and his family to the Lord. What Luis could not have known then, or on this side of eternity, is that August would continue to raise his family in the ways of the Lord. One of August's sons would attend seminary and become a pastor in the

Lutheran church. That son would then have children of his own who grew up to love the Lord, and one of his sons (one of August's grandsons) felt the call of God to evangelize in Africa. That young man, the grandson of August, is a man now known all over the world as Reinhard Bonnke.

Reinhard Bonnke has led more people to Jesus face to face than any other human who has ever lived. Over 70 million people have come to Christ at Bonnke's crusades and his ministry continues to reach millions today. None of the 70 million people saved through Bonnke's ministry would have been saved without the Christian heritage that started with Bonnke's grandfather, August. But August would have never been saved if not for Luis' obedience to the call of God. Because Luis was willing to cross the lake and reach even one person, 70 million people came to know the Lord. I like to think that there is a massive line in Heaven of people waiting to shake Luis' hand and thank him for reaching the one, because his obedience led to their salvation.

## THE REST OF THE STORY

Think back to the story of Legion. The story ends with Jesus commissioning Legion to return home and share his testimony. Legion does that very thing, and Mark records that he traveled around the entire Decapolis preaching the Gospel. This was a hard place to minister. The people in this region wanted nothing to do with Jesus. They had urged Jesus to leave their region the last time that He was there. Despite the opposition he would have faced, Legion faithfully shared his testimony all across the region.

Now, the Bible never again mentions Legion. We don't know what happened to him. We never hear about him again; but we do hear about the Decapolis, that region that had previously rejected Jesus and begged Him to leave. Two chapters later Mark writes this:

*Then Jesus left the vicinity of Tyre and went through Sidon, down to the Sea of Galilee and into the region of the Decapolis. There some people brought to him a man who was deaf and could hardly talk, and they begged Jesus to place his hand on him. After he took him aside, away from the crowd, Jesus put his fingers into the man's ears. Then he spit and touched the man's tongue. He looked up to heaven and with a deep sigh said to him, "Ephphatha!" (which means "Be opened!"). At this, the man's ears were opened, his tongue was loosened and he began to speak plainly. Jesus commanded them not to tell anyone. But the more he did so, the more they kept talking about it. People were overwhelmed with amazement. "He has done everything well," they said. "He even makes the deaf hear and the mute speak."* – Mark 7:31-37

Did you notice a difference? This story takes place in the same Decapolis that only two chapters earlier Jesus had visited in the story of Legion, and the responses could not have been more different. Whereas before, the people of the Decapolis had *begged* Jesus to leave, wanting nothing to do with Him, now the people actually came to Jesus and *begged* Him to stay and heal this man. In fact, in both stories Mark uses the exact same Greek word (*parakaleo*) to describe the people of the Decapolis. In Mark 5 the people were begging Jesus to leave, but in Mark 7 they were begging Jesus to heal and the end of the passage says that they were "overwhelmed with amazement" and couldn't help but share about what Jesus had done.

What's the difference? What changed in between chapters 5 and 7? I have to think that it was the witness of Legion. When Jesus left Legion, Mark tells us that he became an evangelist to his entire region and one man completely changed the spiritual landscape for the whole region. This is the effect of reaching one person. The day Jesus crossed the lake and saved Legion's life, hundreds and thousands of other lives were changed as well. Jesus didn't have the time to travel across the Decapolis ministering the Gospel; He had a job to accomplish on the other side of the lake, but He knew that if He could reach one person, then the potential was there to reach the entire region. Regional transformation occurred because Jesus understood the power of one.

Luis crossed the lake to reach August. Jesus crossed the lake to reach the woman at the well. Jesus crossed the lake to reach Legion. I pray that today you would see the value and impact of reaching even one person. If we try to fix all of the world's problems and save every person we meet, we will be overwhelmed and probably do nothing. But if we will recognize the significance of

53

the power of one, then it will motivate us to cross our own lakes and reach the one. You have no idea who you may be ministering to and the generational and global effect that your testimony may have. Lord, give us boldness to cross the lake and reach the world around us.

# CHAPTER 5

# FROM THEORY TO REALITY

### *THE HUNGER GAMES*

I can't cook. I have a lot of gifts and passions but cooking is not one of them. I mean, sure, I can make a sandwich and I can make myself an omelet, but my cooking knowledge and ability is highly limited. Beyond that, I don't enjoy it. Any time I have to cook I am constantly nervous. I am paranoid at every step. I triple check every instruction to make sure I didn't just ruin the meal. And what takes most people 30 minutes will take me well over an hour. I'm just not a good cook.

I do, however, know the reason for this: I'm spoiled. Growing up, my mom was a miracle worker in the kitchen (with four boys I'm sure there were days where my mom felt like she never stopped cooking). She made 99% of my meals growing up. I never had to worry about what to eat because mom would take care of it. I never had to worry if I would like it because mom didn't know how to make a bad meal. I didn't learn because I didn't have to. And my thought process went something like this, "I could work for decades and still not cook as well as my mom. She's the pro. She's been doing this for years. Plus, for as often as mom cooks, she sure must love it. I would hate to deprive her of that privilege."

So, having enjoyed the luxuries of a great cook, naturally I prayed for the same thing for my wife and, true to His word, God gave me the desires of my heart (Psalm 37:4). My wife, Michelle, is an excellent cook! There was no downgrade when I got married. My mom passed the torch well to Michelle. We have what I consider to be a great cooking system in our marriage: Michelle loves to cook and I love to eat; it's a win-win situation.

As you can see, I've been spoiled, and for this reason, I am a horrible cook and avoid it like the plague. However, there are those rare times when Michelle is working late or out of town and I am put in the undesirable position of having to cook. Whenever this happens, I try to make sure that I know ahead of time so that Michelle can write out the directions for me word-for-word, because without some instructions I am completely lost. For example, if Michelle just called me one day and said, "Josh, I need you to make enchiladas," I wouldn't have the slightest idea of where to begin. I would be completely lost without some sort of direction or step-by-step instructions.

In my experience I have found that most people feel the same way about evangelism as I do about cooking—it's unnatural, it's intimidating and they don't have the slightest idea of where or how to begin. I certainly don't have all the answers, and there is no "one size fits all" process for witnessing, but I would like to at least try to give you some instructions for the recipe of witnessing, so that you would be motivated to move evangelism from theory to reality.

## *KEEP IT SIMPLE*

Growing up my dad always told me that the smartest people in the world were not the ones who sounded smart or who used huge words and confusing concepts. The truly intelligent people are the ones who are able to take difficult concepts and explain them in such a way that even a child can understand. Those are the true geniuses. When it comes to geniuses, Jesus is at the top of the list. Jesus was an expert at communicating the truth of the Gospel in a way that even children could understand. This was the reason He spoke in parables. Instead of describing the Kingdom of God or the heart of the Father in philosophical or abstract terms, Jesus told stories.

One of the common mistakes that people often make when it comes to witnessing is that they overcomplicate things or try to bite off more than they can chew. Witnessing should not be an overly complicated event. You do not need to discuss the intricacies of the incarnation or the mystery of the Trinity in order to witness. If those subjects arise, then address them, but most people aren't wrestling with those questions when they are considering Christ, so don't muddy the waters for them.

One of the great evangelistic ministries in America the past few decades is Campus Crusade for Christ (now known as CRU), founded by Dr. Bill Bright. In 1951 Bright founded this ministry to specifically evangelize on university campuses around the world.[20] He saw a need for evangelism and discipleship on the university campuses because the next generation was being inundated at universities with liberal, secular worldviews that run contrary to the Word of God. In an effort to combat the secularization of the upcoming generation, Bright set out on a mission to win campuses for Jesus. Now, when ministering to University students, you often deal with people who are critical, intellectual and definitely wary of Christianity. So Bright had to come up with what he felt was an effective way of ministering to such an audience. In doing so, and after trying a multiplicity of approaches, you might be surprised by what he chose. He didn't focus on creationism v. evolution. He didn't debate the evidence for God. He didn't compare Jesus to other revolutionaries throughout history. Instead, he took a very simple, yet (what proved to be) highly effective approach. He installed an evangelistic model called the "Four Spiritual Laws," and decades later, this is still one of the most effective means of witnessing. When looking to witness, the Four Spiritual Laws provide you with a great structure of what to cover. These laws are:

1. God loves you and has a wonderful plan for your life (John 3:16; John 10:10).

2. Man is sinful and separated from God. Therefore, he cannot know and experience God's love and plan for his life (Romans 3:23; Romans 6:23).

3. Jesus Christ is God's only provision for man's sin. Through Him you can know and experience God's love and plan for your life (Romans 5:8; John 14:6).

4. We must individually receive Jesus Christ as Savior and Lord; then we can know and experience God's love and plan for our lives (John 1:12; Ephesians 2:8-9; Romans 10:9).

In reality, these laws are about as simplistic an approach as there is in sharing the Gospel, and yet, these laws have helped millions come to know the Lord! One of Christ's many problems with the Teachers of the Law was that they had taken the simple commandments of God and made them severely more difficult. The Old Testament contains 613 commandments that God gave to the Jewish people, but to narrow such a large number down God gave the people the very simple 10 commandments. The Pharisees, though, were not content with the 613 commandments and kept adding to the laws. What started out as clarification for the Old Testament Laws turned into a whole new set of laws found in what is called the Midrash. The Midrash contains literally thousands of additional laws. For example, whereas God made one commandment to not work on the Sabbath, the "Jewish scholars created 39 separate categories of what 'work' means, and within those 39 categories there are many sub-categories"[21] that contain thousands of additional rules, "including how many steps you can take, and how many letters you can write on the Sabbath."[22] It was exhausting.

By the time that Jesus arrived, nobody but the religious leaders could keep track of the intricacies of the law, and trying to follow all of the rules was exhausting. What was Jesus' response? "Instead of thousands of commandments, and even instead of 10 commandments, let's just boil it down to two commandments: Love God and Love People." Jesus preached a simple Gospel, and theologians have spent 2,000 years trying to complicate it. There are certainly audiences where a more academic or heady approach is necessary, but by and large, the best approach is a simple approach. Sometimes less is more.

*TESTIMONY TIME*

When witnessing, it is essential to share the story of Christ and of the Bible, but often the most effective story to tell is your story. People can argue and debate the tenets of the Gospel all day long, but it is difficult to argue with a personal encounter. People like stories, and they like authenticity. When you share your testimony it brings validity to what you say. This isn't hypothesis or conjecture; this is reality. So, if sharing your testimony is key to witnessing it is important for you to know how to share your testimony. Simply put, your testimony is your story. My dad has a great way of helping to create a testimony by simply asking yourself these three questions:

1. What was your life like before Jesus?
2. What event brought you to Jesus (your conversion story)?
3. What has your life been like since Jesus?

Your testimony has power. When Jesus saved you He washed away your sins but He didn't wash away your past. When you accepted Christ your mind was not erased of your life before Christ. You can still remember your past, and that is because the value of your salvation is tied to the depravity of your sinfulness. You were not saved from a life of happiness, joy, peace and perfection. If you were, then the need for salvation would be nonexistent. The reason why we need Jesus is because of what our life was like without Jesus. There is value in remembering where you came from, because it makes you so much more grateful for where you are. Your testimony is the story of Jesus rescuing you from your past and giving you a hope and a dream for the future.

When you share your testimony, walls come down. People that may have once been apprehensive or even critical of you will begin to change as they hear your story. When you become vulnerable enough to share your yesterday, people will become vulnerable with you to share their today. Perhaps the most famous song in Christianity is John Newton's hymn *Amazing Grace.* I love that hymn because it shares a testimony:

*Amazing Grace, how sweet the sound,*
*That saved a wretch like me.*
*I once was lost, but now am found,*
*Was blind but now I see.*

The reason why the grace is so amazing is because it saved a wretch like me. If we only sing of God's amazing grace, but never acknowledge what that grace did in our own lives, we render useless the grace of God. Whenever I share my testimony I am always reminded of God's grace, and I become thankful and grateful all over again.

I was ministering at a youth camp in McAllen, Texas a year ago. Most of the students lived in Mexico but had come to camp in Texas. On the final night of the camp I shared my testimony. I was not rescued from a life of alcoholism and I've never been in a gang (the thought of me being in a gang is laughable), but I certainly have my own story. I grew up in a great home with godly parents and I knew what was right. But, as with many teenagers these days, when I was 12 years old I became interested in pornography. What started out as interest soon turned into an addiction and for two years I struggled with this sin. I knew it was wrong, and I unsuccessfully tried many times to stop on my own, but it was only until one day when my parents found out that everything changed. I repented for my sins and my parents helped me to renew my mind and conquer my sin. I was not perfect overnight, and it was definitely a process of victory, but by the grace of God I am not the same person I was at 14 years old.

After sharing my testimony, I transitioned to the end of the service and asked students to respond to the message. Dozens of students came to the front and bowed at the altar as they gave their lives to Jesus. I was making my way throughout the crowd praying for students when the Lord directed me to a girl in the back of the room. One of the senior girls was standing alone. She was a fun, popular girl and I had gotten to know her throughout the week. I went back to her and asked, "I'd like to pray for you. What's going on?" As soon as the words left my mouth she began to weep, and then she said, "For three years I have struggled with a porn addiction. I have tried to stop many times but it has never worked. I have felt so horrible I have felt so dirty. I have felt so ashamed. For three years, I have kept this sin a secret. I have never told anyone about this... until now. But when you shared your testimony and that you had gone through the same thing that I was going through, you gave me hope. I realized that if God could free you then He could free me and tonight I want to be free." I was overcome by the goodness of God, that He would allow me to be a part of this girl's story. We talked and prayed. I got her connected with one of the female leaders so that she could have accountability. I recently spoke with this girl on Facebook and asked her how she was doing. She told me that she is the happiest she has ever been and the Lord is helping her to win her battle for purity.

As I reflect on that story I thank God that He has the ability to take all things, even my past sin, and turn them into good, for the saving of lives (Genesis 50:20; Romans 8:28). As you think about that story, what caused her to confess her secret sin after three years of holding it in? It wasn't the worship. It wasn't the prayers. It wasn't the Bible stories. It wasn't even my message. It was my testimony. Revelation 12:11 declares that we triumph over the enemy by the "blood of the Lamb, and the word of our testimony." Your testimony is incredibly powerful because:

1. It reminds you of the goodness of God in your life. When you feel discouraged about your day, reflect on your testimony to see from where the Lord has taken you. There is a saying you may have heard in church that says, "I'm not where I want to be, but thank God I'm not where I used to be." Your testimony will cause you to thank God that you're not where you used to be.

2. It reminds the devil of how he has been defeated in your life. Anytime the enemy tries to come against you and bring condemnation and shame in your life, remind him that because Jesus lives in you, he has already been defeated in your life. A quote I love says, "When the devil tries to remind you of his past, you remind him of his future."

3. It provides encouragement to those to whom you are ministering. When you become vulnerable, others will become vulnerable. Your testimony will open doors of opportunity to witness, just as it did for me at that youth camp in McAllen, Texas.

4. It is a weapon that overcomes the attacks of the enemy (Rev. 12:11). When you feel discouraged or tempted use your testimony to overcome the enemy. The devil hates hearing your testimony because it reminds him of how he lost the battle over you.

Your testimony is a weapon, but as with any weapon, it is only useful when it is used. A sword that stays in its scabbard will never defeat an army. A spear that is left at home will do you no good on the battlefield. And your testimony will never help anyone unless you begin to use it.

## THE SAMARITAN WOMAN

At this point, many of you are probably thinking, "Joshua, I understand. Witnessing is a simple task, not a complicated one. I need to share my testimony. But how do I actually *do* this? Am I supposed to just corner someone at Wal-Mart and say, 'Listen to my testimony?'" For the record, I do not suggest cornering someone at Wal-Mart to share your testimony. There is no foolproof, 100% perfect way to witness to someone. Each person and each situation is different, but as with everything, Jesus is our perfect example and in the story of the Samaritan Woman in John 4 He provides us with a great step-by-step process on how to share our faith.

*Now he had to go through Samaria. So he came to a town in Samaria called Sychar, near the plot of ground Jacob had given to his son Joseph. Jacob's well was there, and Jesus, tired as he was from the journey, sat down by the well. It was about noon. When a Samaritan woman came to draw water, Jesus said to her, "Will you give me a drink?" (His disciples had gone into the town to buy food.)*

*The Samaritan woman said to him, "You are a Jew and I am a Samaritan woman. How can you ask me for a drink?" (For Jews do not associate with Samaritans). Jesus answered her, "If you knew the gift of God and who it is that asks you for a drink, you would have asked him and he would have given you living water." "Sir," the woman said, "you have nothing to draw with and the well is deep. Where can you get this living water? Are you greater than our father Jacob, who gave us the well and drank from it himself, as did also his sons and his livestock?" Jesus answered, "Everyone who drinks this water will be thirsty again, but whoever drinks the water I give them will never thirst. Indeed, the water I give them will become in them a spring of water welling up to eternal life."*

*The woman said to him, "Sir, give me this water so that I won't get thirsty and have to keep coming here to draw water." He told her, "Go, call your husband and come back." "I have no husband," she replied. Jesus said to her, "You are right when you say you have no husband. The fact is, you have had five husbands, and the man you now have is not your husband. What you have just said is quite true." "Sir," the woman said, "I can see that you are a prophet.*

*Our ancestors worshiped on this mountain, but you Jews claim that the place where we must worship is in Jerusalem." "Woman," Jesus replied, "believe me, a time is coming when you will worship the Father neither on this mountain nor in Jerusalem. You Samaritans worship what you do not know; we worship what we do know, for salvation is from the Jews. Yet a time is coming and has now come when the true worshipers will worship the Father in the Spirit and in truth, for they are the kind of worshipers the Father seeks. God is spirit, and his worshipers must worship in the Spirit and in truth." The woman said, "I know that Messiah" (called Christ) "is coming. When he comes, he will explain everything to us." Then Jesus declared, "I, the one speaking to you—I am he."* – John 4:4-26

I referenced this story earlier and explained that the rest of the story is that this woman returns to her hometown and shares her experience. The people in the town believe in Jesus because of the woman's testimony and they come out to meet Jesus as well. Salvation came to many in Sychar because of this encounter with the woman. In this story Jesus provides us with a step-by-step model of how to share your faith with someone.

1. Pay Attention (4:6). The story begins with Jesus alone at the well and some translations say it was at the "sixth hour" while others (such as the one above) say it was at noon. This is not a contradiction. Jewish time was different than our time. The Jews didn't begin the first hour of the day at midnight, as we do. Instead, they began at sunrise, or 6 am. So, when John says that it was the sixth hour, he means that it was the sixth hour from 6 am, thus noon. Now, you may be asking yourself, "What does this have to do with anything?"

One of the principles that I learned while studying hermeneutics at Oral Roberts University was that "there is no unimportant information."[23] If the author of the book put it in his original manuscript then it must be important considering how expensive and time consuming writing a document as long as the Gospel of John would have been. If that's the case, then the logical question is, "What is so important about this story happening at noon?" The reason why John mentions this is because no one draws water at noon. Israel is in the Middle East and the desert isn't too cool at noon. "Usually, the town well was outside the town walls, and the women would go to draw water in the early morning or the evening when it was cool."[24] Going in the morning gave the women the water they would need for the day and going again at night would give them enough water to last the family through the night. But no one drew water at noon. So why was this woman? As we will find out, this woman was an outcast. She had had five husbands in a culture that condemned divorce and was currently sleeping with someone who wasn't her husband. The women of the town wanted nothing to do with her and probably shamed her whenever she would draw water with the rest of them. So she would have "went to the well at off-peak times to avoid the scorn and ridicule of the other women of the town."[25]

The first step in witnessing is to simply pay attention to your surroundings. You didn't have to be a rocket scientist to figure out that this woman was an outcast. No normal woman would draw water at noon. Jesus must have been aware that this woman was an outcast, not simply because He was God but because He was observant. Oftentimes we miss opportunities to witness or minister not because we are living in sin or because we don't want to, but many times it is because we are simply not paying attention to the situation around us. You have to be available if you want to be used. Pay attention. Stay alert. I wonder how many times I have missed an opportunity to witness because I was looking at my phone or because I was listening to music. When you intentionally pay attention, you will be amazed at the things you begin to notice.

2. Start a conversation (4:7). Jesus' entry point into the woman's life was not, "You're a sinner on your way to Hell." It wasn't, "Can I tell you the good news?" It was simply, "Could I have a glass of water?" When interacting with a complete stranger, find something natural to start a conversation about. Don't go for the jugular with your first words; just start a conversation. When I fly I try to start a conversation with the person sitting next to me. It's nothing spiritual, it's usually just, "Where are you headed? Where is 'home' for you?" Learn to simply talk to people as Jesus did.

3. Don't judge (4:7-9). If I asked most people for a drink of water, the expected response would probably be that they would give me a drink of water. But when Jesus asked the Samaritan woman her response was, "You are a Jew and I am a Samaritan woman. How can

you ask me for a drink?" The woman was shocked that a Jew would ask a Samaritan for a drink because "Jews wouldn't drink from the same vessels as Samaritans."[26] Samaritans were outcasts among Jews. They were half Jewish and half gentile. The Jews didn't like them because they were half gentile, but the gentiles didn't like that they were half Jewish. So she was shocked when Jesus asked her for a drink. Not only was she a Samaritan but she was also a woman. In this male dominated society, men rarely respected women. Women were seen as second-rate. And not only was she a Samaritan and a woman, but she also clearly had a checkered past, evidenced by the fact that she was drawing water at noon. For any or all of these reasons the woman was probably expecting for Jesus to judge her. Instead Jesus extended love and equality towards the woman as He asked her for a drink. When you witness, don't do anything that would cause the other person to feel inferior or judged. If Jesus didn't, we shouldn't either.

4. Listen to the person (4:9). This is valuable advice in any type of communication, but especially true in the context of witnessing. We often go into a situation with our own preexisting agenda. We have already mapped out how we want our conversation to go, but each encounter is different and we need to read the situation. The best way to do this is by listening. How does the other person respond? Follow their lead; don't push against them. Jesus started a conversation and the woman was immediately ready for a conversation, a real conversation. Jesus may have initially thought that He would engage in more small talk first but this lady wasted no time in getting deep by saying, "You are a Jew and I am a Samaritan woman. How can you ask me for a drink?" Jesus, actively listening, followed her lead.

5. Turn the conversation (4:10). This woman helped along the process but there came a point where Jesus turned the conversation from secular, natural things to spiritual things. Jesus took what they were naturally talking about—water—and turned the conversation towards God—living water. Now, this can get pretty corny pretty fast if you aren't careful. For example, I am not saying a conversation on the plane should go like this: "Where are you headed?" you ask. "Houston," your neighbor replies. You follow up, "Cool, is that your home?" "Yes," he responds. "So you're heading

home to Houston right now. What about when you die? Where will you be headed then? Where is your eternal home?" As I said, that is *not* the way to turn a conversation. Don't get weird about it, but the point is that there comes a time when you must be willing to turn the conversation towards spiritual things. Sometimes, depending on the person and the situation, they may do it, but usually you will have to turn the conversation yourself.

6. Listen to the Holy Spirit (4:16-18). When we read Jesus' stories it is easy to see them as fictional, or far-reaching, but Jesus did what He did not because He was God but rather because He walked in the power and presence of the Holy Spirit, which is why we can model our lives after Him. While talking, the Holy Spirit supernaturally tells Jesus (and equally important, Jesus listens and obeys) to ask about the woman's husband. This is a word of knowledge that the Spirit gives Jesus. There is no way in the natural for Jesus to have known that the woman had marriage problems. Jesus would have naturally seen that the woman was an outcast, but to specifically ask about her husband was a question that could only be known by the Spirit. This question was the perfect question to ask, and the Holy Spirit knew it. He knows the perfect questions to ask people so we must learn to listen and obey His voice. This question ends up being the reason why the woman believes in Jesus. As you are witnessing, listen to the person but also listen to the Holy Spirit. He knows what that individual needs to hear a whole lot better than we do.

7. Don't get distracted (4:19-24). Immediately after Jesus points out that the woman has had five husbands and is living with another man, what does the woman do? She immediately tries to change the conversation to another topic—praying in Jerusalem. Not only that, but she challenges Jesus. She tries to start a debate. When the Holy Spirit begins to convict people, they get uncomfortable. They want to shift the conversation in another direction, they even get defensive and start accusing you of things you haven't done, or they may try to debate with you. They had not discussed Jerusalem. Her accusation had very little to do with their conversation, but she was convicted by the Holy Spirit and wanted to do whatever she could to get off that topic.

Yet, notice how Jesus responds. He does not get offended. He does not yell at her. He does not just quit the conversation. Instead, He acknowledges her question, gives a great answer to it, but steers the emphasis of the conversation back to where it should be—the focus remains on God. He didn't engage in the geographical differences of Jerusalem and Samaria. He did not compare her people's leaders to His. He addressed her question but He then redirected the focus back on God. Don't get distracted or moved from the purpose for why you are having the conversation. People may try to distract you or engage you in a debate, but remember the purpose of your conversation and don't fall into the enemy's trap.

8. Introduce him/her to Jesus (4:25-26). The ultimate goal in having a conversation like this with someone is to give that person an opportunity to meet Jesus. Now, this can come in a variety of ways. You can introduce people to Jesus by giving them a Bible or encouraging them to read theirs if they have one. You can invite them to your church. Or you can simply introduce them to Jesus by sharing your testimony. The key here, though, is that when you leave you want to make sure you fulfilled the purpose of why you started the conversation in the first place—you wanted someone to know Jesus. If that is your goal, then give the person an opportunity to do that.

There it is. Jesus has given us a great model of how we can begin to share our faith today. Now, here is what you need to understand when you share your faith with people: not everyone is going to like it, receive it or understand it. Even Jesus' own disciples were confused as to what Jesus was doing speaking with the Samaritan woman. Some people may look at you funny. You won't always have a good experience, and people won't always get saved, but the reality is that it is not your job to save anyone anyway. That is the Holy Spirit's job. Your job is to tell them about Jesus and hope that that conversation will one day lead to their adoption into the family of God.

### NINETY MINUTES TO LIMA

I had just finished a week of ministry in the Amazon city of Tarapoto, Peru. For a week our team had ministered in this beautiful city that sat in a valley surrounded by cloud-capped mountains. We had ministered in churches, at pastor's conferences, at youth groups, at crusades, for the Peruvian Army, on the radio and on TV. The Lord did amazing things and as I boarded my flight in Tarapoto I began to thank God for all that He had done through our team that week.

As I found my seat, I sat down next to two young men. Nick was 25 and John was 22 and we began to talk. They were from California and our conversation started with sports. It wasn't long, however, until I asked them what they were doing in Tarapoto, Peru. They explained to me that they were on their way home from a two-week spiritual experience. As you can imagine, that piqued my interest. I asked them to tell me about it. They began to tell me that both of them were drug addicts and had tried multiple times to stop but nothing had worked. But then they had heard about this special spiritual experience in the middle of the Amazon where a Shaman would teach them how they could be free from their drug addiction. They explained that the past two weeks they had been cut off from all outside communication so that they could receive therapy for drug abuse by using eastern religious exercises with the help of other, more natural drugs (yes, they were trying to overcome their drug addictions by using drugs; it seemed a little contradictory to me too).

I kept asking them questions about their experience there. I was intrigued, but I was also fishing for information and waiting for the right time to turn the conversation. Eventually I mentioned Jesus. Nick was a Jew and had never really tried Christianity. John had grown up in the church but found it to be more legalistic than anything. We talked the entire 90-minute flight about everything under the sun: God, sin, Heaven, Hell, why marijuana was wrong if God created it, I mean you name it and we probably talked about it. We disagreed on almost every subject but we kept talking. There were times where the conversation would hit a lull or would go off topic, but I was constantly trying to steer it back to Jesus.

As we began our descent into Lima I asked them both if they would be willing to do something for me, "Would you guys give Jesus a chance? It is obvious that you are searching for something to help your pain and bring joy to your life. You have both tried a lot of things, and what I'm asking you to do is to give Jesus a shot." They both said that they had Bibles and I also asked them, "Would you promise me that you would begin to read the Bible with an open mind? What can it hurt, right?" John told me, "Josh, I'm going to do it. I will read the Bible. I'm going to start at the beginning and go all the way through." Nick then told me, "Josh, I want you to know, this has been the best conversation I've ever had. You presented your view of things much better than anyone I've ever known, and you did it in an incredibly respectful way. Because of you, I'm going to give Christianity a chance." I thanked him and asked him to clarify. "Did you just say that this was the best conversation you have ever had? Ever? About anything?" "Yes," he responded, "this was the best conversation I've ever had." I was blown away, and I laughed to myself considering he had just come away from two weeks in the jungle talking about spiritual things, yet our 90-minute conversation topped that.

I wish I could tell you that I led Nick and John in the sinner's prayer. I wish that I could tell you that they contacted me later on and told me that they had become Christians. I wish I could tell you that I'll see them again in Heaven, but I can't. I hope and pray that they will turn to Jesus but I don't know what will happen. Ultimately, though, that's out of my control. I can't save, that is the Holy Spirit's job. As Paul said in 1 Corinthians 3:6, "I planted the seed, Apollos watered it, but God makes it grow." God will do His part, but a seed can only grow once it has been planted and watered. We must do our part in order for God to do His.

## *MAKE DISCIPLES*

Before ending this section on motivations for evangelism I want to make one last point. I have been privileged to grow up learning from my father. He is an evangelist and from the time I was 12 years old I have traveled with him all over the world. We have traveled to some of the most unreached areas on the planet, places like Armoor, India where our crusade director told us that 90% of the people had never even heard the name of Jesus. When we go to these places our model for evangelism is almost always the same: we hold a multi-night crusade meeting for the community. This is usually in a large stadium or open field where tens of thousands of people can come and hear the Gospel. We will bring in bands and have teams do dramas and we make the event appealing to the city (in all honesty, some people come simply because there's a white man from America in town). When the people come, we preach the Gospel and thousands respond to the altar call, giving their lives to Jesus.

Throughout the years I have heard many people criticize crusade evangelism. They described it as inefficient, fruitless, self-serving, emotionally driven, numbers-focused and a disservice to Christianity. Now, there are certainly people and ministries who have taken a similar model and done a disservice to the Body of Christ and the people to whom they minister. There are wrong ways of doing mass evangelistic ministry, but one rotten apple doesn't have to spoil the whole bunch. Just because some have done things incorrectly doesn't mean that somebody can't do it correctly. Furthermore, anyone who has a problem with crusade evangelism must have a problem with Jesus and Peter and Paul. The heroes of the New Testament, including our Savior, often traveled to a city, spoke to a large crowd, and shortly thereafter would go on to another city, so there is certainly a biblical precedent for such a ministry.

The most common problem that I hear that people have with this evangelistic model is that we are leading people in a prayer only to get a big number of decisions, but that there is no real discipleship taking place. I also have a problem with any ministry that has that perspective. However, that is why at every crusade that we have ever done, we have always had a corresponding pastor's conference the same week. We bring in all of the local pastors, regardless of denomination, and train and encourage them to carry on the work of the Lord long after we leave. We are only able to be in a given community for a week or two, but God has purposefully placed pastors and Christian leaders in that community to carry on the work of the Lord. So we train and equip those pastors to do the follow-up work of making disciples, "someone who follows another person or another way of life and who submits himself to the discipline (teaching) of that leader or way."[27] God has called us to make disciples.

*Then Jesus came to them and said, "All authority in heaven and on earth has been given to me. Therefore go and make disciples of all nations, baptizing them in the name of the Father and of the Son and of the Holy Spirit, and teaching them to obey everything I have commanded you. And surely I am with you always, to the very end of the age."* – Matthew 28:18-20

When Jesus gave the Great Commission His command was not to convert as many people as possible. He did not tell us to make decisions. He commanded us to make disciples. For the lost to simply pray a prayer is not enough. Peter likens the new believer to a newborn baby (1 Peter 2:2). What would happen if you took a newborn baby and just left him on the side of the road to fend for himself? It would not be long until he died. If the new believer is like a new baby, then the new believer needs to be trained and cared for and nurtured. People must not just pray a prayer; they must be made into disciples. At our crusades, this is the job of the pastor and it is a beautiful relationship. We can come for one week and help the churches exponentially grow because of what the Lord does at the crusades. Whenever a person prays the prayer of salvation, they fill out a response card that is then distributed to the pastors so that the people are not left as newborns to fend for themselves.

I teach at Victory Bible College in Tulsa, OK and this past year I had a very special student in my class. I arrived that first day of class to see my dear friend Rose. Rose is the wife of our crusade director in Rwanda, Africa. We have been friends with her family since 2000 and here she was in my class. She had traveled from Rwanda to study at Victory Bible College. One day as I was sharing about our ministry to the class Rose raised her hand. I called upon her and she said, "I just want to confirm what Joshua is saying about their ministry. Joshua, you may not know this, but this is just one example of how effective crusade evangelism can be. In 2006 you did a crusade in Cyangugu, Rwanda and because of that one crusade, in addition to the many existing churches that grew exponentially, 34 brand new churches were started." I was amazed! I had never heard that about Cyangugu and I was so blessed by it. But she did not stop there. "It is amazing that 34 new churches started, but what is even more amazing is that 10 years later, all of those 34 churches are still here to this day!" That is the lasting fruit of discipleship.

Making disciples is not a suggestion or a recommendation, it is just as much of a command as any other part of the Great Commission, but this is an often overlooked aspect of ministry. To the detriment of the Great Commission, the making of disciples has often been seen as a secondary priority. However, conversion without discipleship is as effective as a car without gas—you will never go anywhere. Whether you are witnessing to a crowd of 50,000 in India or you are witnessing to a family member at Thanksgiving, our goal must always be to make disciples.

# OBSTRUCTIONS
# TO
# EVANGELISM

# CHAPTER 6

# CONSCIOUS EXCUSES

*CLEANING THE KITCHEN*

I am the oldest of four boys. My brother Jesse is two years younger than me, Daniel is four years younger than me, and Luke is eight years younger than me. I am incredibly grateful that I am very close to all of my brothers. They are truly my best friends. But if you've ever had brothers, then you know that it isn't all just a bed of roses. We had a few rough patches.

My brother Jesse was probably the one who annoyed me the most growing up. There were a number of things which he did that frustrated me, but one of the main ones was how he used to weasel his way out of cleaning! If you know Jesse today, then you know that he is an incredibly hard worker. However, growing up Jesse would do just about anything to get out of cleaning, and there was always one excuse that happened over and over again. After dinner all of us boys were responsible for cleaning up the kitchen, loading the dishwasher, clearing the table, etc. This didn't surprise us. Each night we knew the routine. It was like clockwork. What was also like clockwork, though, was that just as we would begin to clean up after dinner, Jesse would "conveniently" announce, "Hey guys, sorry, I have to go to the bathroom." And for the next half hour Jesse would be in the bathroom reading a book or playing on his phone, while the rest of us cleaned the kitchen. He would emerge from the bathroom to see that all of the cleaning had already been done and state "Oh, thanks for cleaning, guys. Sorry I was gone." Are you sorry, Jesse? Because it sure seems to happen a lot!

Excuses are common. Each day we either give or hear excuses from people. People excuse why they were late to work. People excuse why they got upset. People excuse why they didn't work out. People make excuses for everything. But when it comes to Christians, perhaps the thing that is most excused is why people don't witness. Most Christians would agree that they are supposed to witness. They know that Jesus commanded us to evangelize. But for so many reasons, we so often make excuses rather than make disciples. In the previous section we examined the many different motivations for evangelism, but in this section I want to highlight the many obstructions to evangelism, and the first obstructions to evangelism are conscious excuses. These are excuses we deliberately make about not fulfilling the Great Commission. No matter how frequent these excuses may be, they are no justification for our inefficiency concerning the Great Commission. My prayer is that this section will encourage you to identify any obstructions in your life so that you can effectively move past them.

## *WHAT IF I LOOK STUPID?*

*For I am not ashamed of the gospel, because it is the power of God that brings salvation to everyone who believes: first to the Jew, then to the Gentile. For in the gospel the righteousness of God is revealed—a righteousness that is by faith from first to last, just as it is written: "The righteous will live by faith." –* Romans 1:16-17

Paul is essentially dealing with the "What if I look stupid?" excuse here. He is saying that though many may think the preaching of the Gospel is embarrassing or shameful, I refuse to let that stop me from preaching it. Because the Gospel is the power of God, Paul cannot be ashamed of it. He has a responsibility to share the Gospel, for it is the only answer for this world. Because of this, he does not have time to be ashamed of the Gospel. He must share the Gospel with the unreached.

Imagine that you are walking down the street when suddenly you look to your right and see a building on fire. The fire has started on the base level and while much of the building is not yet in flames, it is obvious that this is a bad fire with the potential to destroy the building and kill the people in it. You quickly look upward and see people on the upper-level stories completely unaware of the fire below. They are cleaning and cooking and playing and going about their regular business without any knowledge of their impending death. What would you do? Wouldn't the natural response be to cry out and try to get their attention? You would hopefully jump up and down, waiving your arms and screaming at the top of your voice in an attempt to warn the people on the upper levels. You wouldn't be concerned that passersby might look at you funny for jumping up and down. You wouldn't be embarrassed that neighbors would hear you shouting and look at you funny. Hopefully, your personal concern for shame and embarrassment would completely disappear in light of the people's need for safety.

All too often shame, embarrassment and other people's opinions keep us from evangelizing. Yet, while we are concerned about what other people may think, people around us are in a burning building! Any shame or embarrassment that Paul may have had in sharing the Gospel was immediately forgotten when he realized the importance of sharing the Gospel. He had a message that could save. How selfish and self-centered he would have been if he kept that message to himself. There are billions of people living their lives in a building that is on fire, completely unaware of their situation, and Christians must put aside any potential embarrassment or shame to cry out and warn the world around us.

## WHAT IF I GET PERSECUTED?

*"If the world hates you, keep in mind that it hated me first. If you belonged to the world, it would love you as its own. As it is, you do not belong to the world, but I have chosen you out of the world. That is why the world hates you. Remember what I told you: 'A servant is not greater than his master.' If they persecuted me, they will persecute you also. If they obeyed my teaching, they will obey yours also.* – John 15:18-20

This is not one of Jesus' most comforting promises. There are many comforting and happy promises that Jesus gives His disciples but this is probably one that the disciples would have preferred not to hear. However, Jesus was not in the business of telling people what they wanted to hear. He was interested in telling the truth. To be honest, if we ask ourselves, "What if I get persecuted?" then we are asking ourselves the wrong question. Look at the passage above; Jesus promised us persecution. One of the marks of a true disciple of Christ is to stand out from the culture. We are supposed to be in the world but not of the world. If there is no identifiable difference between us and the world, then something is wrong.

My wife was telling me a story recently about a girl with whom she works. This girl is a good, Christian girl but Michelle told me that she will occasionally swear (or cuss, as they say in Oklahoma) for emphasis. It is not that she has a mouth like a sailor or that she's always using foul language, but there are times when she is really upset that she will swear to emphasize her point. Michelle said to me, "It's not as though I think she isn't a Christian or that she is this horrible person, but when she does that I think to myself, 'Why was that necessary?' When she speaks that way, she is speaking no differently than the world." And that is the key: our lives are supposed to look different than the world's. But if we speak the same as the world or watch the same movies and shows as the world and listen to the same music as the world, then the world won't notice any difference between us and them. We are called to change the world, but why would the world want to look like us if we look like them? I want to challenge you to live a life that stands out from the world. That is what Jesus did. He spent time in the world, eating with tax collectors and prostitutes, but He never engaged in their sin. He looked ostensibly different from the world, and that attracted the world to change their lives.

In light of this, we should not be asking ourselves, "What if I get persecuted?" Instead we should be asking ourselves, "What am I doing wrong that I'm not being persecuted?" I am as guilty of this as anyone. There are days and times that I choose not to witness because I'm concerned that people will reject me or because I would *rather* watch that show or listen to that music or speak that way, if only to be accepted. But we are called to live differently. When was the last time you were persecuted or ridiculed or shunned for being a Christian? If you can't remember, then it has been too long and it is probably time for you to reevaluate your label as a Christian.

I was recently on a plane flight from Johannesburg, South Africa to Atlanta, Georgia. This was a 16-hour plane ride (for the record, that is a form of persecution in and of itself). As I sat down next to this stranger I thought to myself, "I should share Jesus with her." We began to make conversation and I found out she was a Law Professor. I explained that I was a minister. And that's about where the conversation ended. Why? Well, first of all, I was exhausted and ready to sleep, but more than that, I was a little scared about how the conversation might go. Maybe she wanted nothing to do with Christ? She was a strong, educated woman and if I started asking her questions about Christ, it may have upset her. And I certainly didn't want to do that at the beginning of a 16-hour flight. What really kept me from witnessing was my fear that I could have been persecuted.

As I look back on this experience, I can't help but lament a missed opportunity. I could have had a very powerful and meaningful conversation with this woman about Christ; maybe a conversation that she really needed to have. But I chose not to, and my main reason was because I didn't want to get persecuted. What a lousy excuse.

Jesus did not call us to shy away from persecution. In fact, he went out of His way to mention that if we are doing our jobs correctly, then we will be persecuted. Now, this does not mean that we should unnecessarily cause enemies or seek out persecution, but it does mean that we should not be worried about receiving persecution when it comes, because persecution is the proof of a right relationship with God. And honestly, our persecution in America is not much to be too concerned about anyway. Relatively speaking, we have it incredibly easy. There are Christians all over the world that are undergoing far, far worse persecutions than ourselves for the cause of Christ. I was in eastern Egypt recently where many Christians are fearful for their lives. Worshiping Jesus may end up costing them their jobs, their homes or even their lives. When I compare my "light and momentary troubles" (2 Corinthians 4:17) with the persecutions of others, there is really no comparison. For those living in the western world, persecution is almost laughable.

*Now I rejoice in what I am suffering for you, and I fill up in my flesh what is still lacking in regard to Christ's afflictions, for the sake of his body, which is the church.* – Colossians 1:24

This is one of the most interesting verses in Scripture as people have difficulty thinking that there is somehow something lacking in Christ's work on the cross. This verse is not saying, though, that Christ's sacrifice was somehow insufficient or lacking. Instead, Paul is emphasizing that as the body of Christ, Christ's body is still suffering all over the world. Christ's afflictions are not finished, they continue today in Egypt and Iran and China, just as they did in Paul's own body. Persecution is not to be feared, for through persecution we partner with Christ.

*They called the apostles in and had them flogged. Then they ordered them not to speak in the name of Jesus, and let them go. The apostles left the Sanhedrin, rejoicing because they had been counted worthy of suffering disgrace for the Name. Day after day, in the temple courts and from house to house, they never stopped teaching and proclaiming the good news that Jesus is the Messiah.* – Acts 5:40-42

Our reaction to persecution should be humility. We should be honored to share with Christ in the suffering of His Body, just as Peter and John did after suffering from the Sanhedrin. To be persecuted for Christ, and with Christ, is an honor. And just as persecution did not stop the disciples from ministering, so we must continue to preach the Gospel regardless of what trials we face. Persecution should not keep you from starting to witness, nor should it stop you from continuing to witness. "The world will not offer incentive or encouragement to faithful Gospel proclamation... Therefore the Church must be particularly diligent to safeguard her fidelity to her biblical mandate to take the Gospel to the nations."[28]

## *I'M NOT AN EXTROVERT*

*Moses said to the Lord, "Pardon your servant, Lord. I have never been eloquent, neither in the past nor since you have spoken to your servant. I am slow of speech and tongue." The Lord said to him, "Who gave human beings their mouths? Who makes them deaf or mute? Who gives them sight or makes them blind? Is it not I, the Lord? Now go; I will help you speak and will teach you what to say."* – Exodus 4:10-12

Anyone who knows me knows that I'm an extrovert. I love hanging out with people. I love talking with people and asking people questions. I have little to no shame (which has at times gotten me in trouble) and so going up to a complete stranger and starting a conversation isn't terrifying for me like it is for some people. But I fully realize that everyone is not as extroverted as I am, but is that an excuse not to witness? It didn't exactly work for Moses.

God gave Moses a command to witness, to speak to Pharaoh about Almighty God, and yet his response wasn't exactly agreeable. He didn't like talking. He didn't feel that he was good at talking. And perhaps he thought that excuse would work with God, but it didn't. Instead, God responded that if He had the power to make man's mouth, then He also had the power to help Moses use his mouth well.

When God gave us the Great Commission, He did not put qualifiers on it. God's command to preach the Gospel with others was not only for the extroverted but for all disciples of Christ. It may come easier to some people than to others, but discomfort and difficulty is not an excuse for inaction.

Growing up, I did fairly well in school, but the subject that always gave me the most trouble, and that demanded the most time, was math. I was always so impressed with math geniuses because it was so foreign to me. There were definitely times where I would think to myself, "Why does this even matter? I understand why I should write properly or that learning how the human body works is important, but how is algebra ever going to matter in the real world?" When I began to do my own taxes, though, I learned the value of math. Now, here's what's interesting about taxes: everyone has to do them. In fact, it is illegal not to do them. But let's say that you aren't very good at math and so you don't do your taxes. When the IRS calls you and you explain to them that the reason why you didn't do your taxes was because you weren't good at math, how do you think they will respond? Do you think they will excuse you? Not at all! Just because doing taxes comes easier to some does not mean that those for whom it is difficult are excused from the responsibility.

If you can show me in Scripture where Jesus excuses the introverts from the Great Commission, then I will be happy to excuse you from it too; but you won't find that in Scripture. We must put aside our natural tendencies for the sake of the Gospel. Even the most introverted individual can still strike up a conversation. Even the most introverted individual can make friends. Is it necessary for the introvert to start a preaching ministry? No. You may be shy, but you serve the One who made man's mouth. Could the Lord not help you overcome your natural tendencies for the sake of bringing others to Christ? And in reality, that is one of the primary reasons why Christ sent the Holy Spirit.

When we speak of the Holy Spirit we often think of the baptism of the Holy Spirit and speaking in tongues, which is a great aspect of the Holy Spirit, but it is not the only aspect or even the most important aspect. It is important to note, first of all, that every Christian already has the Holy Spirit. If you accept Christ then you accept the Holy Spirit, regardless of whether you believe in miracles or the gifts of the Spirit.

*Again Jesus said, "Peace be with you! As the Father has sent me, I am sending you." And with that he breathed on them and said, "Receive the Holy Spirit." –* John 20:21-22

This event occurs after Jesus has risen from the dead and now, for the first time, the disciples can accept Jesus as the resurrected Messiah. Paul says that we are saved when we "confess with our mouth that Jesus is Lord and believe in our heart that God raised Jesus from dead" (Romans 10:9). Up until Jesus' resurrection, this was impossible for the disciples. So, in some ways, this is the disciples' salvation experience. At this moment the disciples have the Holy Spirit living on the inside of them, and yet, this is different than the baptism of the Holy Spirit. If they were the same, then why would Jesus tell the disciples to wait in Jerusalem to receive the promised Holy Spirit (Acts 1:5)? Didn't they already have the Holy Spirit? Yes, but they still needed the empowerment of the Holy Spirit.

After receiving the Holy Spirit unto salvation the disciples stayed in Jerusalem and nothing seemingly changed. They did not evangelize. They did not teach. They stayed in the upper room and waited. The Pentecostal event takes place in Acts 2 when, in a spirit of unity, the Holy Spirit enveloped the room and empowered the disciples. Now, if you read the account in Acts 2 you will find that just what Jesus predicted would happen did happen: "You will receive power when the Holy Spirit comes on you, and you will be my witnesses in Jerusalem, Judea, Samaria and to the ends of the earth" (Acts 1:8). Immediately after receiving the baptism of the Spirit Peter stood up and addressed the crowd and gave one of the most powerful sermons recorded in Scripture. His sermon was so powerful that Luke records that 3,000 devoted Jews accepted Christ at that very moment. This is the same Peter who had just a few weeks earlier denied that he even knew Jesus to a young servant girl (Mark 14:66-72). He who was previously intimidated to share his relationship with Christ to one young servant girl was now, in a moment, so transformed that he was sharing it with thousands in the city of Jerusalem, and 3,000 of those were saved (Acts 2:41).

This story shows the most important reason for being baptized in the Holy Spirit: power from on high that will embolden you to fulfill the Great Commission. Peter and all of the disciples, who were previously huddled up in a room in Jerusalem, probably still scared of the Jewish leaders coming to arrest them (John 20:19), were now filled with courage to spread the Gospel, which all of them did! What changed? Those who were previously afraid of even identifying themselves with Jesus then became the most radical disciples of Him, traveling to the uttermost bounds of the earth and even giving their lives for the cause of Christ. What happened? The Baptism of the Holy Spirit!

The Lord knew that there would be many with a natural disposition to not witness or evangelize. And let me be clear, extroversion is no better than introversion, but speaking to people about Christ just comes more naturally to some people than to others. But just as the Holy Spirit empowered Peter, and just as God enabled Moses, so too the Lord is able to empower and enable you to fulfill the Great Commission.

## SOMEONE ELSE CAN DO IT

The opening chapter of Acts tells the story of Judas Iscariot committing suicide after betraying Jesus. In light of this, the disciples present two men as suitable replacements for Judas: Matthias and

Joseph called Barsabbas. Matthias ends up taking Judas' place and goes on to be one of the twelve disciples and do an incredible amount of mission work before giving his life for the work of the Lord. What is amazing is that it is very possible that if not for Judas' betrayal, perhaps Matthias never would have accomplished what he did for the Kingdom of God.

God wants to use you, and He does have a unique plan for your life, one different than He has for anyone else, but if you refuse to be used by Him, then He will find someone else to replace you, just as He replaced Judas with Matthias. Judas was a man that God wanted to use; Jesus had specifically chosen him. But when Judas chose to turn his back on the call of God, he ruined his destiny and God chose Matthias instead. Think about how different Judas' life and memory would be if he had repented and followed the plan of God. Matthias stands for what Judas could have been. We have the choice to be like Judas or Matthias. We can turn our back on the call of God and wind up like Judas, or we can embrace the call of God and live a life of eternal impact like Matthias.

Evangelist Reinhard Bonnke tells a story about how one night he was lying in bed when suddenly he saw a vision. "I saw all of Europe and North America painted with a large brush of evangelism. I asked God what this meant and He told me that He had a work for me to do. What knocked me out of bed and threw me onto my knees is when God told me that I was not His first choice. I was His third choice. He had asked two others who had rejected the call. I immediately said to God, 'You don't have to ask Number Four, Number Three accepts.' After that, God's plan unfolded clearly before my eyes. I was to write a booklet on the power of the cross, called, *From Minus to Plus*, and mail it to every household in all of Europe and North America."[29] The Lord can and will use someone else if you choose not to do it, but why would you want to miss out on the joy of working with the Lord to bring others into the family of God?

The other aspect to this, though, is that when we say, "Someone else can do it," we never know how many people's lives will be cost in the process. Bonnke was the third choice, and praise God for the miracle that happened. Thousands of people came to

Christ and received prayer because of his obedience, but how many others did not because by the time they received the card, it was too late? Hundreds of millions of people could have been reached sooner if one of those first two men had acted! In Bonnke's story, God could have called upon another individual to do the work, but there are times where you are the only one who can do what God has called you to do. You are a unique person placed in a unique situation in this world and there are people that only you can reach. If you don't reach them, perhaps no one else will. You have a responsibility to do what you can where you've been placed. Do not let someone else do your job because you may be the only person for the job.

## IT CAN WAIT UNTIL ANOTHER TIME

*Don't you have a saying, 'It's still four months until harvest'? I tell you, open your eyes and look at the fields! They are ripe for harvest.* – John 4:35

*For he says, "In the time of my favor I heard you, and in the day of salvation I helped you." I tell you, now is the time of God's favor, now is the day of salvation.* – 2 Corinthians 6:2

When I was at university I saw this all the time. For some students it was a way of life. For others it was something they constantly battled. Whenever parents would find out that their child was doing it they were upset. Professors would warn students not to do it. University staff would instruct incoming freshmen to stay away from it. But it was so easy to do, and it seemed like everyone did it. Guys did it. Girls did it. Upperclassmen did it. Freshmen did it. I'm ashamed to admit that there were even times that I did. Yes, I am talking about that evil of procrastination.

While I was dramatizing the issue a bit, the reality is that procrastination is a real problem, and equally so with regard to evangelism. We always think that we have more time than what we actually do. But every fatal car accident is just that—an accident. No one gets into a car and expects to die. No one knows the day he will die. I am not speaking death or negativity, and I'm not trying to scare anyone, but the reality is that people around us are abruptly taken from this earth all of the time. Remember what Jesus said when speaking about the abruptness of the Lord's coming, "If the owner of the house had known at what time of night the thief was coming, he would have kept watch and would not have let his house be broken into" (Matthew 24:43). As I stated earlier, the harvest is ripe now! Paul does not tell us that salvation is tomorrow or that salvation is in a week or a month or a year. Salvation is today!

Why put off until tomorrow what can be done today? This is exactly what Jesus' point was with the disciples. "Do not say four more months…" but how often do we say "four more months?" How often do we make excuses that we can wait, when in all honesty, we don't know for sure? If the devil can't get you to run from the call of God, then he will settle for convincing you to put it off until tomorrow.

I remember another story about Reinhard Bonnke that communicates this point well. A woman came to Bonnke's hotel one day saying that she had heard him preach at the crusade and that she knew she needed to be saved. Bonnke was overjoyed that she had come to him and asked the woman to pray right there to receive salvation. The woman replied, "I'm not sure that I'm ready. This is a big decision for me. I live with my boyfriend and I know I would have to move out if I accepted Christ. I'm just not sure that I am ready to make that decision." Bonnke asked her again but the woman insisted that she sleep on the decision.

The next morning, as Bonnke was eating his breakfast, someone rushed in and said, "Reinhard, I'm so sorry but there has been a horrible accident. Please come." Bonnke exited the hotel where, on the street lay a woman, having just been hit by a car. The woman was the same woman whom Bonnke had met with the night before. She was instantly killed and as Bonnke retells the story, his heart was crushed. He so desperately hoped that that woman was crossing the street to his hotel to tell him that she had accepted Christ, but he does not know that for sure.[30] The story portrays well the reality that none of us are guaranteed tomorrow, and for something as important as eternal life, we must stop using the excuse that it can wait until another time because you don't ever know if you will have another time.

## *I'M TRYING TO BE RELEVANT FIRST*

*Though I am free and belong to no one, I have made myself a slave to everyone, to win as many as possible. To the Jews I became like a Jew, to win the Jews. To those under the law I became like one under the law (though I myself am not under the law), so as to win those under the law. To those not having the law I became like one not having the law (though I am not free from God's law but am under Christ's law), so as to win those not having the law. To the weak I became weak, to win the weak. I have become all things to all people so that by all possible means I might save some.* – 1 Corinthians 9:19-22

My home church is Victory Christian Center in Tulsa, OK. I know that I am biased, but for me, I attend the greatest church in the world. I love my church and am honored to be part of it. I travel to many churches all over the world and I have certainly visited some churches that would do well to be a bit more culturally relevant. I have also been to some churches where it seems like *all* of the focus is on being relevant, even at the expense of the Gospel. There are many churches today whose preachers never open the Bible and whose sermons sound more like self-help lessons than life transformation.

One of my favorite TV shows to watch is *Shark Tank*, which is a show were entrepreneurs and inventors pitch their business ideas to millionaire and billionaire investors who are looking to invest in companies. One of the things that I have learned in watching that show is that it does not matter how good your product is, if you don't package it correctly, no one will buy it. There are many churches and ministers and Christians who have an amazing product, but because it isn't packaged correctly, very few people are buying it. Christians should strive to be on the cutting edge and look for the most relevant ways to reach people. The methods for evangelism and outreach and witnessing can change and adapt from culture to culture and time period to time period, but the message must stay the same. Unfortunately, what I have seen is that there are many people and ministries who sacrificed the message in favor of the method. Being relevant is only good as long as it helps to reach people with the message.

Paul talks about how his methodology changed from culture to culture. Sometimes he stressed the Jewish side of him, if he was trying to reach a Jewish audience. At other times he stressed the non-law part of him, to reach those not under the law. He quite clearly says, "I have become all things to all people." That is important, but that is often where many churches and Christians end. However, Paul's sentence does not stop there. He goes on to say that the reason why he does this is "so that by all possible means I might save some." That is the goal—that people would be saved. In your effort to be relevant, remember the purpose for being relevant—that people would be saved. Thus, if you want to follow in Paul's footsteps of becoming "all things to all people" then follow his footsteps to the very end of the path, which is that all of the methods and relevance is to help people come into the family of God. Relevance is no substitute for repentance.

### I'M BUILDING A RELATIONSHIP FIRST

*He said to another man, "Follow me." But he replied, "Lord, first let me go and bury my father." Jesus said to him, "Let the dead bury their own dead, but you go and proclaim the kingdom of God." Still another said, "I will follow you, Lord; but first let me go back and say goodbye to my family." Jesus replied, "No one who puts a hand to the plow and looks back is fit for service in the kingdom of God." – Luke 9:59-62*

I remember reading this story as a child and thinking, "Jesus, aren't you being a little harsh? This man's father just died. Wouldn't it be ok to let him bury his father first?" It seemed a little heartless of Jesus. But as I've studied this story more, and read commentaries and heard sermons on it, there are a few things that I didn't recognize when I read it as a boy.

First of all, the man seemed to elevate his desire to bury his father over a relationship with Jesus. As Timothy Keller rightly points out, "Notice their language… 'Lord, first, let me do this.'"[31] Jesus is asking the man to make Him his first priority, while the man wants to make Jesus secondary to his father. With Jesus, there is only one position for Him to hold: first.

Secondly, the story never states that the man's father had died. Whenever I read this story growing up, I had always assumed that the father had just died and his funeral and burial were imminent, but there is nothing in the story to indicate that the man's father had died. It is very possible that this man was telling Jesus that he wanted to wait for an indefinite period of time before he would start following him. This certainly changes the perspective of the story.

Lastly, this viewpoint holds credence because it was not customary in the Jewish system for the son to leave his father before his father had died. The son felt an obligation to not do anything until the father had died. This is exemplified in the story of Abraham where God calls Abraham to leave his "father's household" to go to the land God had called him (Genesis 12:1). Thus, when Jesus asks the man to follow him and he responds that he wants to first bury his father, he is essentially telling Jesus he wants to wait until the time is absolutely right before he answers the call of God. But if you wait until the perfect time to do anything, you will do nothing.

As I mentioned earlier, my wife and I recently had our first child. We are incredibly happy, but having a child also comes with its set of challenges and questions. We don't have it all figured out yet. But let me ask you, if I had waited until we had all of our child's college expenses paid for before having kids, how long do you think it would take before we started having kids? If I had waited until I had every potential expense paid for before we had Anna, we would never have had her. There is no perfect time to have a child; you could always be more prepared.

I was ministering in Cairo, Egypt a year ago at a pastor's conference. We had many pastors from four different African countries there who came to learn. It is illegal for us to proselytize Muslims so we couldn't hold any outdoor crusades, but we were allowed to minister in churches and encourage pastors. So that is just what I did. And one of the things I did was implore the pastors to stop waiting for the right time to witness to their Muslim friends, but rather to step out in faith and give people an opportunity to accept Christ. The day after I had preached on that specific subject I had one of our pastors come up to me with a massive smile on his face. He began to tell me that for months he had befriended three separate

Muslim friends but that he was waiting for the perfect time to share Christ with them. As I was preaching the day before the Holy Spirit was working on his heart and told him that today was the day and he shouldn't wait any longer. Immediately after our meetings he went to each of those three friends and shared the Gospel with them and each of them accepted Christ immediately!

The point that Jesus is making here is that the Kingdom of God is advancing now, and if you spend your entire life waiting, you will never accomplish anything for the Kingdom, because it will pass you by. You need only build a relationship for so long until you bring up Christ. Do not wait too long because the risk is far too costly. There comes a time when you must put your hand to the plow and stop making the excuse that you are building a relationship first.

### THEY'RE PROBABLY ALREADY SAVED

*"Therefore keep watch, because you do not know on what day your Lord will come. But understand this: If the owner of the house had known at what time of night the thief was coming, he would have kept watch and would not have let his house be broken into. So you also must be ready, because the Son of Man will come at an hour when you do not expect him."* – Matthew 24:42-44

Not every night, and not even most nights, but every once in a while, it happens. Michelle and I will be lying in bed. I'm just on the verge of sleeping when I hear a voice from the other side of the bed, "Josh, did you lock the front door?" "Yes, Michelle, I locked the front door." "Are you sure?" she replies. "Maybe you should get up and double-check?" So I get up and check to make sure that the door is locked (and it always is). This sort of thing will happen from time to time about whether we turned off the stove or about whether she forgot to turn off her curling iron. Honestly, my wife doesn't forget much at all, but she will question herself that she may have.

Whenever I read this parable about the owner of the house and the robber, I think about Michelle and those situations. Most nights (in fact, probably every night), we wouldn't need to lock the doors to our house. I'm sure we've never had an attempted robbery and that all would be fine even if the doors were unlocked, but why do we lock the door? Just in case. In the unlikely event that someone does try to enter through one of our doors, we have made sure that they are secure.

One of the excuses for why we don't witness is because we think to ourselves that the person is already saved anyway. But what if they are not? Does it hurt to ask? Perhaps it's an inconvenience. You are putting yourself out there, a bit, but the small inconvenience is far better than the potential risk. It is the same reason we pay for car or house insurance. I don't expect to get into an accident (that's why they call it an accident), but if I do, I want car insurance. I believe that my home will never burn down or be destroyed in any way, but in the highly unlikely event that it does, I want to make sure that it is insured. This is the same reason that we witness to people, even if we think they're already saved. There is no harm in simply asking a Christian if he is saved. But there is great harm in not asking a non-Christian if he is saved. Both the risk and the reward are too great not to witness.

## *I LET MY LIFE DO THE TALKING*

*The teachers of the law and the Pharisees brought in a woman caught in adultery. They made her stand before the group and said to Jesus, "Teacher, this woman was caught in the act of adultery. In the Law Moses commanded us to stone such women. Now what do you say?" They were using this question as a trap, in order to have a basis for accusing him. But Jesus bent down and started to write on the ground with his finger. When they kept on questioning him, he straightened up and said to them, "Let any one of you who is without sin be the first to throw a stone at her." Again he stooped down and wrote on the ground. At this, those who heard began to go away one at a time, the older ones first, until only Jesus was left, with the woman still standing there. Jesus straightened up and asked her, "Woman, where are they? Has no one condemned you?" "No one, sir," she said. "Then neither do I condemn you," Jesus declared. "Go now and leave your life of sin." – John 8:3-11*

One of the common liberal views about Jesus today is that He was much more concerned with loving people than He was about dealing with people's sin. The liberal view would like to superimpose its personal views of Jesus onto the biblical picture of Jesus to say that Jesus really isn't concerned, for example, with whether someone is homosexual. He is concerned with making sure that everyone is loved and that no one feels judged. They will use stories like the one above to "prove" their point. They argue that the religious leaders represent the Bible-believing right wing, who are so quick to judge and condemn anyone. Jesus is much more liberal and lenient, though. He didn't condemn the woman's sin, they say, instead He made sure that she felt loved and accepted.

Jesus certainly emphasized the difference between condemnation and forgiveness. He was not interested in the woman paying the death penalty for her adultery because He was already on His way to the cross to pay the penalty for her sins. Furthermore, He would not allow the religious leaders to stone her for her sin while they had unresolved sin in their own lives. But Jesus also didn't condone her sin. He very clearly instructed her that while He didn't condemn her, He was also not fine with her adulterous way of life. He didn't leave her to continue in her sin, nor did He simply let His righteous life do that talking for Him, instead He gave a very clear command to "Go now and leave your life of sin." His command was not only instructive but also empowering. The grace of God empowers you to walk in the freedom of the atonement. Jesus did not find her life of sin acceptable. Jesus cared enough about her to encourage her toward repentance.

There are many who would have preferred for Jesus to simply send her off without giving her a command to leave her life of sin; but that's not how Jesus worked. Jesus was not concerned with making people feel better about their sin; He wanted them to be *freed* from their sin! In order for that to happen He knew it would demand more than just living a good, exemplary life. When Jesus gave the Great Commission He did not say to "Go into all the world and live the Gospel." He said, "Go into all the world and preach the Gospel." Living a good life is good, and part of the Christian life, but evangelistically we are called to do more.

Early Church father, St. Francis of Assisi, once said, "Preach the Gospel at all times and when necessary use words." I fear that many Christians have become much more content to "live the

Gospel" rather than "preach the Gospel," and while they do not have to be mutually exclusive, in many regards, they are.

"Preach the Gospel at all times and when necessary use words," a saying commonly attributed to Francis of Assisi, has become axiomatic to many Christians. In its purest form it is a call for consistency between words and deed. Too often, it has become an excuse to avoid evangelism. Far from a legitimate biblical strategy for kingdom expansion, it has become an ointment to assuage the consciences of those not interested in sharing the gospel with others. Unfortunately too many Christians find it easier to share food occasionally than to share Christ."[32] – Todd Miles

## I'M FOCUSED ON THE PHYSICAL RATHER THAN THE SPIRITUAL

*Religion that God our Father accepts as pure and faultless is this: to look after orphans and widows in their distress and to keep oneself from being polluted by the world.* – James 1:27

Let me begin by saying that I like this verse. I do. It's a wonderful reminder about our need to make sure that our religion is more than just theoretical but that it is acted out in the way that we care for the poor, for example. That being said, this verse has become the hallmark verse for many ministries and churches. Again, not that that's a bad thing, but caring for orphans and widows, while important, is not the overarching theme of the New Testament. Nor is it the emphasis of Christ's ministry or teachings.

Not only has this verse been emphasized, but it has also been interpreted with a very narrow view. The verse simply says to "look after" orphans and widows in their distress, but most people have interpreted that to mean to only care for their physical needs (i.e. food, clothing, shelter, etc.). But wouldn't the truest form of religion be to look after the spiritual health of the orphans and widows? Absolutely! Yet, all too often many Christians and Christian ministries only focus on the material needs.

I am certainly not against humanitarian work, and it is important to feed the poor, clothe the naked and build orphanages, but only insofar as they lead to Jesus. As I stated in chapter 3, churches, orphanages, food ministries and any other humanitarian work is not the end but rather a means to the end. The end is Christ. The goal must be to help people come to know Jesus. Meeting the physical needs of people is amazing and should continue to happen, but there are many ministries and organizations that start out by saying that the physical will make room for the spiritual, but they often stop at the physical. If an organization is offering only food or clothes or shelter or medicine, it's not as much a Christian ministry as it is the United Nations.

Yes, the world needs ministries and organizations that meet the physical needs of people, but more than that, the world needs ministries and organizations that reach the spiritual needs of people. The reality is that the majority of the money that is given to overseas missions is given primarily to relief and development activities. In fact, "seven of the top 10 North American mission agencies by income are devoted almost entirely to relief and development."[33] From 2001 to 2005 the total income donated to overseas ministries grew by 27.5%. During that time, "American agencies focused on evangelism/discipleship saw combined income grow by 2.7 percent during those four years; those focused on relief/development saw theirs grow by a whopping 74.3 percent."[34]

The need for social reform and justice is great, but the need for life transformation is even greater. Social issues, as significant as they are, are no substitute for the Gospel. "Hunger, poverty, sickness, and death are evidences of a fallen world. Christ came to redeem that world and inaugurate His kingdom... As such any good works of service must be done with an explicit identification with Jesus Christ, not with a vague or unspoken nod"[35] to a higher power or out of the goodness of the human heart. Just as it was with Jesus, may our focus always be centered on people's spiritual needs, first and foremost.

## I DON'T HAVE A PASSPORT

*"Whoever can be trusted with very little can also be trusted with much, and whoever is dishonest with very little will also be dishonest with much."* – Luke 16:10

There are many people who think that because they are in America, a "Christian" nation, then they don't need to witness as much as they would, say, in Iraq. Now certainly there are more Christians here than in Iraq (by population and by percentage), but there are also more non-Christians here than in Iraq. Around 40 million people live in Iraq. Approximately 320 million live in America. Where do you think there are more non-Christians?

If you've ever been on a mission trip then you know that on a mission trip it is much easier to be evangelistically minded. You put aside your inhibitions and limitations and distractions for the sake of ministering to the lost. For one week you are always on alert, ready to witness at the drop of a hat. But then when you return to home a week later, it's as if you turn it off and just go back to your regular way of life. I'm as guilty of this as anyone. But my encouragement to all of us is to be soul winners in your home like you would on a mission trip. In fact, that is where God wants you to start. The Kingdom of God states that in order for you to be trusted with much you must first prove yourself faithful with little. When I meet with aspiring evangelists or ministers, one of the first questions I ask them is, "What ministry are you doing right now in your church or in your community?" People often think God can't really use them evangelistically unless they go to the nations, but you must be faithful with a neighborhood before God will give you a nation.

*But you will receive power when the Holy Spirit comes on you; and you will be my witnesses in Jerusalem, and in all Judea and Samaria, and to the ends of the earth. –* Acts 1:8

Jerusalem is where the disciples were when Jesus gave them this command. For many of them, Jerusalem was their hometown. When Jesus gave the Great Commission, Jesus did not demand that the command be only fulfilled outside of the confines of your hometown. Yes, this message must be preached to the ends of the earth, but it must also be preached in Jerusalem. Jerusalem was the disciples' hometown. Judea and Samaria were their home regions. The command to evangelize is not just for the uttermost bounds of the earth, for if every evangelist in New York City evangelized outside of New York City, then New York City would remain unevangelized. The great healing evangelist, Oral Roberts, said it like this: "Go into every person's world."

The lost surround you. They are at your work, in your neighborhood, and in your family. Those who surround you are just as much in need of the Gospel as anyone else, so make it your ambition to fulfill the Great Commission both locally and globally, but realize that neither will happen until you "Go."

It is important to note that the Great Commission begins with the word, "Go." This is because the rest of the command is dependent upon that first step. In my experience, sinners do not typically come knocking on your door, and if they do, it's probably not because they're looking for Jesus. We must initiate. We must make the first step. But you do not need a passport in order to start going. For you, the Great Commission begins in your hometown. And once you have proven yourself faithful in Jerusalem, God will expand your borders to Judea, and then Samaria and then to the ends of the earth. But it begins as you go.

### I DON'T KNOW WHAT TO SAY

As I write this I am only recently removed from the hardest season of my life. My wife's mother, Sharon, had battled liver problems since she was two years old. For decades her liver had failed her, despite living a good life. Multiple times in the past 20 years she was admitted to the hospital, and the doctors had essentially given up on her, giving her no hope for a recovery. Each time Michelle and her family would acknowledge the facts from the doctor but would choose to believe the truth of God's Word instead. They prayed for her healing and time and again she was healed.

The past few years things started to decline at an accelerated pace to the point that she was going to need a liver transplant. There were a number of different options presented to her and we were hopeful that perhaps she would get a new liver. In fact, we were only a few weeks away from what we hoped would be an opportunity for a liver transplant when my mother-in-law became unresponsive and went into a coma. The doctors found bleeding on her brain and coupled with her already failing liver, gave us a very negative prognosis. But we prayed. For one week we lived in the hospital, praying over mom. Quoting the word. Anointing her with oil. Singing songs of freedom over her. So many others joined in faith for us for her supernatural healing, just as we had seen demonstrated before.

On April 29, 2015 my mother-in-law received her ultimate healing and went to be with her Savior in Heaven. It is difficult to put into words how much this hurt. My wife and our family hurt so badly. We grieved (and continue to grieve). And even though we have the assurance of seeing her again, there is still a massive void that remains. Along with the void, we were left with many questions. There have been many late nights where I have held Michelle as she wept and asked the hardest and most difficult questions I have ever been asked. I certainly don't have all of the answers, but in the moments of not knowing what to say, I have been so grateful for the help of the Holy Spirit who always knows what to do and say. Very often there is nothing I can say, and my job is to simply hold Michelle and mourn with her (Romans 12:15). But then there are times when I feel led to speak, and my words provide comfort and strength for Michelle, and I realize that those words were not my own but rather because of the leading of the Holy Spirit. In those moments when I truly don't know what to say, the Holy Spirit is there to help and guide me.

*"When you are brought before synagogues, rulers and authorities, do not worry about how you will defend yourselves or what you will say, for the Holy Spirit will teach you at that time what you should say."* – Luke 12:11-12

I'm not sure what your life is like but I know that for me, I don't frequently meet with presidents, governors or synagogue rulers. And yet, if brought before them, the promise from Christ is that I can have confidence that the Holy Spirit will guide me to know what to say. If that is true for the leaders of nations, how much more is it true with my friends or coworkers or neighbors? Additionally, when Jesus gives this encouragement, it is in the context of a difficult, persecuted situation. It was not simply that the disciples were fearful that they might look stupid in front of the Sanhedrin or that they may not know what to say in front of the political leaders—these men were concerned for their lives. One misspoken word could warrant the death penalty. And yet, the assurance from Christ is that in that difficult situation the Holy Spirit is present to give you the words to speak. That same assurance is ours as we do the work of the Lord.

Now, do not misunderstand me. Some people take this too far and think that the Holy Spirit will do all of the work and that they don't need to worry about anything. As a result, they don't prepare, they don't study and they don't do anything to make themselves ready to be used by God. We do have a part to play. God washed away our sins, not our minds. We have been given a brain and books for a reason. Knowledge is not acquired by osmosis. Knowledge is acquired by focused diligence. Prepare as much as you are able to prepare yourself for the Great Commission, but then also rely on the Holy Spirit. The Holy Spirit can only bring to your remembrance what you have already committed to memory (John 14:26). You can't remember something you did not previously know. So too the Holy Spirit cannot help you remember something you did not spend the time to learn. Invest now what you want to reap later. If you want to reap a prepared and capable life in the context of evangelism, then invest into that dream and calling today. The Holy Spirit's supernatural guidance and preparation go hand in hand. It is not an either/or philosophy; it is a both/and.

## *WHAT IF I DON'T HAVE THE ANSWER?*

*A second time they summoned the man who had been blind. "Give glory to God by telling the truth," they said. "We know this man is a sinner." He replied, "Whether he is a sinner or not, I don't know. One thing I do know. I was blind but now I see!"* – John 9:24-25

This is one of my favorite stories in Scripture. Jesus met a man who had been born blind and gave the man a gift he would never forget: he gave the man his vision. The man was ecstatic and began to rejoice, telling everyone that he had been healed. The Pharisees heard about this miracle and because the man had been healed on the Sabbath, they were infuriated and demanded to know who had healed the man. The blind man didn't know Jesus and despite being questioned, he had very little he could offer the Pharisees. So the Pharisees called the man's parents to validate that this man was, in fact, blind at one point. They confirmed it but had no explanation for how this had happened. Once again the Pharisees called upon the man and asked him about the Healer and whether or not He was a sinner; and the man's response is one of my favorite answers in Scripture: "Whether He is a sinner or not, I don't know. One thing I do know. I was blind but now I see."

Some of you really need to hear this next statement: It's ok if you don't know the answer. It's important for you to hear that. We often think that in order for us to be effective evangelists, we have to know all there is to know about every subject. The reality is, though, no one knows all there is to know about anything, even those who study a given subject for their entire lives. If we knew it all and had all the answers, then what would be the point of the Holy Spirit? The Holy Spirit is our Teacher (John 14:26), but if we already know everything then we do not need a Teacher.

Furthermore, it is not your job to have the answer to every question or to be an expert on every subject. In fact, I find it incredibly refreshing when a leader is humble enough to admit that they don't have all of the answers. And the reality is that it is not your job to have every answer. It is your job to introduce people to the Answer. The man who was healed of his blindness was not educated. He didn't attend seminary. He didn't have all of the answers, and he even admitted as such. But that did not keep him from testifying to Jesus and what Jesus had done for him.

It is not a defeat to simply say, "I don't know." In fact, it has the potential to help a great deal. People are often much more comfortable and willing to discuss with a person who doesn't act like he knows it all. We should not be intentionally ignorant (see the previous point), but we should also not let our lack of knowledge keep us from sharing what we do know. When you admit that you don't know the answer, you create an opportunity to find the answer together. For example, if you are witnessing to a Muslim man about the difference between Jesus and Muhammad and he asks you a question that you don't know the answer to, the best way that you can respond is to simply say, "That is a great question and to be honest, I haven't researched that question, but I would love to find the answer. Why don't we work together to find the answer?" Think of the opportunity this gives you to walk through the Scriptures with an unbeliever. Not only that, but because the "gospel is true, it can stand up to the toughest questions and most vehement criticism. We do not need to have all the answers. A simple 'I do not know' response is not a rejection of Christ, nor is it a denial that an answer to a specific question exists."[36]

The Great Commission is not only given to seminary students or pastors or CEO's of non-profit organizations. The Great Commission is given to everyone who calls himself a disciple. It is a mandate from the very mouth of God, and yet so often we find excuse after excuse to distance ourselves from that commission and to justify our inaction. Instead of choosing one of the many excuses I have outlined in this chapter (or another one that comes to your mind), consciously decide to devote your life to the work of the Lord today. Yes, if you want an excuse, you can find one, but you won't find one that is good enough to stand up against the command of Scripture.

# CHAPTER 7

# SUBCONSCIOUS EXCUSES

## I DON'T HAVE WHAT IT TAKES

*One of those days Jesus went out to a mountainside to pray, and spent the night praying to God. When morning came, he called his disciples to him and chose twelve of them, whom he also designated apostles: Simon (whom he named Peter), his brother Andrew, James, John, Philip, Bartholomew, Matthew, Thomas, James son of Alphaeus, Simon who was called the Zealot, Judas son of James, and Judas Iscariot, who became a traitor.* – Luke 6:12-16

In the 21st century it is easy to think that one must have a degree in order to complete the call of God. Society tells us that someone must have a certain level of experience or education in order to fulfill the mission that God has for him or her. And yet, the Bible promotes a very different message. God chooses 7 and 8-year-old kings like Joash and Josiah to lead the people of Israel. God picks a teenage boy as the one to face off against Goliath and deliver the Israelites from the Philistines. The Son of God is not born in a palace or in the temple, nor is He born to a family of notoriety or prestige; instead Jesus is born in the humblest of places to a peasant teenage girl. The message of the Bible is that God is not concerned about appearances or qualifications. Jesus is concerned about what's in your heart, and with His help, all things are possible.

Perhaps this is no truer than in Jesus' decision-making regarding His disciples. Luke tells us that Jesus spent the entire night praying to God for His disciples before He chose them. And yet, in the eyes of the world, Jesus could not have chosen a more unqualified, irrational group of individuals than the 12 that He did. If I were Jesus, I would want the absolute best and I probably would have gone to the Temple to find them. I would have approached the

Rabbi and said, "Who are your top students? The ones who have memorized all of the Old Testament, the ones who are always here serving, the ones who have demonstrated knowledge and aptitude in theology. Those are the ones I want." Maybe I would have gone to the seminary and asked them who their top students were—those are the ones I want. Or perhaps I might have visited the most prominent marketing firm in Jerusalem and say, "Who are you brightest and most hardworking young employees or interns? I need some men who are going to come up with some cutting-edge commercials and a state of the art website and who are really going to be able to market me and my new book (it's called the Bible, and I'm confident it could be a be a *New York Times* Bestseller)!" I may have even asked the head of the military who his best officers were. If I ever needed some bodyguards, the military would be a great place to look. That's probably the way that I would have went about doing it, but that's not how Jesus did it.

Jesus spent an entire night praying about who to pick to fill His inner circle. This is an exclusive group if there ever was one: the opportunity to learn from the Messiah. Those are important positions to fill. But Jesus picks some of the most unlikely people to fill those positions. To begin with, He chooses a tax collector—Matthew was a Jew so the Romans hated him, but he worked for the Romans and cheated people out of their money, so the Jews hated him. Not exactly the public relations move I would have expected. Then there's Nathanael. He is a racist! When he hears that Jesus is from Nazareth he asks, "Nazareth? Can anything good come from there?" (John 1:46). Nathanael was against Jesus purely because He was from Nazareth. Then you've got the Zebedee boys, James and John. For starters, Jesus did not find them in the Temple studying the Torah. He found them fishing on the lake, which was not typically the profession of the brightest individuals. Secondly, these guys were out of control. Their nickname was the "Sons of Thunder" because they were always causing a commotion. For example, one time, Jesus sent His disciples ahead of him to a Samaritan village to get things ready for His arrival, but the town rejected Him. James' and John's response would be hard to believe if it weren't in the Bible, "Lord, do you want us to call down fire from Heaven to destroy them?" (Luke 9:54). That was their question! Can you imagine a similar encounter today? "Pastor, we went to this hotel to get our rooms and the people there were very unwelcoming. Do you want us to go and light the hotel on fire?" And, of course, there is Peter, who probably had more questionable statements and actions than any of the apostles.

When I think about the apostles I think about how strange Jesus' choices were. He stayed up all night to choose these men? They were certainly not the men that I would have chosen, and yet, I am so glad that He chose those that He did. Jesus did not call the most qualified or the most intelligent or the most skilled to fulfill the Great Commission. The men that He chose to entrust the message of the Gospel with were not the obvious choices, but this only confirms what Paul wrote when He said, "God chose the foolish things of this world to shame the wise; God chose the weak things of the world to shame the strong" (1 Corinthians 1:27). In the eyes of the world the disciples certainly didn't have what it took to be the leaders of the Christian Church, but the Lord worked with them and equipped them to change the world.

Most people would never announce that they don't have what it takes, and many people may not even realize that they think that way, but by the way that they live their lives they demonstrate that they don't believe that they're good enough to be used by God. For those who feel that they have nothing to give, take a page out of the life of those same apostles.

*One day Peter and John were going up to the temple at the time of prayer—at three in the afternoon. Now a man who was lame from birth was being carried to the temple gate called Beautiful, where he was put every day to beg from those going into the temple courts. When he saw Peter and John about to enter, he asked them for money. Peter looked straight at him, as did John. Then Peter said, "Look at us!" So the man gave them his attention, expecting to get something from them. Then Peter said, "Silver or gold I do not have, but what I do have I give you. In the name of Jesus Christ of Nazareth, walk." Taking him by the right hand, he helped him up, and instantly the man's feet and ankles became strong. He jumped to his feet and began to walk. Then he went with them into the temple courts, walking and jumping, and praising God. – Acts 3:1-8*

Peter and John came to the temple that morning with absolutely nothing in their hands. In fact, when the paralytic specifically asked them for money, they could not help. In the natural, they did not have anything to help the man. Yet their response 2,000 years ago still serves as an example for us today. Peter and John realized that even when they had nothing, if they had Jesus, then they had everything! And because of that revelation they were able to look at the paralytic and say to him, "Silver or gold I do not have but what I have I give you...Jesus Christ!" Today, you may feel as though you have very little to offer God as it pertains to the Great Commission, but if Peter and John are any indication, the Lord specializes in using people who are unqualified in the eyes of the world. If the disciples proved anything, it is that with Christ, you have what it takes.

## I DON'T WANT TO

*They went to a place called Gethsemane, and Jesus said to his disciples, "Sit here while I pray." He took Peter, James and John along with him, and he began to be deeply distressed and troubled. "My soul is overwhelmed with sorrow to the point of death," he said to them. "Stay here and keep watch." Going a little farther, he fell to the ground and prayed that if possible the hour might pass from him. "Abba, Father," he said, "everything is possible for you. Take this cup from me. Yet not what I will, but what you will." – Mark 14:32-36*

As horrible as this excuse sounds, it is one of the most common. Most people would never admit that they feel this way, but if we were honest with ourselves, many times we would just rather not evangelize. We often refuse the call of God on our lives simply because we would rather not do it. The reality, though, is that our relationship with Christ will often require us to put aside our flesh. In fact, being a Christian demands constant crucifixion of the flesh. The flesh would prefer to sleep in on Sunday mornings rather than wake up to go to church. The flesh would prefer to not give tithes and offerings and instead keep all of our income.

People often ask me why I travel to the places that I do. They ask, "Wouldn't it be easier if you just ministered in North

America?" Ministering in America is certainly not without its challenges, but I have found the discomforts to be greater overseas, in the places that we go. Ministry is difficult enough on its own, but it becomes increasingly more difficult with things like jetlag, dirty accommodations and a less-than-ideal diet. So, why would we go? The reason has, and always will be the same: it is out of a deep love for God and people. The Lord has asked us to fulfill the Great Commission and that may mean certain levels of discomfort, but the opportunity to bring others into the family of God is always worth whatever discomfort it may cost. If we are going to be true disciples of Jesus, it will often require us to do what we may naturally not prefer to do, but it will always be well worth it.

Jesus, as perfect as He was, still had to put aside his own desires for our sake. Jesus didn't want to go to the cross, but He willingly laid aside His preferences for us. When we witness, especially when we don't want to, we lay aside our preferences for someone else's. There is nothing more selfish than keeping the cure from the one who needs it. When Jesus took up the cross, He laid down His personal feelings. When we witness, we take up that same cross in order to reach this world. The love of Jesus drove Him to the pain of the cross. The love for the lost must also drive us to fulfill the Great Commission.

## *I'M TOO BUSY*

*Jesus entered Jericho and was passing through. A man was there by the name of Zacchaeus; he was a chief tax collector and was wealthy. He wanted to see who Jesus was, but because he was short he could not see over the crowd. So he ran ahead and climbed a sycamore-fig tree to see him, since Jesus was coming that way. When Jesus reached the spot, he looked up and said to him, "Zacchaeus, come down immediately. I must stay at your house today." So he came down at once and welcomed him gladly. All the people saw this and began to mutter, "He has gone to be the guest of a sinner."*

*But Zacchaeus stood up and said to the Lord, "Look, Lord! Here and now I give half of my possessions to the poor, and if I have cheated anybody out of anything, I will pay back four times the amount." Jesus said to him, "Today salvation has come to this house, because this man, too, is a son of Abraham. For the Son of Man came to seek and to save the lost." –* Luke 19:1-10

Have you ever taken the *Strengths Finder* test? If not, the *Strengths Finder* test essentially works to identify your most dominant personal traits so that you can be aware of where you are strongest, and the things for which you need to be aware. One of my strongest characteristics is that of an achiever. An achiever takes "great satisfaction from being busy and productive,"[37] An achiever feels as if "every day starts at zero. By the end of the day you must achieve something tangible in order to feel good about yourself."[38] This describes me very well. While it is good to work hard, it also has the potential to be a problem. An achiever will often draw much of his self worth from the things that he accomplishes. Our society is full of achievers where we glorify busyness; and I fall victim to this mindset far too often. Our culture has given us so many things to do and has celebrated those who are busy, where we feel guilty if we aren't as busy as someone else. This busyness has a crippling effect on many people, though. If I am not careful, my need to be busy will wear me out. I won't get the sleep or the rest that I need. I won't spend the quality time with my wife that our marriage requires. And often the busyness of our lives, even the busyness of ministry, will get in the way of spending time with Jesus.

The story of Zacchaeus is one of my favorite stories in Scripture, and one of the reasons is because it shows so much about how Jesus lived His daily life with a focus on people. As Jesus was passing through Jericho the people began to flock to Him, and for good reason. Jesus was practically the most popular man in the world. Everywhere He went He drew a crowd. Everything He did was catalogued. If there was a busy man, Jesus was it. It would have been incredibly easy for Jesus to ignore Zacchaeus in the tree. It would have been very easy to disregard him because of His schedule. But Jesus didn't allow His busyness to get in the way of Zacchaeus' moment with Him.

Jesus always left room for divine interruptions. If you read the Gospels you will find that practically all of Jesus' miracles were unplanned. Jesus never entered a town on the prowl for the local blind man so that He could heal him. Jesus didn't intentionally tell 5,000 men to forget their lunches so that He could work a miracle. Jesus didn't tell the disciples to boat in the middle of a storm so that He could calm the wind and the waves. The miracles of Christ were not scheduled, but the opportunity for them was. We must never let our schedule become so concrete that we do not allow for divine interruptions. If Jesus had allowed His busy schedule to dictate His life, then Zacchaeus, and countless others, would have never had an experience with Jesus. I wonder how many times I have missed an opportunity to share the Gospel because my life was too busy. If your schedule is too busy to allow for divine interruptions, then your schedule is too busy.

*Yet the news about him spread all the more, so that crowds of people came to hear him and to be healed of their sicknesses. But Jesus often withdrew to lonely places and prayed.* – Luke 5:15-16

There are so many people, in ministry or otherwise, who do not know how to rest. Perhaps the most overlooked of the Ten Commandments would be the fourth, to remember the Sabbath and keep it holy. How often do we actually observe the Sabbath, though? The American culture has created an environment where busyness is praised. We are addicted to being busy, to the point that vacation and rest have become taboo. A study done by MasterCard discovered that in 2013, 429 million vacation days went unclaimed, with the majority of those being paid vacation days.[39] And of those who took vacation days, the study showed that 61% of people continued to work while on vacation.[40] Not only are we not resting, even when we say we're resting, we are working.

As with everything, Jesus is our perfect example, and the Gospels describe Jesus as a Man who took rest seriously. As the Son of God, He certainly had no shortage of work to be done, but He recognized that in order for Him to be effective in ministry, it required retreating from ministry in order to rest. In the story above, the crowds flocked to Jesus asking Him to heal them. It would have been easy for Jesus to see the needs of the people and feel compelled to minister, but instead Jesus withdrew to rest and pray. And this Lukan example is not atypical. Luke writes that this was Jesus' habit; He *often* withdrew from the crowds. We too must learn to often withdraw from people and work and social media for the purpose of rest. We must fight the American addiction of being busy and slow down.

"I have so much to do today that I'm going to need to spend three hours in prayer in order to be able to get it all done."[41] – Martin Luther

May our schedule never become so busy that we cut out the necessary time with the Lord and our family. Luther's statement is challenging, but also inspiring. Luther knew that in order for Him to do everything He had to do, He needed to take the time to rest. My pastor, Paul Daugherty, preached a message on this recently where he said, "We are not forsaking our responsibilities when we rest. It is for the sake of our responsibilities that we rest."[42] Rest well so that you can work well. Rest is designed to help us succeed, while overworking ourselves will limit our effectiveness. If you've ever spoken to someone who is nearing death, I can guarantee you will never hear him say, "I wish I would have spent more time in the office. I only wish I would have spent more time staying up late at night working. I really regret all of the time I spent with my wife and kids on vacation." Our regrets will not be because we weren't busy enough; it will be because we were too busy.

## I'M TOO DISTRACTED

Continuing with the story of Zacchaeus, I am amazed at Jesus' ability to stay focused. Not only did Jesus allow for divine interruptions but He also made a point to prepare for them by refusing to be distracted. Think about it: Jesus' busy schedule was not the only thing that could have kept Him from meeting with Zacchaeus. In fact, the easier and more likely possibility for this story is that Jesus would have simply missed Zacchaeus. Hundreds of people surrounded Jesus as He made His way through Jericho. People would have been pressing against Him and asking Him for various miracles. There were distractions literally all around Him, and then there was Zacchaeus sitting in a sycamore tree. Luke doesn't tell us that Zacchaeus was shouting at Jesus or waving at Him trying to get His attention. It wasn't Zacchaeus who reached out to Jesus; it was

Jesus who reached out to Zacchaeus. It would have been incredibly easy for Jesus to miss Zacchaeus based solely on the distractions that surrounded Him, but He didn't.

This world is constantly fighting for our attention. Social media, world news, sports, entertainment and people are constantly distracting us. In fact, oftentimes even good things distract us and cause us to miss those divine interruptions. The distractions come in a variety of ways and many times they aren't negative things, but sometimes small distractions can turn into big mistakes. Let me give you an example.

As I have said before, my wife is an amazing cook, but even the best cooks must put away distractions in order for the meal to turn out well. Towards the beginning of our marriage Michelle had made us dinner. It was a pasta dish where the sauce recipe asked for a large amount of parmesan cheese. I don't know what Michelle was doing. Maybe she was watching a show on her iPad. Maybe she was singing. Or maybe she was just distracted by her own thoughts. Whatever it was, the point is that she was distracted. And as a result, when Michelle read that the recipe called for a lot of "parmesan," she read it as "parsley" and proceeded to put in lots of parsley. I'm not sure if you know what parsley tastes like—before that night I know that I didn't—but I can assure you that I know what it tastes like now! The phrase "a little goes a long way" certainly applies to parsley, so if a little goes a long way, then a lot goes a lot farther than it should. I took that first bite and was instantly hit with a much stronger flavor than I had expected. Now I was in a predicament. I could fight my way through the meal and eat it as if nothing was wrong, so as to keep the peace. I could say something and risk hurting her feelings. Or I could simply wait it out and hope that her plate of pasta tasted the same as mine. I anxiously watched as Michelle took her first bite and was relieved when I saw her face. She spit out her food and said, "Did you taste this?" "Yes," I responded, "and I'm so glad you taste the same thing that I do so I didn't have to fake it." We threw out the pasta and ate sandwiches instead as we laughed about the simple yet significant difference between parmesan and parsley.

While the story is lighthearted, and ultimately the distraction only cost us some pasta, the story proves a point. Distractions often cause us to miss God's divine interruptions for our lives. How many times have we missed an opportunity to minister to someone because every free moment we have is spent looking down at our phones? Let us learn from Christ's example and keep our eyes focused on the world around us so that we are never distracted from an opportunity to minister.

## *I'M TOO HOLY*

This is probably the least likely excuse that someone would verbalize, but in reality, it so very often keeps us from reaching people. I was just recently having lunch with a friend of mine who is the youth pastor in the inner city. When he began as youth pastor six months ago the youth group had a whopping four people. The senior pastor told him that if he would grow the youth group he would go from part-time to full-time youth pastor. In six months he had grown that youth group from 4 to 45 and seen transformation in so many of the students. It has been incredibly hard and time-consuming work, but to see students' lives changed, it has been time well spent. You would think that the church members and the senior pastor would be thrilled for such rapid growth, right? Wrong.

As I mentioned, the church is in an area of town that struggles economically, and while the majority of the congregation are elderly, white, upper class, the community surrounding the church is not. As a result, the entire youth group is comprised of African-American students, many of which deal with incredibly difficult home lives. If you could hear the stories of what so many of these students have to go through, you would be appalled. My friend recently had a meeting with the senior pastor about increasing his pay considering how rapidly and exponentially the youth group had grown. The senior pastor responded, "Well, you didn't grow the youth group the way I had hoped." What he meant was that he was interested in a youth group with white, suburban kids who brought their wealthy parents to church. He wasn't interested in growing the church. He was interested in growing the budget, and the poor, lower class students were costing him money.

He told me a story about how one Wednesday night two of the teenage boys walked forty-five minutes one way in the heat of the summer just to get to youth group. They arrived early, earlier than my youth pastor friend, who was still picking up other students. When the students arrived, though, the ushers at the church wouldn't allow the boys into the air-conditioned church until the youth pastor arrived. They had walked forty-five minutes in the Oklahoma heat just to come to youth group, and when they arrived they were turned away because they weren't the type of students that the church really wanted. To hear a story like that broke my heart and infuriated me at the same time. I was reminded of Jesus with the Pharisees. Wasn't that one of Jesus' main problem with the religious leaders? They were too holy to reach out to the tax collectors and prostitutes?

When you look at the story of Zacchaeus you can see that Jesus was not too holy. Remember that Zacchaeus was a tax collector, hated by the community. He was an outcast from society. The religious leaders of the day would certainly have nothing to do with him because of their "holiness." They would not stoop down to Zacchaeus' level. They certainly would not pick him out of a crowd to ask to go to his house for dinner. This was completely unreasonable. Jesus was doing the unthinkable. Jesus did not consider Himself too holy to spend time with the outcast. Jesus was not too holy to have dinner with sinners. Thankfully Jesus was willing to spend time with sinners, because if not, salvation would not have come to Zacchaeus' house.

I have had the opportunity to travel all over the world preaching, and some of the saddest experiences I've ever had have been my conversations with internationals concerning other preachers. I remember one such time in India where we were working with a new crusade director for the first time. He picked us up from the airport and brought us to a really nice hotel, even by American standards. The next morning when he came to pick us up we thanked him for the nice hotel but we told him, "We don't need to stay in a hotel like this. We are content to stay where you stay, even in your home. If it is good enough for you, then it is good enough for us." He was shocked. He said, "Thank you for saying that. I have worked with many well-known preachers and even this beautiful hotel is never good enough for them." He then proceeded to tell me a story about a well-known minister whom he had hosted. He brought this minister to this hotel as well and shortly after dropping the minister off he received a call. The minister had found a piece of hair in the bathroom sink and demanded to be moved to a new hotel. Aside from being upset with the minister, I was devastated that someone bearing the name of Christ had acted in such a disrespectful way towards our crusade director.

On another trip, I was having dinner with all of the pastors after one of the crusade nights. They had invited our team to eat with them at one of the pastor's homes after the service, and of course I agreed. Now, I should let you know that while I love food, the one food that I cannot stand is Indian food. And yet, I have been to India nine times! Sometimes I ask the Lord, "Why can't you send me to Italy or Mexico or Greece? I love those kinds of food!" But, if the Indians are offering me food, I will do my best to receive and enjoy their generous gift. As I was eating with my hands I looked up from my plate to see the pastors staring at me. I wondered if I had something on my face. "Is everything ok?" I asked. The pastors said to me, "Thank you for eating with us. The western preachers never eat with us. It means a lot to us that you would eat our food with us." Jesus went out of His way to eat with Zacchaeus. He was not too religious that He couldn't eat with a tax collector like Zacchaeus. How much more should we be willing to stay in bad hotels or to eat with foreign pastors?

There are many pastors and church leaders who take on the attitude of a superstar. There are certainly times where men and women of God have to distance themselves and they need time to themselves, but if you are too good or too big or too holy for the people to whom you are ministering, something is wrong. My home church, Victory Christian Center, is one of the largest churches in America and it would be very easy for my pastor, Paul Daugherty, to take on the superstar attitude; but he doesn't. One of the things that I love about my pastor is that though there may be thousands of people in the service with multiple exits out of the sanctuary, unless He is ministering to someone at the altar, at the conclusion of each service he will run to the back doors to greet people as they leave. That is the heart of Jesus. How can you be my pastor if you don't even know me? In John 10 Jesus says that there are sheep who don't know the shepherd's voice, but I believe that there are also many shepherds who don't know their own sheep's voices because they are too good or too holy to spend time with them. Ministry is not about being a celebrity; it is about being a servant. Never become too holy to spend time with sinners. Even the most holy man alive was not too holy for that.

Sometimes the most often-used excuses for why we don't fulfill the Great Commission are subconscious ones that we would rarely identify or admit to having, but they are incredibly devastating to the expansion of the Gospel. None of us are perfect and I am certainly guilty of many, if not all of these excuses at one point or another. But instead of dwelling on our mistakes, let us repent and identify them as areas of growth. The world is desperately in need of our message, not our excuses.

# CHAPTER 8

# INCORRECT EVANGELISM

## *NINJA WITNESSING*

As I have mentioned previously, I grew up in a very evangelistically minded home, for which I am incredibly grateful. As a result, some of the things that we would do for "fun" growing up were really quite unique. For example, I remember a time where, for a few weeks, we had been going over a Bible study on the importance of one-on-one evangelism and learning how to do it. Well, one day my dad had obviously felt that it was time for us to put into practice what we had learned so he dropped us four boys off at Wal-Mart and told us to come back to the van once we had witnessed to someone, and then he would take us all to eat. Free food was just about all the motivation that teenage boys needed to share the gospel so we went in and did some one-on-one evangelism.

One specific evangelistic exercise that we would do, growing up, was to give out tracts (little brochures that communicate the gospel). Now, giving out tracts was fun, but only for so long. At 8, 10 and 12 years old, giving out tracts got old pretty quickly. So dad had this ingenious idea where we would become tract ninjas. We would go to the mall with a handful of tracts and enter the bathrooms. We would then proceed to enter each bathroom stall and roll out just a little bit of the toilet paper, place a tract onto the toilet paper, and then roll it back up. That way, the next unsuspecting patron to the stall would roll out his paper and have the gospel dropped right in front of him. We were creating an evangelistic environment right there in those bathroom stalls.

I look back on those stories and laugh, while at the same time thanking God for giving me a father who emphasized the importance of evangelism. That being said, for some of you, the words "evangelism" and "witnessing" have some very negative connotations. And the reasons for those feelings may be quite justified. From what I have found, the primary reason why people have a problem with witnessing or evangelism is because they may have either experienced evangelism done incorrectly. This creates an obstruction to evangelism that keeps us from doing what we are supposed to do. In order to know how to correctly evangelize, it is sometimes helpful to know how *not* to evangelize.

## FIRE AND BRIMSTONE

*Or do you show contempt for the riches of his kindness, forbearance and patience, not realizing that God's kindness is intended to lead you to repentance?* – Romans 2:4

As with most things in life, there is a need for balance. If proper theology and mission is a road, it is a narrow one with large ditches on either side. It is very easy to fall into a ditch on either side of the road. And when there is no balance, our theology and mission veers to one side of the road and we fall into an unfortunate ditch. One of the ditches when it comes to the Gospel is the fire and brimstone message. We have probably all experienced or heard of a "fire and brimstone" preacher. I define this type of message as one where Hell and condemnation are emphasized over and above the grace and love of God. This message is usually devoid of any good news.

Now, there is nothing wrong about preaching about Hell, in fact, most of what we know about Hell comes straight from the mouth of Jesus Himself. As you will see in my next point, I have no problem with preaching on Hell and sin and the need for repentance. The problem arises when we emphasize Hell at the expense of Heaven. There are many preachers who focus so heavily on how sinful we are without mentioning Jesus' sacrifice. They focus on how much God hates our sin without mentioning how much He loves us. They focus on how our sin will lead to unimaginable and eternal torment in Hell without mentioning the glorious eternal home for those who accept Christ. There is value in making the sick aware of their sickness and of the outcome of that sickness, but if all we do is emphasize the sickness and its consequences without also mentioning the cure, then we have missed the point altogether. The word "Gospel" literally means "good news," but the message that some preach doesn't sound like good news at all.

Think about the very term "good news." Good news implies that there must be another type of news as well, a different, contrasting type of news. If all news was good news then there would no need to call it "good;" by default, it would simply be "news." So, in order to make the good news good, we must first make someone aware of the bad news. The problem is that some preachers only focus on the bad news—we are sinners, we are destined for death and torment in Hell for eternity—and fail to mention the other news, the part that makes the Gospel good news. Salvation should not be the result of a scare tactic. Salvation should be the result of a deep desire to accept the good news in substitution for the bad news. Do not scare people into the kingdom, because fear has never motivated anyone towards love. Furthermore, if people make decisions out of fear, they can just as easily change their mind. If someone is scared into salvation, more than likely they will also be scared out of it.

This is why I get upset with certain street evangelists. If you are on a corner preaching the whole Gospel, I applaud your courage and devotion to evangelism. If you are approaching people and engaging them in a one-on-one conversation that ends with you sharing about Christ's sacrifice, I commend your passion to win the lost. One of the great evangelists of our world today, Ray Comfort, does an excellent job of winning people to the Lord on street corners and in one-on-one evangelism. I have no problem with that. But that is very different than a man shouting through a bullhorn, "You're all sinners! You're going to Hell! God is disgusted with you and your sin!" Where is the good news in that?

In the verse referenced above, Paul quite clearly states that God's kindness leads men to repentance. The Greek word translated as "kindness" is *chrestos*, which can also mean "goodness, kind, loving."[43] The grace of God was "designed and adapted"[44] to lead people to repentance. It is *that* type of kindness that God has demonstrated unto us for the purpose of salvation. Emphasizing fear or doom is not what leads men to repentance. It is the whole

Gospel—which climaxes with the love and kindness of God—that brings people to salvation. As you share the Gospel, be careful to make sure that it is actually good news, both to the hearer and to Heaven.

## HYPER-GRACE

*What shall we say, then? Shall we go on sinning so that grace may increase? By no means! We are those who have died to sin; how can we live in it any longer?* – Romans 6:1-2

Throughout the 18th, 19th and the beginning of the 20th century, many of the American pastors and evangelists preached a "fire and brimstone" gospel. This created a lot of fear and legalism in the Church and the general public categorized Christianity as judgmental and hardhearted. This was not the heart of God, and well-meaning Christians desired to change this by emphasizing the love and grace of God. While there is certainly nothing wrong with the love and grace of God, in many ways we have now fallen into the other side of the ditch in the 21st century. Imagine a large grandfather clock that has a huge pendulum swinging back and forth. For decades, and even centuries, the pendulum was on one side, and now the pendulum has swung to the other side. If fire and brimstone is one side of the ditch, hyper-grace is the other side of the ditch.

The Bible is very clear about God's attitude towards sin. He hates sin. But the reason why He hates sin is because of what it does to people. It is out of His love that He hates sin. The hyper-grace message, though, would prefer to not talk about sin; yet Jesus talked about sin quite a bit. The hyper-grace message often ignores the teaching on Hell. But the Bible doesn't do that. In fact, Jesus talks about Hell twice as much as He does about Heaven.[45] I am not saying that you must preach on Hell more than Heaven, but to completely throw out any mention of Hell flies in the face of the Scriptures. Jesus, Paul and all of the New Testament writers make it quite clear that sin and Hell are not taboo topics but rather topics of the utmost importance because they make us aware of our need for Christ.

One of the hallmarks of the hyper-grace gospel is to overemphasize the grace of God. Now, let me be clear, the grace and love of God is unbelievably amazing. When done properly, it really cannot be overemphasized enough. The problem comes when the love and grace of God are elevated to the highest position with no balance of God's other characteristics. God is Love (1 John 4:8). No Bible-believing Christian would ever deny that or even diminish that. But He is not *only* love. Scripture also describes Him as just, jealous, righteous and holy. Just as bad news without the good news is incorrect evangelism, so good news without first mentioning the bad news is incorrect evangelism. One of the common pitfalls in the Church today is to preach all grace, or hyper-grace, to the point that God's judgment and holiness are devalued, or forgotten altogether.

If you were to describe God in one word, what would that word be? If you were to identify God's primary characteristic, what would you choose? The vast majority of people in the world today would respond with "love." And yet, when describing God, love is not the most commonly used word in Scripture. It is "holy." In fact, when Isaiah, and then later the apostle John, had a vision of Heaven, they saw God surrounded by angels. These angels had one job: night and day they would worship God by declaring the same thing over and over again. Eternally they cry, "holy, holy, holy." But how often do we think of God as holy, set apart and coming back for a pure and spotless bride?

When I think about the world in which we live today, I am struck by how many people abuse the grace of God. There is no sense of righteousness or holiness or sanctification. They view the grace of God as a license to sin and freedom from guilt. Yet Paul opens Romans 6 by declaring that just because the grace of God is present does not mean we should take advantage of it by sinning. In fact, the grace of God doesn't permit you to sin; instead it empowers you not to sin, just as Jesus demonstrated with the adulterous woman in John 8. When He told her to go, He didn't overlook her sin or condone her sin; He imparted His grace to her that empowered her to say "no" to sin!

*In the presence of God and of Christ Jesus, who will judge the living and the dead, and in view of his appearing and his kingdom,*

*I give you this charge: Preach the word; be prepared in season and out of season; correct, rebuke and encourage—with great patience and careful instruction. For the time will come when people will not put up with sound doctrine. Instead, to suit their own desires, they will gather around them a great number of teachers to say what their itching ears want to hear. They will turn their ears away from the truth and turn aside to myths. But you, keep your head in all situations, endure hardship, do the work of an evangelist, discharge all the duties of your ministry.* – 2 Timothy 4:1-5

The apostle Paul wrote two letters to Timothy, one of his many sons in the faith. Timothy was a pastor trying to guide and disciple his congregation. In the last letter that Paul wrote, he wrote addressing Timothy's culture and time period, but it is as appropriate now as it was then. We would do well to learn from Paul's words as it seems as though he could not have known our time period and culture any better:

1. Paul begins by noting that God is judge, a judge who is going to judge the "living and the dead," in other words, everyone. Before giving His charge, Paul makes it clear that what he is about to say he says with the approval of God and with the presence of God firmly on his mind. The following verses should be read in light of the fact that God is more than just love; He is a judge.

2. Paul wants Timothy, a young preacher, to preach the Word. The first thing Paul instructed Timothy to do was to preach the Word of God. There are many churches that you can visit today, some of them even popular ones, and there is no mention of the Word. Or maybe the minister will open with the Bible but never mention it again, as if the introductory Bible verse was nothing more than obligatory. A true minister must preach the Word, not what his congregation necessarily wants to hear. When it comes to evangelism and witnessing, we must preach the truth of the Word, regardless of how inconvenient, uncomfortable or socially unacceptable it may be.

3. Be prepared in season and out of season. When it comes to evangelism, you must always be ready. You must be in a constant state of readiness because you don't know when you will need to share Christ or defend your faith. Jesus was not given a heads up

about the woman with the bent back showing up to the synagogue. Jesus was not given time to prepare for the woman with the issue of blood. Jesus didn't receive a warning that Nicodemus was coming to ask Him questions. He was just always ready; we must be too.

4. Correct, rebuke and encourage. That's 67% of the "negative" and 33% of the "positive." Many sermons you hear today are happy and uplifting, but totally devoid of any correction, rebuke or conviction. You can't just spoon-feed your congregation what they may want to hear. A child who is never disciplined is in danger. Regardless of what society may tell you, to not discipline your children is doing them a massive disservice (Proverbs 23:13-14). You must correct them and rebuke them if you are going to see them grow; but be sure to do so with "patience and careful instruction." As Paul says elsewhere, we must always "speak the truth in love" (Ephesians 4:15).

5. Perhaps the part of the passage above that sounds the most like our society is the third verse where Paul writes, "For the time will come when people will not put up with sound doctrine. Instead, to suit their own desires, they will gather around them a great number of teachers to say what their itching ears want to hear." That is exactly what is happening today. People who don't want to be convicted of their sins are turning to people and preachers and churches that will preach a radical grace message, one not based on sound doctrine but rather on personal preference, giving them a license to sin. Instead of changing their actions, they would rather change their church or their friends.

6. After all of these other commands, Paul tells Timothy to "do the work of an evangelist." The world in which we live needs more people doing the work of an evangelist. And what is that work? One aspect of that is just what Paul outlines here. Correct evangelism is preaching the whole Gospel. It is holding to sound doctrine that will correct, rebuke and encourage. It will not only preach the grace and love of God, but also the holiness and justice of God.

*For the wages of sin is death, but the gift of God is eternal life in Christ Jesus our Lord. –* Romans 6:23

On the road of salvation there are two oft-visited ditches of "fire and brimstone" and "hyper-grace." The solution is to find balance between the two and travel down the middle of the road. Perhaps no better verse sums up that balance than the one above. Paul makes the Romans aware of their need for Christ by declaring that sin has a price tag: death. Yet, after making them aware of their depravity, Paul makes them aware of the unmerited and undeserved gift of God in Jesus Christ. May our communication of the Gospel always contain the message of this verse.

## FAKE CONVERSION

My favorite part of every church service is always the end. That isn't because I don't enjoy church and am anxious for it to be over, it is because I love the altar call. I love seeing people make a public decision to follow Christ. In my many years of volunteering and service in the local church, I have often been an altar counselor, meeting people who respond to the altar call so that I can pray with them. It is always a privilege to pray with someone. And yet, after doing it for many years, I have noticed something. Whether at youth group or in young adult ministry or regular church services, I found that I would often see the same people responding to the altar call week after week. I would find myself praying with the same people month after month.

Now, it wasn't that I had a problem praying with the same people or that it was even wrong for people to weekly repent of their sins, but I was confused. Why did the same people need to respond week after week? There were times I would personally follow up with a person with which I had prayed and would encourage him to live for the Lord. I would text him daily to make sure he wasn't in sin. And all too often I would hear back from him about how he had fallen and had to get "re-saved" again the next week. It wasn't that they weren't worth my time or that they needed to be perfect and never sin, but Jesus said that we should be able to notice a Christian by the fruit that he bears (Matthew 7:16) and there seemed to be a lack of fruit. At times it was very frustrating and exhausting for me to just try to help these people to live for the Lord. And, while

I would never say it, the thought would cross my mind, "Are they even saved?"

"It is my opinion that tens of thousands, if not millions, have been brought into some kind of religious experience by accepting Christ, but they have not been saved."[46] – A.W. Tozer

"The vast majority of members of churches in America today are not Christians. I say that without the slightest fear of contradiction."[47] – D. James Kennedy

Is this true? Is there such a thing as fake conversion? And if so, how does this happen? This is related to the points discussed above in that during the past 50 years there has been an overemphasis on the grace of God and de-emphasis on the judgment and law of God. We cannot fully appreciate the grace and mercy of Christ until we first understand the law and judgment of God. The reason why the vast majority of people who get saved backslide or turn their backs on Christianity or have to keep going back to the beginning is because an improper gospel has been presented to them.

*Brothers and sisters, I could not address you as people who live by the Spirit but as people who are still worldly—mere infants in Christ. I gave you milk, not solid food, for you were not yet ready for it. Indeed, you are still not ready.* – 1 Corinthians 3:1-2

*In fact, though by this time you ought to be teachers, you need someone to teach you the elementary truths of God's word all over again. You need milk, not solid food! Anyone who lives on milk, being still an infant, is not acquainted with the teaching about righteousness. But solid food is for the mature, who by constant use have trained themselves to distinguish good from evil.* – Hebrews 5:12-14

The reality is that there are many in the Church who are at a place of infancy (or worse) when they should be teachers and leaders. There is a lack of maturity because there has been a lack of biblical teaching. Many Christian ministers, evangelists, teachers and preachers have presented a gospel where the love, joy and grace of God has been offered without first mentioning the depravity of man and the necessity of forgiveness from a just God. In order to raise up disciples, we must preach the "whole counsel of God" (Acts 20:27), not just the parts that we find to be comfortable and comforting. In Paul's letter to the Romans, Paul outlines the type of format by which to present the gospel:

1. Chapters 1-4 deal with sin, justification and the faithfulness of God
2. Chapters 5-8 deal with the life of the justified
3. Chapters 9-11 is a parenthetical teaching on Israel
4. Chapters 12-16 deal with practical ethics

What you will find when you read Paul's opening 4 chapters to the Romans is that he begins by explaining the wickedness of man and the punishment for sin. He begins with this emphasis. It is only after sin is exposed for what it is, and humanity's peril is emphasized, that the message of the cross not only becomes relevant but essential. It is very easy to preach a gospel that sounds and feels good yet provides our audience with nothing more than false hope and a false understanding of God. It is imperative that when we preach the gospel we take Paul's example and begin with sin and its consequences.

Suppose that someone runs up to you and joyfully tells you, "I've got good news for you: I want you to know that I paid your $25,000 speeding ticket!" What? You would be thoroughly confused and probably respond, "That's not good news. That's nonsense. That doesn't make any sense. I don't have a $25,000 speeding ticket!" You wouldn't be grateful for that person; you would think he is crazy. Not only that, but the interaction would also probably offend you. This person is insinuating that you so severely broke the law that you have incurred a $25,000 fine when you are convinced you haven't broken any law. This man has not helped you; he has offended you and caused you to think he is foolish or worse.

But what if the interaction started out differently? Suppose the same man ran up to you and said, "You don't realize it but yesterday you violated a horrible traffic law. You were driving in a 55 mph area when you started approaching a school zone for the blind. There were ten large signs posted next to the road as you approached the school zone area. Each sign stated that the speed limit was 15 mph and was strictly enforced. The penalty for violating this school zone for the blind was severe. You didn't notice or chose to ignore those signs and traveled through that school zone at 55 mph, and the resulting fine is $25,000. Here's the good news: I just got back from the courthouse and I have paid the entirety of your fine." Now your response would be completely different. Since you have some context and explanation, you would no longer be confused or offended; you would be unbelievably grateful! In order for you to truly appreciate the payment for your penalty, though, you had to first hear about the broken law and its consequences, otherwise the message is offensive, confusing and irrelevant.[48]

So often the gospel is presented to someone by simply saying, "Jesus loves you and died for you" or "Jesus paid the price for your sins." However, by itself these phrases will be foolishness and offensive—foolishness because the message of the cross is foolishness to the sinner (1 Cor. 1:17), and offensive because you are insinuating that the person is a sinner. But if you take the time to follow the steps of Jesus and open up the law of God to the person, he will be made aware of his sin and then his need for salvation. The Gospel will no longer seem foolish or offensive; it will be life to him—the power of God unto salvation. This is the purpose of the law. Too often we view the law as evil or outdated for the New Covenant believer, but that is not the case.

*Now we know that whatever the law says, it says to those who are under the law, so that every mouth may be silenced and the whole world held accountable to God. Therefore, no one will be declared righteous in God's sight by the works of the law; rather, through the law we become conscious of our sin.* – Romans 3:19-20

Preaching the law is not legalistic or oppressive. The law provides the sinner with an opportunity to know what sin is. It is only by the law that we know what is sinful. Sin is driving 55 mph through a 15 mph school zone. The law is the 10 signs stating that the speed limit is 15 mph. It is not the law that is sinful; it is the law that helps us to see our sinfulness. The law is necessary to inform the sinner of his sin.

*What shall we say, then? Is the law sinful? Certainly not! Nevertheless, I would not have known what sin was had it not been for the law. For I would not have known what coveting really was if the law had not said, "You shall not covet." But sin, seizing the opportunity afforded by the commandment, produced in me every kind of coveting. For apart from the law, sin was dead. Once I was alive apart from the law; but when the commandment came, sin sprang to life and I died. I found that the very commandment that was intended to bring life actually brought death. For sin, seizing the opportunity afforded by the commandment, deceived me, and through the commandment put me to death. So then, the law is holy, and the commandment is holy, righteous and good. Did that which is good, then, become death to me? By no means! Nevertheless, in order that sin might be recognized as sin, it used what is good to bring about my death, so that through the commandment sin might become utterly sinful.* – Romans 7:7-13

We would not have even known what sin was if it were not for the law. Now, did the law make us sinful or cause us to be sinful? Not at all! Paul makes it clear here that the law is holy. The law acts as a schoolmaster (Galatians 3:24) to bring us to God. The Law teaches us what sin is so that we do not do it. The Law does not cause us to sin; it simply exposes the sin in our lives.

Have you ever dusted before? Dusting was always one of my least favorite chores growing up. I can remember dusting certain rooms and I had thought I had removed all the dust. I would ask my mom to come in and inspect my work. On occasion, I would do this having dusted in a darker room. When my mom would come in she would open up the curtains, exposing much more dust that I had missed. There was dust in the air, dust on the table and dust on me. I had not noticed it until the window was open and the light shone into the room. Now, did the sunlight coming through the window cause the dust? Did it create the dust? Not at all. The light simply exposed the dust that was already present. The law does not make us sinful; the law exposes the sin in our lives so that we can get rid of it.

When Christians stopped preaching about sin and judgment and using the Law to demonstrate the need for salvation, people stopped seeing their sinfulness and their need for Christ. In light of this, Christians had to find a new way to appeal to people. How were people going to come to Christ? So, instead of saying, "God loves you, but you have sin in your life that has separated you from God, and Jesus is the only way for salvation," the message became "Come to Jesus, who will give you life, joy, happiness and fulfillment." Yes,

He will do all of those things, but there is a massive problem in promoting Jesus this way.

Imagine that two men are on a plane when the flight attendant comes to one of the men and says, "Sir, will you put on this parachute? It will make for a far more happy, joyful and fulfilling flight. Please, put it on." The man puts on the parachute and notices the weight of the parachute. The weight of it begins to hurt his shoulders. He finds the parachute to be bulky and he can't lean back comfortably. He also notices that there are a number of people around him staring at him and making fun of him for wearing the parachute while seated. The flight attendant comes down the aisle with boiling hot coffee and trips right next to the passenger. Because of the bulkiness of the parachute he can't get out of the way in time and the hot coffee spills on him. In disgust the man jumps up, rips off the parachute and tells the flight attendant, "You promised me this would improve my flight but it didn't do that at all! I'm done wearing this parachute."

The flight attendant approaches a second man and this time says, "Sir, there is a problem with this plane and at some point there is a very good chance that we are going to have to jump from 25,000 feet and your only hope for survival is this parachute. Will you put it on?" This second man quickly puts on the parachute. He barely notices the bulkiness or discomfort of the parachute because he is so grateful to have this parachute. Other people's laughs and criticism do not bother him because he is aware of the parachute's necessity for survival. Even if coffee is spilled on him, his response will not be to rip off his parachute because he knows that it is the one thing that can save him.

When we tell people to come to Jesus simply because He will give them joy and fulfillment, what do you think they will do at the first site of discomfort or persecution? Jesus most definitely brings joy unspeakable and the most fulfilling life imaginable, but it also comes with a cost. He said He came to bring a sword (Matthew 10:34). We are aliens in this world (1 Peter 2:11). We will be ridiculed and hated because of Christ (Matthew 10:34). We will suffer many things for the sake of Christ (Matthew 24:9). Yet, we endure all of this because we know of the judgment (and life) to come. Instead of telling people to put on a parachute to enjoy the flight, we must tell them to put it on because of the impending fall. The message of salvation is not one of happiness, but of holiness. Happiness and joy are great fruits of holiness, but we must stop using them as the motivation for holiness. If we only put on Jesus because of how He can improve our "flight," then at the first moment of hardship or persecution, we will just as readily take Him off. Until we are made aware of the impending fall, we will not appreciate the parachute that is Christ.[49]

In an effort to make the Gospel sound more appealing to the world around us, we have made it into something it is not. We have left out the reason for the cure and only offered the cure so as to not offend people with the bad news. But if the bad news is not first given, then the good news makes no sense and loses its value. As Christians, our goal is not to preach a message that excites or pleases the world. Our goal is to preach the "whole" gospel in order that some might truly come to know Christ.

"Biblical evangelism, as seen in Scripture, is law to the proud and grace to the humble (James 4:6). You never see Jesus give the grace and love of the Gospel to a proud person. With the law He breaks the proud heart, and with the Gospel He heals the broken heart."[50] – Ray Comfort

In Luke 10 the Bible tells about an expert in the law who came to test Jesus. Jesus gave him the law. This was a proud man. He was challenging Jesus by asking Him how to inherit eternal life. Jesus responded by asking, "What is in the law?" Jesus' response to this proud man was to give him the law. The man responded, "Love God and love your neighbor." Then Luke rightly tells us that the man wanted to justify himself by asking, "Who is my neighbor?" The man was fine loving some of his neighbors, but not all of them. As a result, Jesus tells the parable of the Good Samaritan to break down the man's pride. He gave law to the proud.

However, when it came to humble people, Jesus did not spend time expounding on the law. He gave grace. Nicodemus acknowledged the truth of God's word and came honestly asking questions (John 3). He received the grace of the gospel. Nathanael had no deceit or guile in him, and he received the gospel of grace (John 1). This is same for the Jews at Pentecost, who were cut to the heart by the message of grace (Acts 2). They knew the law; they did not need to be reminded of it again. Instead, they needed the freedom and forgiveness found in the grace of the gospel.

"That is why there are so many mushroom converts. Converts who just spring up out of nowhere and then disappear. Because they do not have a conviction of the law."[51] – George Whitefield

"The first duty of the minister is to preach God's law and show the nature of sin."[52] – Martin Luther

"Satan, the god of all dissension stirs up daily new sects. And last of all, which of all others I should never have foreseen or once suspected, he has raised up a sect such as teach that men should not be terrified by the law, but gently exhorted by the preaching of the grace of Christ."[53] – Martin Luther

*"Not everyone who says to me, 'Lord, Lord,' will enter the kingdom of heaven, but only the one who does the will of my Father who is in heaven. Many will say to me on that day, 'Lord, Lord, did we not prophesy in your name and in your name drive out demons and in your name perform many miracles?' Then I will tell them plainly, 'I never knew you. Away from me, you evildoers!'"* – Matthew 7:21-23

The reality is that there are many in our churches who hear a sermon but are not hearing the full message of the Gospel. It is seed that falls on rocky ground or on the road or where there are thorns. There are those who put on a show and act like they are saved. They may talk the lingo. They may perform the actions. But they are nothing more than fake converts. As Christians, we must battle the popular and comfortable position of preaching only a one-sided gospel. Incorrect evangelism is to preach only law or only grace. The world does not need a watered down gospel; it needs the full gospel. It needs the simple gospel. It needs the balanced gospel that proclaims the sin of humanity but the grace of God demonstrated through the cross. Preaching the whole gospel will produce true disciples, not fake converts. Lord, give us the strength to preach that gospel.

## *MANIPULATION*

Growing up, our TV watching was regulated. My brothers and I were not allowed to watch whatever we wanted and there were many times where we were only allowed to watch for a certain amount of time. For example, I remember when I was around 10 years old and each of us boys were given three hours a week to watch TV. We could use those hours to watch whichever shows or movies we wanted to watch. At 10 I had just begun to get interested in sports and each week there were a number of sporting events I wanted to watch, but I only had three hours for the whole week. There was no way I was going to be able to watch all of the sporting events that I wanted to with only three hours. And then I had an idea. Even though I only had three hours, my eight- and six-year-old brothers, Jesse and Daniel, each had three hours as well. I realized that if I could convince the boys to use their three hours of TV time on my sports, I would be able to see a lot more of my sports. Now, you may be wondering how I convinced an eight-year-old and a six-year-old to use their TV time on sports instead of cartoons? Honestly, I was very manipulative. It's not necessarily something of which to be proud, but ten-year-old Josh knew how to manipulate his brothers into thinking that they would rather watch regular season hockey than Bugs Bunny.

Let me be clear, I am not condoning my actions as a ten-year-old, but when it comes to sports or cartoons, my manipulation was rather harmless (though, if you ask my brothers they will still speak loathsomely of those days). However, when it comes to the work of the Lord, manipulation is a very big deal. Unfortunately, there are many ministers who often use manipulation today. They manipulate or trick people into salvation. They use emotion in order to cause people to make a decision for Christ. Yet, our end goal is not to count how many people come to the altar, that is fine to do, but not if we stop there. That is only the beginning. As I said a few chapters earlier, our job is not to fill altars but to fill Heaven. The problem with some mission work is that it ends at the beginning. Making a decision to follow Christ is the starting line, not the finish line.

Discipleship is the goal. Responding to an altar call is the entry point. We must not manipulate people into simply praying a prayer because that is not the end goal. Furthermore, it is not the example of Christ, but rather of the devil. The devil's ways are cunning and shrewd and deceptive. Manipulation is a tactic used by the enemy, so Christians should want nothing to do with it. Not only that, but we are called to walk in the steps of our master: Jesus.

Jesus was the least manipulative person who has ever lived. He had the utmost respect for the human will. Certain people know what things to do or say in order to generate a response, but it is important to show real maturity by demonstrating restraint. Just because you *can* do something, does not mean that you *should* do something. Jesus' life was full of restraints. When Satan tempted Jesus in the wilderness, He demonstrated great restraint. It was true omnipotence for Jesus to not turn stones into bread but rather to demonstrate restraint so as to not do that. In one of the greatest books I have ever read about the person of Jesus, author Philip Yancey writes:

"God's terrible insistence on human freedom is so absolute that he granted us the power to live as though he did not exist, to spit in his face, to crucify him. All this Jesus must have known as he faced down the tempter in the desert, focusing his mighty power on the energy of restraint. I believe God insists on such restraint because no pyrotechnic displays of omnipotence will achieve the response he desires. Although power can force obedience, only love can summon a response of love, which is the one thing God wants from us and the reason he created us."[54] – Philip Yancey

This mindset is further demonstrated in Jesus' interactions with people. Not once will you find Jesus manipulating or convincing people to be saved; quite the opposite. Jesus looked at the rich young ruler and loved him as he walked away, even unsaved. Jesus knew Satan was trying to sift Peter like wheat, yet instead of forcing him not to, he simply prayed that he would not. Even though Jesus was fully aware that Judas would betray him, he did not force him otherwise, for his value of human liberty would not allow him to intervene in Judas' situation. On the cross, Jesus demonstrated this beautiful restraint once again by rejecting the call to come down from the cross. Throughout his ministry, when the Pharisees would ask for a miracle or for a sign, Jesus would only do what His Father said, not what would impress the religious leaders. "'Take up your *cross* and follow me,' Jesus said, in the least manipulative invitation that has ever been given."[55] If Jesus is our great example, then let us learn from Him in this way also. Jesus never succumbed to the desire to either manipulate or force people into making a decision. We must not either.

# THEOLOGICAL
# IMPLICATIONS

# CHAPTER 9

# THE FOUNDATION

### *GRADUATION*

I had the privilege of going to university. I know not everyone may consider that a privilege (I agree that the idea of paying thousands of dollars to do homework doesn't sound very appealing), but it is a blessing to attend university. I studied at Oral Roberts University and loved my time there. I was in the school of Theology & Ministry and majored in biblical Literature with a concentration in New Testament Studies. I had classes in Systematic Theology, Luke/Acts, Hermeneutics, biblical Greek, Church History, Pauline Epistles and many more. I loved my classes, but as I entered my senior year there was one specific class that got me a little scared.

In order to graduate, my major required that I write a Senior Paper. This paper was long, much longer than any I'd written before. And it had to be well researched. I couldn't just write what I wanted; I had to have sources, and lots of them. And it had to be formatted correctly. There were a lot of requirements and it was a bit of a daunting task, but if I was going to graduate I was going to have to write this paper. There was just one problem: I had no idea what to write. I prayed about it. I thought about it. I talked with family and friends and professors about it. I wanted to write on a subject that interested me. I also wanted to write on a subject that had meaning and value. Finally I landed upon my topic. The topic excited me. I thought it addressed a very important issue, and yet I didn't feel like there was a whole lot written about it. I felt that it was a topic that had major implications and thus, it was worthy of my time and attention. Not only that, but with my upbringing and experience, it was a topic that affected me directly. I was going to attempt to answer the question, "What happens to those who have never heard the Gospel?"

I immersed myself in books. I read articles. I was late to far too many of Michelle's meals while working late in the university library. And I studied the Bible in such a thorough and comprehensive way in order to answer this question. As the son of an evangelist, and having led many mission trips to very unreached areas, it was not the first time I had considered the question. In fact, it was a question I had really wrestled with from time to time. I felt it was a very legitimate question and one of incredible importance, and as I researched and wrote my paper, the significance of that question became much more real to me.

In many ways, that paper was the springboard for this book. As I researched the topic and discussed the topic and wrote about the topic, I was struck by the necessity of sharing about it. This question deeply impacted my view of the Kingdom of God and the Kingdom of Darkness. It brought new meaning to the necessity of proclaiming the Gospel. It impassioned me to fulfill the Great Commission. What was once only a class standing in between me and graduation had become so much more.

As I begin this third section of the book, I want to once again go back to senior year. Up until now this book has hopefully encouraged you and motivated you to love God and love people through the proclamation of the Gospel. The call to fulfill the Great Commission is as loud as ever, and hopefully the previous chapters have inspired you to do just that. But before finishing this book, I want to kick it up a notch. I want to challenge you. I want you to think. I want you to wrestle with the Scriptures. I want you to go beyond the surface and consider the theological implications of the Gospel. The longer I was in university, the more challenging and demanding the content was. However, it also became more and more rewarding. Before "graduating" from this book, I want to tackle some of Christianity's tough questions. I want to walk through the theological implications of the Gospel. I certainly don't claim to have all of the answers, but I do believe that the Bible does, and as we enter this section, my prayer is that the Holy Spirit would bring revelation and illumination on these all-important subjects. How we treat these subjects and how we answer these questions will affect not only our lives but the lives of countless others.

## *INTOLERANT JESUS*

One of the hallmark cries of the world today is that of tolerance. If you watch the news, if you're on social media, if you read blogs, then you know that the culture of the 21ˢᵗ century preaches a message of tolerance. The American public has elevated tolerance above virtually every other quality, insisting that true love incorporates tolerance. Tolerance, simply defined, is the willingness to put up with something even if it goes against your beliefs. There are many churches and ministers and "Christians" who are calling the Church to be more tolerant. They cry, "Be willing to compromise. Why do you have to be so exclusive and judgmental? Doesn't love accept people just as they are?" From legalized drugs to homosexuality to divorce to postmodernism to blended religions, the world is telling Christians to tolerate it all. Stop judging. Stop opposing. Stop the intolerance.

Those demanding tolerance often appeal to Jesus. "Wasn't Jesus tolerant?" they ask. "He accepted tax collectors. He hung out with prostitutes. He redefined the laws of the Sabbath. He changed the status quo. It is more important that we love and accept all people and become tolerant of their views and lifestyles since that's what broad-minded, tolerant Jesus would have done." Are they right? Is the church too closed-minded? Does becoming more like Jesus mean becoming more tolerant?

The reality is that many people confuse Jesus' evangelistic efforts with tolerance. Not once will you find Jesus condoning the acts of the tax collectors; instead He reached out to the tax collectors in order that they might find salvation, as Zacchaeus did (Luke 19). Jesus never tolerated sexual immorality, quite the opposite. When the woman was brought to Jesus having been caught in the act of adultery, He did not accept her sin. He condemned the Pharisees for their hypocrisy but He didn't overlook the woman's sin. Instead, He gave her a clear command to go and never sin again (John 8). Many today view Jesus as a beacon of tolerance, but when it comes to the issues of sin, salvation and eternal life, He was as intolerant as they come.

*Enter through the narrow gate. For wide is the gate and broad is the road that leads to destruction, and many enter through it. But small is the gate and narrow the road that leads to life, and only a few find it.* – Matthew 7:13-14

The message of the Gospel is not all-inclusive. When it came to salvation, Jesus preached a very specific message. He wasn't interested in preaching a message that would make everyone happy; He was interested in speaking truth. Christianity can't change its true colors, and its true colors are fairly clear—there is a very narrow path to truth. Wide is the road that leads to Hell, because there are many ways to get there; but there is only one way to salvation: through Jesus Christ.

Our world would often prefer for us to be tolerant rather than truthful, but truth is always better than tolerance. I travel a lot, and whenever I drive to a new city I am so thankful that I live in 2015 where I have a built-in GPS on my phone. Traveling to new places is so much easier now than it was back in the day. But let's suppose for a minute that I don't have my phone and I am traveling to New York City from my home in Tulsa, Oklahoma. I get on the interstate and start traveling in the direction I feel like traveling, which happens to be west—I am going in the complete opposite direction of New York City. A few hours into my trip I stop at a gas station and start talking with an employee there. I tell him, "I'm heading to New York City!" Surprised, he responds, "Wow, that is a long way from here! Where are you coming from?" "Tulsa," I reply. At this, he gets a strange look on his face. He knows that I am traveling in the wrong direction. I am headed for the Pacific Ocean not the Atlantic Ocean. He replies, "Sir, I hate to tell you this, but you're heading in the opposite direction. You need to turn around and head east." "What? I reply. "Why are you telling me this? I can go whichever way I want. Why can't you just be tolerant of my way instead of trying to correct me or make me go the way that you think is best?" If I ever responded that way when put in that position, I give anyone full permission to slap me. You see, when a person is lost, tolerance does them little good. Tolerance will only keep me going in the wrong direction. I don't need tolerance. I need truth.

I am grateful that when a pilot lands a plane, he is very narrow-minded. He does not think he can land it anywhere in any way. He is very specific and narrow in his approach—he shoots for a very narrow runway upon which to land. I'm thankful for that. When it comes to science and math, there is no room for tolerance. If you try to tell a mathematician (or any human, for that matter) that 2+2=5, he will be corrected. Yet, the world in which we live would rather that we be tolerant of that unique viewpoint than speak the truth and bring correction.

The message of Christianity can be viewed by many as a specific Gospel taught by an intolerant Master, but that is not a bad thing. If I were diagnosed with cancer, I would not want a tolerant doctor interested in hundreds of different ways of treating it. I would want a doctor who knew the one, specific way to treat my illness. When it comes to our sin, there is only one cure, and His name is Jesus.

## IS JESUS THE ONLY WAY?

There are many today who view the Bible as a book of fables with a lot of good advice. These same people admire Jesus. They celebrate Him as a good, moral teacher who helped a lot of people, and they claim to like His message of love and acceptance. While most of Jesus' words are generally accepted by the majority of Christians, and even many non-Christians, there is one statement that has been the cause for a great deal of scrutiny throughout history, but particularly in recent history. In John 14:6 Jesus declares, "I am the way, and the truth, and the life. No one comes to the Father except through me." This well-known statement has caused, and continues to cause, a great deal of disagreement due to its exclusive nature. When Jesus declares that He is "the way," He is not only identifying Himself as the way but He is also eliminating any other way as legitimate. It is with this assertion that many take issue.

There are a great number of people who would argue that while Jesus was a good moral teacher, He was not God, nor did He ever claim to be God. But the Bible goes to great lengths to explain that Jesus was, in fact, God. In the prologue of his Gospel John writes, "In the beginning was the Word, and the Word was with God, and the Word was God" (John 1:1). Here it is made abundantly clear that Jesus is not only related to God but is, in fact, God in the flesh. Later, in John 10:30 Jesus quite clearly says, "I and the Father are one." Jesus doesn't seem confused about whether He is or is not God; He knows quite well who He is.

Not only that, but as God, His words carry power. In John 12:49-50 Jesus says that whatever He says is just what the Father has told Him to say. Thus, whenever Jesus speaks, He does so authoritatively. This includes His statement in John 14:6. Thus, anyone who claims that Jesus was simply a great moral teacher yet never claimed to either be God or to be the only way to God must choose between two possibilities, for this verse leaves no opportunity for both to be true. If one argues that Jesus never claimed to be the only way to salvation, then this statement makes Him out to be a liar or a lunatic, neither the qualifications for a good moral teacher. If these words are real, though, then Jesus cannot simply be a good moral teacher since He has claimed deity and exclusivism.

Those who maintain that Jesus was still only a good moral teacher then consider this statement to be a mistranslation, and that what Jesus really meant is that His way was simply one of many ways to attain salvation. You will hear this sort of argument a lot. Whenever people find a passage of Scripture or a verse that doesn't fit into their worldview, they chalk it up to mistranslation. "Jesus didn't really say that. If you knew the original translation, it means something completely different." Not only is this a cop-out answer but it is also incorrect.

Even an elementary reading of this passage in the Greek makes the message quite clear. In biblical (Koine) Greek the indefinite article is never mentioned; there is no word for it. "If a Greek writer wanted a word to be unspecified (i.e. equivalent to our English a, an), then that writer would leave off the definite article."[56] Thus, if John had wanted to communicate that Jesus was only *a* way to God, instead of *the* way, then he would have had to not include the definite article whatsoever. Even this, though, would not make Jesus' statement indefinite, since "some nouns are definite whether or not they have a definite article. [And] there are many instances where anarthrous (a word without a definite article) words are definite."[57] In other words, by simply looking at the original Greek, one should be able to tell quite easily what Jesus' original intention was because if the definite article is present, whatsoever, then there is no doubt that Jesus was declaring that He was not just *a* way but *the* only way.

I realize that not everyone reading this book has studied Koine Greek, however I do think that it is important to incorporate it and other academic arguments when defending our faith. It is encouraging to know that our faith in Christ and His Word can stand up against the scrutiny of science, history, linguistics, archaeology and reason. With that in mind, let's take a closer look at John 14:6.

The Greek translation of this verse reads as follows: Ἐγώ εἰμι ἡ ὁδὸς καὶ ἡ ἀλήθεια καὶ ἡ ζωή· οὐδεὶς ἔρχεται πρὸς τὸν πατέρα εἰ μὴ δι'ἐμοῦ. In the Greek this passage contains the Greek definite article, ἡ, in all three instances. As was discussed above, even with the absence of the definite article each of the words— way (ὁδὸς), truth (ἀλήθεια) and life (ζωή)—could have very well been translated definitively, but by John including the definite article, he is overemphasizing the point that Jesus is the only way to the Father. This is John's way of putting an exclamation point on Jesus' statement, eliminating any provision for salvation by any other means besides Christ. "Any hint at universalism, syncretistic patterns of salvation, or reaching the Father through any other means than Jesus is here completely eliminated."[58] There may be no one who says it better, though, than one of the greatest authors in history, C.S. Lewis:

"I am trying here to prevent anyone saying the really foolish thing that people often say about Him: I'm ready to accept Jesus as a great moral teacher, but I don't accept his claim to be God. That is the one thing we must not say. A man who was merely a man and said the sort of things Jesus said would not be a great moral teacher. He would either be a lunatic — on the level with the man who says he is a poached egg — or else he would be the Devil of Hell. You must make your choice. Either this man was, and is, the Son of God, or else a madman or something worse. You can shut him up for a fool, you can spit at him and kill him as a demon or you can fall at his feet and call him Lord and God, but let us not come with any patronising nonsense about his being a great human teacher. He has not left that open to us. He did not intend to."[59] – C.S. Lewis

The basis for this book, and for Christianity, is wrapped up in this truth: Jesus is the only way. That, in and of itself, is a very exclusive statement. It is an intolerant declaration. We are ruling out all other options for salvation. We are eliminating all other modes of salvation. We are saying that Jesus, and Jesus alone, is the way to salvation. There are many who have a problem with this. This intolerant, exclusive Jesus does not fit the preferred message of many, but our job is to not make Jesus fit the mold of the world, it is to make the world fit the mold of Jesus. Anyone who wants to claim that Jesus was not God, and never claimed to be, will have to look to somewhere other than the Bible to do so. The message of Scripture, and the very words of Christ, attest to the truth that Christ alone is the gateway to salvation. With that foundation, we can now turn our attention to the question, "What happens to those who have never heard the Gospel?"

# CHAPTER 10

# ROMANS 1

## *INTRODUCTION TO ROMANS*

As I began to tackle the question, "What happens to those who have never heard the Gospel?" I was determined to not find my own answer but rather the biblical answer. I certainly came with my own preconceived notions, but I wanted to let the Bible speak for itself. There are two common approaches to studying the Bible. One is exegesis, which is essentially allowing the text to speak for itself. Exegesis is the process of looking to the text in order to determine a belief. Eisegesis is the opposite process. Eisegesis is when someone comes to the text with a preconceived belief and looks for fragmented verses in order to fit the preconceived belief. It is very easy to take an eisegetical approach to Bible study, but that is an abuse of good hermeneutics. All heresies and cults that find support for their incorrect belief systems in Scripture are a good example of the dangers of eisegesis. Thus, when it came to addressing this question I was intent on conducting good exegesis.

There are probably two passages, more than any other, that deal with this issue and they are both found in the beginning of Romans. It is oftentimes difficult to fully understand the meaning of any passage of Scripture without first gaining some background information on the book itself and examining the context in which the passage in question is contained. Thus, before examining these two passages in Romans, it is important to examine this letter and the context of the passages more closely.

Considering the fact that the epistles were originally letters written to specific congregations at a specific time in history, the context surrounding such information is helpful in understanding the purpose and meaning of the letters. The Apostle Paul took three missionary journeys and it would seem that Paul wrote this letter towards the end of his third missionary journey, probably while he was staying in Corinth, having dealt with many of the Corinthian Church's problems. Internal evidence points to Corinth as the place of provenance. For example, Paul stayed at the house of Gaius (16:23), which is perhaps the same Gaius who was baptized by Paul in Corinth (1 Cor. 1:14). Furthermore, he mentions that Macedonia and Achaia helped him in his collection for the Jerusalem Church, which also seems to indicate that he wrote Romans from Corinth. There is "corroborating evidence for this in Acts 20:1-6, which relates that Paul stayed in Greece (Achaia, where Corinth is located) for three months"[60] (Acts 20:3). This would give Paul plenty of time to write to the Romans, and it also fits the content of the letter. Having finally finished his missionary work in the east, "his face is now definitely turned towards the west, for he plans not only soon to visit Rome but to proceed with further missionary work in Spain (Rom 15:24, 28)."[61]

It would seem, then, that Paul was probably writing from Corinth, which would have certainly influenced his letter to the Romans. When examining the situation of the Corinthian Church through 1 and 2 Corinthians, you can quickly see that this Church dealt with some problems. This church had had some serious moral and church struggles, as is clearly evidenced in 1 Corinthians. Paul had to warn them against some of the most depraved acts such as prostitution, incest, adultery, greed, homosexuality, slander and more. If writing from Corinth, this knowledge would certainly have motivated Paul to write to Rome with a strong sense of conviction. He would have wanted to emphasize sin and the need for repentance so that the Romans wouldn't fall into the same traps as the Corinthians. Thus, it does not take Paul long to point out that the Romans are sinful apart from Christ and desperately in need of salvation.

Secondly, the fact that this letter was written either at the end or near the end of his third missionary journey, after having traveled as a missionary for the past 14 years,[62] is significant. This would certainly have influenced the evangelistic content of the first few chapters of Romans. Paul's motivation to write about the guiltiness of man is to make the Church aware of the need to evangelize, and after having finished his third missionary journey, Paul would certainly have the unsaved on his heart as he writes. It is this same heart for the unsaved that drives his desire to travel to Spain (Rom 15:24), for "Spain probably had not yet been evangelized."[63] It seems as though Paul's desire was to stop in Rome on his way to Spain, in part to encourage the Church to also partake in his evangelistic efforts to their own people, for Rome was a cosmopolitan city with its population comprised of individuals from all over the world. So it would seem that the location from where Paul wrote, the context from which he wrote and the people to whom he wrote all helped influence the content of his letter, particularly the passages to be examined.

Finally, before moving on, there is something to be said of the literary structure of Romans. The beginning of the letter is set up to describe doctrinal issues, while the latter part of the letter contains more practical issues. The first four chapters provide teaching on the sin of humanity, the justification purchased by Christ and other doctrinal issues related to both Jews and gentiles alike. "Justification is treated in 1:18-4:25, and the condition and life of the justified in 5:1-8:39,"[64] with a parenthetical teaching on Israel in 9:1-11:36 to follow. The end of the book then deals with practical ethics as well as Paul's desire to minister westwardly, and then final greetings. The literary structure of the book, then, indicates that in his opening chapters Paul wants to establish the essential message of the Gospel before explaining the sanctification of the saved and the practicality of a life lived in Christ. The passages to be discussed thus provide the foundation not only for the study of this paper but also the foundation for Paul's entire letter. His argument is that one cannot live the Christian life until salvation has been received, and Paul does not assume salvation to be received until one is made aware of his need for it. While this introduction of Romans only begins to scratch the surface of understanding the intricacies of this letter, it has hopefully given you a working understanding of the situation(s) surrounding the content to be examined. Not only that, but it also describes Paul's position on the unsaved and unreached as he writes.

*ROMANS 1:16-18*

Much of the Christian world today focuses on the love and grace of God, attributes that are certainly deserving of focus and praise. However, if we are not careful we can begin to think that those are the *only* attributes of God; or that they may be the most important ones. However, God describes Himself in far more words and terms than just love and grace, and yet these have been exalted at the expense of the examination of God's judgment and wrath. While modern Christianity may eschew these characteristics, the apostle Paul does not. Instead, Paul couples the more tenderhearted characteristics of God with the harsher ones. This is demonstrated in verses 16 and 17. While the main part of this chapter primarily focuses on verses 18-23, "the postpositive conjunction γὰρ, 'for,' introduces this section of the letter as a substantiation of the theme stated in 1:16-17."[65] In other words, the word "for" (which appears in the New King James Version) begs the question "why?" It points us backwards. This is important as it definitively links this section to the prior verses. Whatever verse 18 says it says with verses 16 and 17 in mind.

In those prior verses Paul declares that he is "not ashamed of the Gospel...for in it the righteousness of God is revealed through faith for faith" (Rom 1:16a; 17a). In other words, Paul desires to make mention of the Gospel because in this way salvation is offered to the unsaved. As Paul puts aside any inhibitions he may have to share the Gospel, the revelation of the Gospel is made possible. Paul is not ashamed to share the Gospel, despite the fact that he has already undergone numerous persecutions and come close to death. Why is he unashamed? His reason is quite simple: unless he proclaims the Gospel, he is convinced that salvation is impossible.

Standing in contrast to the revelation of the Gospel, though, is another revelation. Paul writes, "For the wrath of God is revealed from heaven against all ungodliness and wickedness of those who by their wickedness suppress the truth" (Rom. 1:18). The word Ἀποκαλύπτεται in Greek is translated here as "revealed" but it could also be translated as "disclosed," having the meaning of a cover that has been taken off of something, exposing it to the world. The idea here is that God has allowed His wrath to be exposed to the whole world just as His righteousness has also been exposed to the whole world.

In addition to this, the verb is in the "continuous present tense,"[66] indicating the continuous nature of each revelation. The force of a continuous verb is that it is not just a one-time event but, as the name implies, it continues to happen. God did not simply at one time reveal His righteousness and then at another time reveal His wrath; rather, both His righteousness and wrath are continually being revealed. Thus, "the continuing revelation of the wrath of God is an expression of His personal righteousness (which also "is being revealed") and its opposition to human sinfulness."[67] The repetition of the "present tense verb 'revealed' is proof of a double revelation—of righteousness (17) and of wrath (18)."[68] These two characteristics stand in contrast because in many ways, they are so much alike. It is the righteousness of God that causes His wrath, for if God were not righteous then there would be no need for wrath against unrighteousness. One of the great $20^{th}$ century theologians, Karl Barth, simply describes it by saying "the wrath of God is the righteousness of God—apart from and without Christ."[69] It is clear from these verses that God has chosen to reveal both His righteousness and His wrath. Not only does this provide two distinct positions, but in so doing, it also eliminates any other positions. In other words, if there is one group of people who are declared righteous, and a second group who are declared unrighteous, with no other alternatives presented, then, logically, these are the only two possible groups. There is no grey area with God—one is righteous or wicked, good or evil, in Christ or apart from Him.

Now, there are many who would argue that even while the unreached may "know" God through creation, they do not reject Him deliberately but rather out of ignorance. First of all, if ignorance was the reason for a person's rejection of God, that does not render the person excused from punishment. For example, perhaps a man is driving the posted speed limit of 35 mph but suddenly comes upon a school zone where the speed limit drops to 25 mph. The man, however, was distracted while driving and happened to miss the school zone sign and continued to drive at a speed of 35 mph. A police officer notices the man traveling 10 mph over the school zone speed limit and pulls the man over. The man is confused as to why he has been stopped, thinking that he had been driving the posted speed limit the entire time. The police officer, however, informs him that he was driving 35 mph in a 25 mph school zone. How would the man most likely respond? Probably by stating that he did not realize that the speed limit had changed; he would plead ignorance as his defense. And how will the police officer respond? "Oh, sir, I am so sorry then for stopping you. If you did not know the speed limit then how could you have driven the correct speed? Certainly I cannot give you a ticket, as you were ignorant of your error." I highly doubt any officer would respond in that way. Instead the officer would explain to the man that while his ignorance may have played a part in his lack of knowledge, his actions still warrant a ticket. It is the man's responsibility to know the posted speed limit and it is the police officer's responsibility to enforce the speed limit, regardless of this man's, or any other driver's ignorance.

To argue that an unsaved or unreached person does not deserve to go to Hell based on his ignorance is the same sort of foolish (and ignorant) argument demonstrated in the story above. Even if someone is ignorant of his sin, he is still sinful, and that sin demands punishment. It is man's responsibility to obey the law of God, and it is God's responsibility to enforce that law. Ignorance is no excuse for the unrighteous to not be saved, it is an unfortunate circumstance—the most unfortunate circumstance—but it is not an excuse for sinful humanity, just as it is not an excuse for the speeding driver. The appeal for the ignorant to be acquitted simply does not work.

If this were the end of the matter, it probably wouldn't make you feel too much better. God set it up so that people would unknowingly sin and then get sent to Hell because of it? That doesn't seem very fair. The Bible, however, does not suggest such a scenario. Not only does the Bible say that the unrighteous are not ignorant, it actually specifies that the unrighteous are deliberately sinful. It is not as though the unrighteous simply stumbled into their sin, instead Paul writes that they have "suppressed the truth." The word "suppress" is from the Greek word κατεχόντων, meaning "to hold down" or to "hinder." "Paul affirms that human beings have not lost this sense of God's power and deity, but he declares that they have chosen to suppress this truth, instead of honoring God and giving him thanks."[70] In essence, this is a deliberate act of unrighteousness. Sin is an active event, not a passive one. This is integral in understanding the wrath of God, for it is not poured out on the ignorant. Nor is it poured out on those who simply stumble upon it. Instead, the wrath of God is poured out against those who have knowledge of God, yet blatantly suppress that truth. This sin is not accidental; it is intentional. And yet, despite this, even in the midst of the wrath of God, God's mercy is still demonstrated, for "God's wrath is directed against all the godlessness and wickedness of men, not against the men as such. God hates sin and judges it, but loves sinners and desires their salvation."[71] This is why God sent His Son, so as to make provision for every unrighteous person. Even in discussing His wrath, God's love and mercy is clearly evident.

In these verses, then, there are a number of incredibly important points. First of all, Paul was not ashamed of the Gospel because he knew the unsaved must hear it to be saved. Secondly, both God's righteousness and wrath are continuously being revealed to humanity. The unsaved are not merely ignorant as they suppress the truth with their sin. Sin is an active event, not a passive one, and it incurs judgment. However, God's wrath is poured out not on mankind but against mankind's wickedness. Lastly, God has made provision for the sinful in their sin so that they might be rescued; all that in just three verses.

### ROMANS 1:19-20

While the first few verses describe that the righteousness and wrath of God are present in the world, the next few verses discuss *how* they are present. Verse 19 states "For what can be known about God is plain to them, because God has shown it to them." The first thing to notice here is the very first word of the verse: διότι. This word is a "combination of two common conjunctions: *dia* (on account of) and *hoti* (because). It has the sense of 'in as much as' or 'in light of the fact.'"[72] Therefore, in light of the fact that knowledge of God has been made plain to the whole world, Paul says that God "is justified in exercising his wrath toward humankind for suppressing that knowledge."[73] What is evidenced here is that humanity, not just the saved world, knows about God, for God has made it plain to the world. Now there is something to be said about this knowledge, for if knowledge about God is equivalent to knowing God (as in salvation), then this passage seems to support universalistic teachings, since this knowledge is made plain to everyone. What, then, is this knowledge that is made so plain?

The phrase τὸ γνωστὸν τοῦ θεοῦ is translated as "what can be known about God" and is really the point of discussion. It is knowledge of God that is identified elsewhere in Scripture as the means by which salvation comes (1 Tim 2:4). If this is what Paul means, then salvation comes to all people at all times, for this knowledge has been made plain to the entire world. If this were the case, though, then what sort of motivation would Paul even have to share this Gospel? If everyone already knows God, then there is certainly no need for Paul to risk his life to share the Gospel. It would seem, then, that this would support some alternate understanding, and the text supports such an alternative.

Knowledge that brings salvation, as used in 1 Tim 2:4, for example, is the word ἐπιγινώσκω, meaning "knowledge" but also meaning to "acknowledge, indicate that one knows."[74] In other words, there is some action that must accompany knowledge in order for salvation to occur. Saving knowledge is more than just an awareness of God. It is an acknowledgement of God that produces an action, namely repentance. The word found in Romans 1:19, though, is the simple adjective γνωστὸν, which can be simply translated as "known" but "it does not follow that it may not be used in the stricter sense of 'knowable, 'what may be known' where the context favors that sense...[and] there is more room for this stricter use here as the word does not occur elsewhere in St. Paul"[75] and does occur in "the LXX [Greek translation of the Old Testament] in the sense of 'knowable, what can be known.'"[76] So the phrase would more likely mean the 'knowability of God,'"[77] or what is "able to be known"[78] about God. This knowledge is "sufficient to make man responsible, but is not by itself sufficient to accomplish his salvation…it is characteristic of man in his sinful state that he knows much more truth than he translates into fitting response."[79] Thus, when Paul speaks of the knowledge of God, he does not mean that all humanity is automatically saved, but instead that the truth of God's existence is made available to all people, and Paul explains this phenomenon in the following verse.

## *AURORA BOREALIS*

While I currently live in Tulsa, OK, I was born and raised in Canada. I love Canada. There are a lot of things to love about Canada. The people are friendly. It has the best view of Niagara Falls. And the country loves its hockey, even more than Texas loves its football. There is a lot to love about Canada, but one of the things that I don't miss about Canada is the cold. I lived in southern Canada. We didn't live in igloos or have pet reindeer, but it was still very cold during the winter.

While there were definitely times where I would have gladly traded in a snow-covered front yard for a beachfront view, the Canadian winter is very beautiful in its own right. Perhaps the most beautiful part of all, though, is the Northern Lights, the Aurora Borealis. I didn't see them often, but I distinctly remember the moments when I did. I was 20 and I was preaching at a youth camp in Canada. It was late and we were gathered around a fire outside in the forest. While singing campfire songs one of the students pointed to the sky and shouted, "Look!" There in the sky was one of the most beautiful sights I had ever seen—dancing green lights more spectacular than any fireworks display. If you've never seen them, google them right now and look at some pictures; they are incredible! And yet, pictures don't do them justice. As I stood there looking at this picturesque scene I couldn't help but think about how amazing my God was. As I gazed upon the beauty of creation, my mind was directed toward God. No one told me to think about God. No one instructed me that if, or when, I saw the Northern Lights I need to think about God. It was a natural response. Looking at creation, I couldn't help but acknowledge that the beauty of the world could not have happened by random chance; this was an act of someone far greater and more powerful than I. I, along with David, had to declare, "The heavens declare the glory of God; the skies proclaim the work of his hands" (Psalm 19:1). That is natural revelation. It is revelation about God through nature. Looking at the ecosystem and animals and the complexity of the human body and the Northern Lights, how could one not believe that there is a God?

## *NATURAL REVELATION*

In Romans 1:20 Paul declares, "For since the creation of the world God's invisible qualities—his eternal power and divine nature—have been clearly seen, being understood from what has been made, so that people are without excuse." While there is an "infinite qualitative difference"[80] between God and humans, God has chosen to make His existence known to the world, specifically through "his eternal power and divine nature." Just as Psalm 19:1 states, "The heavens are telling the glory of God; and the firmament proclaims his handiwork." God "made the stars so beautiful that from them he might be known as their great and wonderful Creator."[81] In other words, "the Creator left behind clues or 'tracks' in creation from which all persons can logically reason"[82] that there is a God. Natural revelation is perhaps no more biblically evident than here in this passage, where humanity constructs "a doctrine of God without appeal to faith or special revelation but on the basis of reason and experience alone."[83] This knowledge of God is gained from "creation, independent of God's special revelation,"[84] a method particularly independent from "the revelation in Jesus dChrist and whose method differs from the exposition of Holy Scriptures."[85] This knowledge of God does not come from the message of the Gospel or from reading the Bible; it comes from creation.

This natural revelation serves as a law for the entire world, both the righteous and the unrighteous, both the aware and unaware, as they are not truly unaware, for "Paul clearly does believe that when humans look at creation they are aware, at some level, of the power and divinity of the Creator."[86] There is no excuse for humankind before the judgment seat of God. One cannot say that he did not know the truth, for the natural law convicts him, even apart from the spiritual law. And for those who would argue that God's invisible qualities are too unnoticeable as to provide a verdict against humanity, Saint Augustine responds this way: "Invisible things are seen in a special and appropriate way. When they are seen they are much more certain than the objects of the bodily sense, but they are said to be invisible because they cannot be seen by mortal eyes."[87] Thus, invisible does not mean more difficult to identify, rather just impossible to view in the physical, yet increasingly more common than the physical. In essence, Paul's argument is that all who have ever lived, whether being aware of God or any specific law whatsoever, are held accountable for their sin, since God has made Himself known to them through natural revelation. This knowledge is not enough to save—for it differs from a saving knowledge of Christ—but it is enough to condemn, as is clearly evidenced in the text.

Now hold on. Doesn't that sound a little unfair? Some would argue that only a cruel God would make the unevangelized "without excuse" based on their knowledge of God through natural revelation. For while natural revelation proclaims the existence of God, "concerning what that God is to us, nature is altogether silent."[88] It seems unfair for God to make Himself known through revelation without offering salvation by means of that same revelation, particularly since that revelation leaves no room for excuse. If that were the whole story, then I agree, it would be hard not to see God as cruel. That, however, is not the whole story.

This is not the instance of a father disciplining his son for no good reason or for something that the son did not even know about. This is instead a case of the son acting in blatant disregard to the father's warnings, and receiving the just punishment for his actions. This is like a son who is told by his father to take out the trash when he gets home from school. This message is reiterated the entire trip home as billboards, street signs, flashing marquees, bumper stickers, smoke signals, advertisements in window-front stores, even airplanes pulling message banners all keep on giving the same command to the boy: take out the trash. Once he gets home there are phone messages on the answering machine, text messages, emails, tweets, Facebook posts and television commercials all once again reminding him of the same thing: take out the trash. And yet he does not take out the trash. "That is how plainly God has made knowledge of himself available to the human race,"[89] according to this passage.

The clause "so they are without excuse" is really quite interesting and the real crux of the argument. There are those who argue that this clause should be translated "'that they may be without excuse,' expressing purpose and not merely result."[90] God made Himself plain in order that men may be without an excuse. In other words, "the design of God in giving so open and manifest a disclosure of his eternal power and divinity in his visible handiwork is that all men might be without excuse."[91] The problem with this rendering is that it portrays God as simply out to "get" the unrighteous. His only reason for making Himself aware to humanity was so that He would have a way to condemn the sinful. This view, though, contradicts the nature of God, "who desires everyone to be saved and to come to the knowledge of the truth" (1 Tim 2:4). If this were the correct rendering, then someone would certainly have a strong argument in favor of the cruelty of God.

There is, however, another rendering, and one that more rightly agrees with both the syntax and the context of both the passage and the letter. The clause "so they are without excuse" ends v. 20, and is obviously linked to that verse, but it is also closely related to v. 21 and "gives the reason why those concerned are without excuse."[92] This clause is the last of the three clauses in v. 20 and εἰς τὸ "denotes here not direct and primary purpose but indirect, secondary or conditional purpose."[93] While God made Himself aware to the unrighteous, which inevitably left them without an excuse, this was not the purpose for providing natural revelation but was rather a byproduct of His real purpose. God knew that man would sin (Rom 3:23), and while He "did not design that man should sin...He did design that if they sinned they should be without excuse: on His part all was done to give them a sufficient knowledge of Himself"[94] in order that they may search for Him. This is a very different view of God, for this view says that God made Himself aware to the sinful in order that an opportunity for repentance may be provided, and while this left them with no excuse concerning their knowledge of Him, this was not the primary purpose for natural revelation but rather a byproduct of it. In short, natural revelation was not given to us for our condemnation; it was given to us to lead us to justification. If it is an indirect byproduct of v. 20, though, then it is most likely a direct product of v. 21.

If you look at the 21st verse you will see that it directly refers to the same people as those in v. 20, but this time convicting them by virtue of their own sinfulness, not just by natural revelation. Paul explains that, "though they knew God, they did not honor him as God." Simply put, they sinned. More specifically, they were filled with pride and committed idolatry. Despite knowing God to be God, the pride of the unrighteous willingly chose to reject Him. Furthermore, they did not give Him the honor due His name and turned their attention somewhere else, constructing an idol in place of the only true God.

As with any passage of Scripture, it must be examined within the context of the letter in which it is written, and it is within this letter that Paul time and again identifies sin as that which separates man from God and condemns him unto death. If sin is what condemns humanity, as Paul argues thoroughly in this letter, then it is not cruel for God to make Himself plain through nature; instead this is a blatant act of love. Humanity simply left to its own sinfulness is already condemned. The fact that God also provides evidence of Himself through nature only strengthens the case against the unrighteous since not only are they without excuse based on their actions (sin)— God's direct intention—but they are also without excuse based on their knowledge of God (natural revelation)—God's indirect intention. Due to their sin, men are without an excuse concerning their guiltiness. But due to natural revelation, men are also without excuse concerning their knowledge of the truth. Thus, while the phrase "so they are without excuse" could rightly be applied to v. 20, it is more so applied to v. 21, based on the syntax, the context, and in keeping with God's nature to reach out to humanity in order to save it from its sins. Thus, it is not the cruelty of God that makes Himself known through creation; instead it is His love. This is yet one more effort to beckon man unto repentance. For God did not "set so vast a system of teaching before the heathen merely to deprive them of any excuse, but so that they might voluntarily come to know him."[95]

*ROMANS 1:21-23*

Paul explains that humanity is without excuse before God because, while having knowledge of God, they chose not to honor or give thanks to Him but instead turned their worship to something (or someone) else. It should be noted that the word "knew" in v. 21, γνόντες, is derived from the same root word as the word "known" in v. 19. Thus, this knowledge of God, within the context of this passage, once again refers to the knowability of God, not the saving knowledge of God. This is evidenced in the fact that even though humanity had this knowledge it did not lead to salvation. Humanity is without excuse because, "though being in possession of this knowledge they did not render to God the glory and the thanks which the knowledge they possessed ought to have constrained."[96] Thus, every person, whether a Catholic priest or a tribal man in the denseness of the Amazon jungle having never heard the name of Jesus, are both at fault because of their own sins. "Sinful humanity suppresses the truth about God by silent ingratitude"[97] and is without excuse by the virtue of the sky, the trees, and the very breath that it breathes.

It is obvious in v. 21 that knowledge of the Creator, even knowledge of Him as the true God and Savior, is not sufficient to come into relationship with Him. Instead, honor, thanksgiving and worship are the required responses. This is not a ridiculous requirement, for should not the created thank the Creator? "Human beings were made to know, worship, love and serve their Creator. That always was and always will be the way to healthy and fruitful human living."[98] It is not just enough to acknowledge God's existence. Instead, the creature is obligated to thank the Creator just as the nurtured is obligated to thank the nurturer. It is not just enough to acknowledge that the nurturer exists.

Imagine that a child is born to loving parents but is tragically separated from his parents at the age of two. The child grows up and eventually finds out who his parents are, but does not reach out to them. He watches them from a distance. He looks at their Facebook pages, but he never communicates with them. Does he have a relationship with them? No. You see, simply acknowledging that he has a parent but making no effort to create a personal relationship with that parent, is not enough. Knowledge is not equivalent to relationship. So it is with Christ. It is not simply enough to acknowledge His existence, even if the existence that you acknowledge is that of Creator, Savior and Almighty God.

Whether you are a sports lover or not, most people in USA know who Michael Jordan is. He is, arguably, the greatest basketball player of all time. There are many who watched Jordan's career closely. They know what jersey numbers he wore. They know where he went to university. They know what teams he played for. They know how many championships and MVP's he won. They know his statistics. They have many stories about Jordan. They know all about him, but they do not know him. They have no personal relationship with him. Knowledge of him and his career and his stories is not the same as having a personal relationship with him. It is the same with Jesus. There are many who know the stories about Jesus. They can quote you what He said. But they do not have a personal relationship with Him; they do not know Him. That is similar to what is happening here. James declares that even the demons believe in God, yet that knowledge does not lead them to salvation (James 2:18). It is no different for humanity. In order for relationship to occur one must glorify God and worship Him as his personal Creator, Savior and Lord, not just acknowledge that He exists.

Not only does Paul say that the unrighteous have not acknowledged God but he makes it clear that they have instead acknowledged and worshiped something else. While "knowing the truth, they decided to worship something else which they knew was not true, so that hiding from God they might worship idols. A cloud of error covered their hearts"[99] and "they unwisely invested in wood and stone."[100] Knowing of Him they should have been all the more prone to worship Him and to offer their lives as sacrifices to Him. Instead they sacrificed their lives on the altar of idolatry, succumbing to the foolish desires of their darkened hearts in true futility.

The significance of this passage in light of the question regarding those who have not heard the Gospel is that the unreached world has been given knowledge that there is a God, a knowledge that brings condemnation. Yet, what is equally significant in this passage is that that knowledge does not lead the lost to repentance and, specifically, to right relationship with God. Instead, Paul continues by saying, "Claiming to be wise, they became fools; and they exchanged the glory of the immortal God for images resembling a mortal human being or birds or four-footed animals or reptiles" (1:22-23). Paul demonstrates that while all people have knowledge of God, they dishonor Him by worshiping something else. "Humans, instead of worshiping God as the source of their life, give allegiance to nonhuman creation. The earth, instead of being ruled wisely by God-fearing, image-bearing stewards, shares the curse for the sake of idolatrous humankind,"[101] the curse of idolatry that began with Adam and has continued throughout history.

Paul's argument is that since people worship creation, they are further condemning themselves and acting in insubordination towards God. For, they would not worship something if there were not an innate knowledge that there is something or someone that should be worshiped. Sadly, they have acted as ἐμωράνθησαν, "fools." What is interesting about this word choice is the connotation that surrounds this word. Obviously it can and does mean just as it is translated: fool. But it can also mean insipid, without sufficient taste to be pleasing, particularly when referring to food. In other words, ἐμωράνθησαν is to have made a decision to exchange the most tasteful and satisfying meal for one with no taste whatsoever; as a man who loves food, I can tell you that that is a foolish decision. And yet, it is even more than that. Mention of this term also implies something of the fact of what is tasteful. This word insinuates that the unrighteous have chosen something that they have deemed tastier than the truth of the Gospel. This is a rejection on the "grounds of taste rather than intellect."[102] Even though all logic and reason and intelligence says to do one thing, emotion says to do another, and humanity has chosen what is tasty rather than what is right.

The error made by the unrighteous would seem unfathomable to us, if it were not for the fact that each of us have also made the same mistake time and again. The sins described here are sins of idolatry, where something has been exalted to the place that only the Lord should fulfill. Paul explains that while immortality could have been worshiped, mortality was chosen instead. Where incorruptible could have been worshiped, corruptible was worshiped instead. The unrighteous used the wisdom they had received from God to construct an idol instead. "What is 'exchanged' in idolatry for the 'glory of God' is 'likeness' (ὁμοιώματι) and 'image'(εἰκόνος) of something merely human or less than human."[103] Instead of worshiping the Creator, they blatantly chose to worship the created by making "these likenesses the objects of worship; *these* they exchanged for the glory of God."[104] It would, to a lesser extent, be like me choosing to reject to love my wife so that I could, instead, love a picture of my wife!

In this passage of Scripture Paul describes a whole host of things but what is clearly demonstrated in Rom 1:16-23 is that the unrighteous are without excuse. Those who argue in favor of universalism will not find support from this passage as it draws a clear-cut line between the unrighteous and the righteous. Furthermore, those who would argue that ignorance is the defense for those who have not heard the Gospel are reading their personal preference into Scripture, for this passage clearly explains that even in the most rural of places, knowledge of God is made evident through natural revelation, a knowledge that provides one with a desire to search for the true God. The sin of the unrighteous is what condemns but the knowledge of the Creator is what leaves one without an excuse.

This passage also demonstrates that humanity does not act in ignorance, for it deliberately rebels against God. When false gods are constructed and worshiped, it demonstrates the awareness of humanity to the one true God. You can go to some of the most obscure places on the planet and still find people worshiping something, for God has "set eternity in the human heart" (Eccl. 3:11b). God has made Himself known through creation as a way of beckoning the unrighteous to search for the truth. All too often, though, the truth is either substituted for a cheap imitation (a likeness or an image of the authentic) or is not clearly presented by us, the Church. Paul emphasized that he was not "ashamed of the Gospel" right before mentioning the depravity of man. Why? Because he understood that mankind was condemned, and if he were too ashamed of the Gospel to share it, then mankind would not hear, and thus not be saved. So Paul had to put aside his flesh, which could cause fear or embarrassment regarding the Gospel. Instead he had to choose to do the right thing and preach the Gospel, regardless of how difficult it may be. Paul saw the Great Commission as worthy of his life, for he knew that the eternity of humanity was at stake.

# CHAPTER 11

# ROMANS 2

*BIBLE ROULETTE*

Do you remember the first time you flew on a plane? I was 12 years old and unbelievably excited! My dad and I were going to Dubai, United Arab Emirates for a ministry trip and I was finally old enough to go with him. This was a year after the tragic 9/11 terrorist attacks on the World Trade Center in New York City, and so airport security was at an all-time high. As a result, before arriving to the airport my dad gave me a few lessons about proper airport conduct. I was not to make any jokes about bombs or blowing things up. I wasn't allowed to mention guns or fireworks. For example, dad told me, "Let's say we see our neighbor, Jack, in the airport. Do not yell out to him, 'Hi, Jack' because that sounds the same as 'hijack.' Or let's say the airport security wants to check your bag, which has been packed very tightly with clothes. As they unzip your bag, do not say, "Don't open that bag, it will explode!'"

These examples are more farfetched and comedic than reality, but the point is this: context is critical. In virtually every other context it would be totally fine for me to yell "Hi, Jack" without fear of being arrested, but not in the airport. In almost every other instance there would be no danger in me warning someone about opening up my packed suitcase, but in the context of airport security, that's a big problem. Context dictates to us what is appropriate and right, and that certainly applies to the Bible.

Growing up as a preacher's kid, my brothers and I played some of the most ridiculous games. We would have sword drills, where one of us would say a Bible verse and the rest of us would see who could find the verse the fastest. We played Bible charades all the time where one of us would act out a scene from the Bible and the rest of us would have to guess. There was another game that we played that I now affectionately refer to as "Bible Roulette." We would close our eyes, flip open the Bible and point at a verse as a way to get a "word from God." As kids we would mainly do this to have fun, and I'm not denying that God couldn't use this method to speak to someone, but I would never recommend this as a good hermeneutical exercise, and the reason is context. To simply take one verse, one paragraph, or even one passage by itself is to oftentimes miss the point. Thus, the context of a passage is so important, and that is why there is great value in looking at the context of a Scripture.

This next passage to be examined is close to the Romans 1 passage, not only in subject matter but also in proximity, as it is only a few paragraphs away. This is important, for there are times where one passage of Scripture will be used to support another, even though the context of the two passages are quite dissimilar. While this is certainly not always the case, with these passages being so close to each other, the same mindset, the same authorial intent and the same context can be assumed. For this reason, there is no need for me to give another introduction to this epistle, or to even discuss the context too in depth since that has already been done in the previous passage. That being said, there is some text that falls between these passages and it would be helpful to briefly examine this to give us a clearer understanding of the upcoming text.

After mentioning that the unrighteous have chosen idols in place of God, Paul specifies those idols, describing some of the sinfulness into which the unrighteous have fallen (most notably, homosexuality). Chapter 2 then begins by referring back to the discussion of the unrighteous, but Paul also chastises the Romans. It would seem that there were among their number those who judged the unrighteous for sins of which they themselves were equally guilty. These people have seemingly acknowledged God's forgiveness at some point but have chosen to continue in their sinful ways. To this Paul asks some rhetorical questions, "Do you despise the riches of his kindness and forbearance and patience? Do you not realize that God's kindness is meant to lead you to repentance?" (Rom 2:4). Once again Paul emphasizes that it is God's kindness and love that desires for mankind to repent and be saved. Yet, God is not simply love, He is also just, and Paul declares that if one does not act uprightly and live holily, then God's wrath will also be demonstrated. As a way to instruct his readers on how to know whether one is in right relationship with God, Paul explains that one's actions are an indication of one's heart. In other words, if the heart is good then the actions will be good. So also, if the heart is bad, the actions will be bad. Paul explains that this rule is not just for one people but for Jews and gentiles alike, "for God shows no partiality" (Rom 2:11). This sets the stage for Romans 2:12-16.

*ROMANS 2:12-13*

This passage is one of the more difficult passages in Scripture and has been the topic of much confusion throughout history. These confusing issues will be discussed but they are most easily understood when a very clear reading of v. 12 is first examined. Paul writes, "All who have sinned apart from the law will also perish apart from the law, and all who have sinned under the law will be judged by the law." Here Paul mentions two groups of people: those under the law and those apart from the law. The context further describes these groups as Jews and gentiles. It is important to recognize that in this context a Jew refers to an Israelite who knows the law, while a gentile refers to "a heathen barbarian who does not have the law, who has no personal relationship with God, who is ignorant of God's statutes."[105] A gentile does not refer (as is often the case) to a non-Jew who has accepted Christ as Savior (which would include myself and most of us in the world). This is an important definition in understanding this text. The second thing to mention in this passage is the similarity between the two groups. The following verses contain many contrasts between the two groups but this verse focuses on two vital similarities. Both groups sin and, as a result, both groups perish. Everything else in this passage must be read in light of these two facts. When people are confused by this passage, it is oftentimes because the verses are not considered in light of v. 12. Thus, it is only natural to begin with this verse as the precedence for the passage.

As I mentioned, this verse describes two different groups of people. Now, the sentence immediately preceding v. 12 states that God is no respecter of persons. That does not, however, mean that God's judgment towards all persons is the same. Paul makes this clear as he mentions two distinct groups in two different situations—the Jews with the Law and the gentiles without it. Initially, any Jew reading Romans would think his possession of the Law was a good thing, and indeed it is, for possessing the Law makes it easier for one to obey the Law. The problem, though, is that there are many Jews who consider their possession of the Law as sufficient for salvation. That is not the case. Paul goes on to say that very thing in v. 13 when he writes, "For it is not the hearers of the law who are righteous in God's sight, but the doers of the law who will be justified." In other words, "while it is true that there is no respect of persons with God, it is also true that he has respect to the different situations in which men are placed in reference to the knowledge of his law."[106] God provides a classification for two groups of people: those that have the Law and those who do not. This is precisely the question we are attempting to answer. What is the eternal destination for those who have not heard the Gospel? Is there a standard by which those who have not heard will be held accountable? This is the question that Paul is answering in this verse. He is essentially dividing all people into one of two classifications: either they have the Law (are made aware of the Law), or they do not. The Romans 1 passage painted humanity with a large, all-inclusive brush stroke. All people have sinned. All people are guilty. All people have a natural knowledge of God. This passage, though, makes a division of persons where humanity is separated into two groups: those who are aware of the Law of God and those who are not.

In these first couple chapters Paul has mentioned both the Jews and gentiles in tandem, often speaking of "the Jew first and also the Greek" (Rom 2:9). As was briefly stated earlier, the Jews oftentimes see their having the Law as a positive thing, as "a diatribe against Gentiles."[107] While it is certainly positive for the Jews to have the Law, "the mere possession of the law gives the Jew no position of advantage; it only determines the standard by which he will be judged."[108] For Paul argues that while both groups are judged, they are judged differently. God will not judge the gentiles according to the written, Mosaic Law for that Law was not made available to them. God's favor and forgiveness is just as impartial to humanity as is His judgment. For this reason, it would be showing favoritism to offer the same grounds of judgment for those who have the Law as those who do not, and since God does not show favoritism (Rom 2:11), then a separate set of criterion is used based on the situation of the unrighteous. "People are held accountable for such knowledge of the truth as was accessible to them, not for what was not accessible."[109]

This same teaching of different judgments is seen elsewhere in Scripture. Jesus chastised some of the cities of His day—Chorazin and Bethsaida—for not believing and declared that "it will be more bearable for Sodom of the day of judgment than for you" (Matt. 11:24). Similarly, in the parable of the faithful and unfaithful slave in Luke 12, Jesus describes two men who both disobey the Master and receive a penalty, but notice the difference: "That servant who knows his master's will and does not get ready or does not do what his master wants will be beaten with many blows. But the one who does not know and does things deserving punishment will be beaten with few blows" (Luke 1247-48a). This means that for the unrepentant person possessing the written (or spoken) Law, judgment will be severe. Also severe will be the judgment of the unrepentant who do not possess the Law, just not as severe.

This is an important distinction that cannot be overstated. The gentiles are still held responsible for their sins. Remember the key verse of the passage: "All who have sinned apart from the law will also perish apart from the law." "Gentiles who sin will perish, but the Law of Moses will not be used as a standard of judgment against them."[110] Gentiles are not excluded from judgment based on their ignorance of the Law, for that would be unfair favoritism on God's part. "The key is that both have equally sinned, one outside and the other inside the Law, and so both must suffer the consequences of that depravity,"[111] for "sin unchecked leads to perdition one way or another."[112] The only difference has to do with the degree of the judgment. The gentiles are not "excused from God's judgment,"[113] but they "will not be condemned for failure to conform to a law-code which was not accessible to them,"[114] for to do that would be like an evil teacher who grades two students the same who have not been given the same opportunity to succeed.

## MATH CLASS

Suppose a teacher instructing her third grade math class was preparing her students for an upcoming test. Now imagine that this teacher preferred one student (Charlie) to another (Joel). One day after class the teacher took her favorite student, Charlie, aside and gave him all of the answers to the upcoming test. Charlie now had the opportunity to study the anticipated questions and answers, and even memorize them to make sure that he aced the test. Joel, however, was not given the answer key and came into the test completely unaware of the upcoming questions. Of course Charlie scored much better than Joel, who did not receive help. When grading the tests, though, the teacher, despite knowing that Charlie had received the answers while Joel had not, graded the tests by the same standard. Would that not be an unfair standard by which to compare the students, considering one had an advantage while the other did not? In fact, couldn't you argue that that teacher had acted unethically by showing favoritism to Charlie and not to Joel? Of course! The teacher would be acting unfairly and holding one student to a standard that does not compare to the other.

This is how some view God and His attitude toward those who have not received the Law or heard the Gospel, and they cannot help but think that a good God would do such a thing. The natural extrapolation for them, then, is that if one is unaware of the Law of God, and unaware of the Gospel, then one is exempt from judgment. In other words, if a student is unaware of an upcoming test because he did not listen in class, then that student shouldn't have to take the test—this is the perspective of many concerning the unreached. That, however, is not what Paul explains here. Instead, what Paul explains is much more like the following example.

Suppose a teacher instructing her third grade math class was preparing her students for an upcoming test. The teacher had been preparing her students for weeks for the test. She had provided visual aids and examples to help convey the mathematics concepts to her students so as to prepare them for the test. She had also informed her class that while there were varying degrees of rewards for doing well on the test there were also varying degrees of punishments for failing the test. Then suppose that the teacher gave one student (Charlie) all of the questions and answers to the test to study and prepare for the test. The only condition was that the student would be held accountable for that knowledge. Charlie would be held to a higher standard since he had been given the answers ahead of time. The time came for the test and while many of the students did well, two of the students failed. The first student who failed, Joel, had no excuse. The teacher had provided visual aids and examples of what to expect on the test and how to prepare, and yet he had still failed and he would receive a punishment as a result. The second student, though, was Charlie, the student to whom the teacher had given the questions and answers to the test. Charlie also had no excuse, but even more so than Joel, for he had been given the questions and answers. Which of the two students failed? Both. Which of the two students would be punished? Both. Which of the students has an excuse? Neither of them does. Now, which of the two students will receive a harsher punishment? That answer should be quite simple, as it is the one to whom the questions and answers were given beforehand.

This story is more like what Paul conveys here. Paul makes it abundantly clear that both groups, Jews and gentiles alike, have sinned, and the punishment for that sin is death. Both students received a failing grade, neither is excused from doing poorly on the test. The degree to which the sinful are punished, though, is determined by whether or not they possessed the Law. "The Gentiles are not excused from God's judgment, but they will not be judged according to the standard (the Mosaic Law) that was not given to them,"[115] just as the punishment for the student receiving the answers prior to the test will be greater than for the one who did not, for the standard by which the teacher measured that student was greater than the one by which the second student was measured.

In addition to the fact that it would be unethical of God to hold the same standard against those possessing the Law as for those who do not, Paul provides another reason. He states, "For it is not the hearers of the law who are righteous in God's sight, but the doers of the law who will be justified." In other words, "possession of the law, even that given by God to his chosen people through Moses, will not save such people from divine wrath, unless that law is observed."[116] Simply put, you can't just talk the talk; you must walk the walk.

The primary point that Paul is making in this verse is that to be "a hearer of the law" is vastly different than to be "a doer of the law." The word translated as "hearer" is the word ἀκροαταὶ, which is either translated as "hearer" or "listener" in the New Testament. What is interesting about this word is that while it only appears in the New Testament four times, every time it also appears with the word for "doer", ποιηταὶ. Besides this reference in Romans, this association is also found in James 1:22,23, 25.[117] Those verses describe the same sort of event described in Romans 2:13, namely that a hearer stands in contrast to a doer. While one is simply aware of the reality, the other acts upon it. For the word ποιηταὶ, while rightly translated as "doer," could also be translated as "a keeper or an obeyer."[118] This accurately conveys the point that Paul is making, and reaffirms the point that Paul made in the first chapter. Just as knowledge of God is insufficient to lead man to salvation, so too, simply hearing the Law is insufficient to lead man to salvation. There must be corresponding action, evidence that the Law has been obeyed. This is not the final step in the discussion of the law, though, for there is another point to which Paul now turns his attention.

*ROMANS 2:14*

Paul continues to teach on the judgment of humanity by once again referencing the law. He writes, "When Gentiles, who do not possess the law, do instinctively what the law requires, these, though not having the law, are a law to themselves" (Rom 2:14). Now, the first thing to identify here is that this verse does not include all people not possessing the law. "There is no definite article before ἔθνη; so it means 'some Gentiles,' not necessarily all Gentiles."[119] This is an important distinction for we should not think that Paul is applying this verse to all who do not possess the law. Again, what the "law requires," literally, "'the (things) of the law,' means some of the precepts of the law, not necessarily all that is prescribed by the Mosaic Law. Paul does not imply a perfect observance of the Mosaic law by such Gentiles."[120] It would be easy for one to read this verse and assume that Paul is describing all gentiles everywhere obeying the totality of the law, but the Greek does not support this. In other words, Paul is saying that if such a gentile were to exist— not that one does—then the following would be true. Paul is only speaking hypothetically, as if the law could be fulfilled and as if the Gospel had not come. But Paul knows that there is no one righteous, not even one (Rom 3:9-10; 20-21).[121]

Beyond that, the more important point is that Paul is mentioning a law separate from that which he had previously been referencing. In order to fully understand Paul's point, the differentiation between these two laws must be identified. Thankfully, "the context shows clearly when the word 'law' means 'the Mosaic Law' and when it means 'the natural law.'"[122] (For the purpose of this book, when referencing the Law of Moses I will capitalize the word "Law" while when referring to any other law, I will not capitalize the word "law.") Verse 14 describes those individuals who were mentioned in the first clause of v. 12, who sinned and perished apart from the law. As has been clearly explained in the previous section, God has chosen to not hold the Mosaic Law against those who do not possess it since He does not show favoritism. That ignorance of the Mosaic Law (or of the Gospel) does not exempt one from being judged, it just changes the standard by which one will be judged. The standard for these people is what Paul identifies in v. 14.

Paul has already made it clear to all people, including those who do not possess the law, that knowledge of God leaves no room for excuse. Furthermore, Rom 2:12 and 3:23 demonstrate that these people have also sinned, and the just punishment for sin is death. All of this is taken into account regardless of knowledge of the law. The question now becomes, though, whether or not this is fair. God has been fair by making Himself known to all people, and God has also been fair by not holding the Law as a standard against those who do not possess the Law. Yet, despite both circumstances, those people are still held accountable for sin. In other words, even though God has been made known, has right and wrong? These people are condemned because of their sin, but is that a fair condemnation if they don't even know what sin is? It is to these questions that Rom 2:14 provides an answer.

Paul explains that even though one may not possess the Law, he is aware of the law of morality, a universally instinctive law. One does not have to teach someone that murder is wrong, regardless of the culture. For a man to take a gun and put a bullet through the head of a five-year-old boy would be considered wrong in any culture. One does not need to educate even the most primitive of cultures of this sin. There are probably pockets of society where murder is seen as a good thing, but these are highly rare cases where the society has so hardened its heart that it is no longer able to differentiate between right and wrong. Murder is an extreme example to be sure, but it helps to emphasize the point that there is some sort of an innate law by which humanity is governed. If one can agree that all societies view the murder of the innocent as wrong, then one must also agree that there is some instinctive, inherent understanding of morality, for how else could one come to such a conclusion?

Paul is arguing for an absolute law, "not relative or psychological, but absolute and objective,"[123] one that even goes beyond the Mosaic Law. This is a law that holds all men accountable, particularly those not possessing the Mosaic Law or any concept of Jesus. Where the Law of Moses is unknown, it is to this "law to themselves" that Paul appeals. God is not unfair in judging those apart from the Law for the sins that they committed, for they are still aware that they are committing sins, for "even in detail they do that which is demanded by the law, thus showing that the work of the law is written in their hearts (2:14ff.)."[124] They may not have as full an understanding (hence a lower standard and a less severe punishment), and they may not call it sin, but they are just as sinful, breaking the law of God along with the rest of the world. "The fact is that the gentile is not really outside the sphere of the law, though he is of course outside the sphere of the Law of Moses."[125] Whatever culture or time period or family or experience we may be from, the absolute law of morality governs each of us.

## ROMANS 2:15-16

Paul further explains the inherent law in v. 15a, "They show that what the law requires is written on their hearts, to which their own conscience also bears witness." Paul "spells out in greater detail the rather vague phrase φύσει τα του νόμου ποιῶσιν."[126] This is not simply a law with which they are familiar, but this is a law that is at the very core of who they are, one that they cannot ignore, for every time that a sin is committed, their conscience confirms it. Now the word for "confirms", συμμαρτυρούσης, is derived from the word μαρτυρέω, which means "witness," and while συμμαρτυρούσης carries with it this connotation, it is more accurately translated as "to testify in support, [to] confirm, [or to] witness along with."[127] This word is only used four times in the New Testament, but three of those times occur here in Romans. Romans 8:16 says that the Holy Spirit bears "witness with our spirit that we are the children of God." Then in Rom 9:1 Paul uses it again saying, "I am speaking the truth in Christ—I am not lying; my conscience confirms it by the Holy Spirit." In both instances Paul uses the same word in a context that indicates a knowing of what is right and wrong and whether one is or is not a child of God. Thus, the conscious law of the gentile is also identified as a law whereby right and wrong can truly be known. In addition to this fact, this word is a present, active participle, which speaks to the continuous nature of the conviction. What Paul is saying is that man's conscience does not just once bear witness to the law of morality, but that this is an ongoing process. The conscience of man is constantly convicting man of his sin and urging him to do right. This is the sort of law that God has provided for all men, and it is by this law that the unreached will also be judged.

Romans 2:15b-16 continues the discussion and provides a semi-conclusion to the passage. Paul writes, "...and their conflicting thoughts will accuse or perhaps excuse them on the day when, according to my gospel, God, through Jesus Christ, will judge the secret thoughts of all." Here Paul explains that the law on the hearts of humanity has power to either condemn or excuse the unreached on the Day of Judgment. Now, these phrases can complicate or confuse people, as is demonstrated by beliefs such as Universalism and Christian Inclusivism. So the first thing to recognize, once again, is the context in which these verses are stated. Remember, v. 12 provides us with a basis for the rest of the passage. It denotes that Paul is talking, from the beginning, about two groups of people, both of which are sinners, perishing either by the Law or apart from the Law. "Paul is not speaking here of the righteous only but of all mankind."[128] The context further indicates that these people are sinners, as evidenced by Rom 3:23. That being said, Paul indicates that if those not having the Law were to obey the law written on their hearts, then that would be sufficient for salvation, since they have provided a law to themselves that has the power to excuse them before God. The problem, though, is that such an instance is downright impossible, for, "while the course of his argument goes on to indicate that, one who was a 'doer' of the law would be justified, yet, since no one does it perfectly, there is no justification that way."[129] Whether the Law of Moses or the law of the conscience, the law is insufficient to save since no one can follow it perfectly.

So while the unreached could, in theory, be saved apart from the Law or any knowledge of the Gospel, that possibility is put to rest in light of the fact that "all have sinned and fall short of the glory of God" (Rom 3:23). Sin condemns all men and the conscience of man is insufficient to save. Yet, the Law of Moses is also insufficient to save apart from Christ. One of the primary points of the book of Hebrews is to demonstrate that the Mosaic Law was insufficient and that Christ's sacrifice was absolutely necessary for salvation (Heb. 10:1-10). Thus, the law as a means of righteousness—whether the Mosaic Law or the law of the conscience—cannot be kept completely and thus cannot lead to eternal life and fellowship with God. There are no true doers of the law. "Indeed, it is out of the question that the way of the law should lead to salvation, since this would render the Christ event pointless and would give the last word to man's spiritual boasting."[130] If simply following the law—any law—was sufficient, then surely God the Father would not have subjected His Son to such great wrath. Surely Jesus would not have emptied Himself and willingly handed Himself over to torture and death. The incarnation, life, death and resurrection of Christ were absolutely necessary for the salvation of humanity because neither the Law of Moses nor the law of morality were able to be fully kept or obeyed by a human, except for Christ Himself.

Since Jesus is the means by which salvation and righteousness come, Jesus is the one to stand in the presence of God on the Day of Judgment. This is a fact that Paul reiterates throughout his letters. What is more relevant to this discussion than Jesus' presence at the Day of Judgment, though, is the fact that there is a Day of Judgment. The phrase representing the Day of Judgment, "clearly refers to the eschatological day of judgment. Such a use of ἡμέρα is well attested in Paul."[131] The Universalist would many times argue that there is no such thing since all will go to Heaven. There is no need for judgment if all receive the same verdict anyway. Paul says the opposite. After establishing that there is a Day of Judgment, Paul notes that there are two verdicts that will be given; one will either be accused or excused by the law, and as has been previously explained, since the law is impossible to completely obey, then all will receive the same verdict—guilty. As if all of this were not already bleak enough, Paul takes it one step further with his last clause. Perhaps someone reading Paul's letter were to make it through all that has been discussed and still have some inclination that perfection of the law was possible by virtue of deeds, for Paul did specify in v. 13 that the actions of man determined his obedience to the law. But it is made even more difficult since God "will judge the secret thoughts of all" (Rom 2:16d), not just our actions.

Whereas Paul had previously provided the actions of man as a way to determine whether or not one was righteous, he has now taken it one step further by including the thoughts of man. Not only that, but the thoughts are not constrained only to blatant or voiced thoughts, but even those thoughts which no other human will ever know, those "secret thoughts." Paul makes it quite clear that "it is not only the overt actions of men that are to be judged but the hidden things of the heart"[132] as well. This is exactly what Jesus taught at the Sermon on the Mount where He equates hatred to murder, and lust to adultery (Matt. 5:21-30), demonstrating that a sin in the mind of a man is no less evil than one which is acted out. In other words, Paul is further padding his argument by showing that the law that condemns men to Hell is impossible to follow perfectly, which is the standard in order to spend eternity with a perfect God. How dark and depressing this message would be if not for the redemptive work of Christ! Yet, true appreciation for Christ's work is not fully realized until man's depravity is fully realized. The free gift of God, eternal life found in Christ, is only appreciated when there is first a realization that "the wages of sin is death" (Rom 6:23).

This passage, taken out of context or flippantly examined, could easily cause one to either complicate or confuse the issue. Yet, when thoroughly and objectively examined, it shows once again the story of the Gospel and the necessity for the Gospel message to be delivered. Man's sinfulness, evidenced from the blatantly public acts all the way to the privately thought ones, is made abundantly clear. Both laws, whether the one applying to those who are aware of a specific Law and those who are not, bring no excuse for humanity, since perfection is unattainable through the Law. Both the Law and the sin of man condemn humanity, and the verdict is death. Thankfully, though, this is not where the story ends. God has instituted His plan of salvation, even before the creation of the world, so that communion with Him may be possible. This is the Gospel, the Good News, but it is only Good News if it is made to be news; it is only helpful when it is known.

I believe the question of what happens to those who have not heard the Gospel is one of the most important questions that the Church can ask and it is for this reason that I have spent so much time analyzing, exegeting and examining these two passages in Romans. These passages, perhaps more than any others in Scripture, deal with this topic. I have done my best to be objective and honest about what they say, not just on a surface level but at the very depth of the text. I didn't do this to prove my point. I did this because I wanted to identify what Paul's theology, and thus Christian theology, teaches concerning those who have never heard the Gospel of Jesus Christ. What is the eternal destination of those who have never heard the Gospel? These passages give a very clear answer that apart from the Gospel, humanity is going to Hell. Whether one has heard the Gospel or not, he is still sinful and needs to hear and believe the Gospel in order to be saved. This position is called Christian

Exclusivism and is supported biblically. While the Bible may teach Christian Exclusivism, there are many in the world, even those who call themselves Christians, who teach a very different belief system. I want to examine those beliefs and see how they hold up to the scrutiny of Scripture.

# CHAPTER 12

# HERESIES

*UNIVERSALISM*

As we look carefully at some of the most common and destructive heresies (as it relates to the Great Commission), it is important to note that heresies are deceptive. Many who believe in these heresies may agree with orthodox Christianity on a number of points but they disagree on one point; the problem is that that point is non-negotiable. Within Christianity there are a number of beliefs where Christians differ. Most of these beliefs are minor, negotiable subjects, but there are certain beliefs that are not, and unfortunately many of these heresies have infiltrated the Church and the lives of Christians, significantly hindering the Great Commission and mission work around the world. There are many heresies that are certainly destructive and must be addressed, but for the purpose of this book, I want to deal with those that are most problematic as it pertains to missions, and the first is Universalism.

Universalism, simply put, "is the belief that ultimately all men will be saved."[133] There are essentially two forms of universalism. 1. Jesus and Christianity are not the only way to God. 2. While Hell may exist, and God may indeed allow the unrepentant to go there, they will not remain there for forever.

The first form of universalism is the most severe. This form says that Jesus and Christianity are not the only way to God but that there are many ways to God; so many ways, in fact, that every person everywhere will be saved regardless of what he believes. The basis for this belief lies in the fact that one cannot truly know the divine plan of God and whether Jesus is the only way. While those holding to this position may assert that Jesus was a wonderful man setting a wonderful example, they will not place Him "in a unique or even normative position in regard to other great figures of history and other ways of salvation."[134] This position sees the exclusive Christian as an enemy, and that in order to come to a place of love, the world "must purge Christianity of the exclusive-mindedness and intolerance that follows from a belief in Christianity's uniqueness."[135] The Universalist argues that "Christianity is absolute for Christians, and the other world faiths are likewise absolute for their own adherents,"[136] essentially providing a relative absoluteness where Christianity is only one of the many ways to God. In other words, a Christian gets to Heaven by following Christ but a Muslim gets to Heaven by following Muhammad and a Buddhist gets to Heaven by following Buddha.

The Bible, however, does not support such a belief as both the Old and New Testaments provide a differentiation between the true religion and the false religions. The first two commandments given by Moses make it abundantly clear that Yahweh is the only God (Exodus 3:5a). His "covenant with the Abrahamic people requires their undivided loyalty,"[137] certainly ruling out other means as a viable possibility for salvation.

The Universalistic arguments can be divided into two sections: theological arguments and biblical arguments. As it pertains to Christianity, they highlight aspects of Christianity that, at first glance, seem to support their belief. I am a firm believer that any good defense of one position requires thorough examination of the opposing position. Yes, I believe that Universalism is heretical, but I think it is only right to give Universalism a fair shot in defending its point. So, let's take a look at its arguments, beginning with the theological arguments.

1. The Love of God. Yes, it was before my time, but The Beatles are perhaps the most famous rock band of all time, and one of their most famous songs is "All You Need Is Love." It may have been popular and sold a lot of records, but it's actually not true (not that you were looking to The Beatles to determine your theology). However, most Universalists would probably have no issue with the song. Those who hold to a universalistic worldview often argue that a loving God could not send someone to Hell; no matter how sinful a life that person had lived. Universalists argue that the love of God

is so overwhelmingly powerful that it would not allow anyone to go to Hell. God's love for people is unconditional, absolutely, but unconditional love does not allow for "whatever goes." To only focus on 1 John 4:8 is to miss the fact that the Bible also describes God as holy (Lev 11:44), jealous (Exod. 20:5) and faithful (Deut. 7:9). Paul argues that the "wrath of God" has been revealed, or poured out, on the world. Paul goes on to say in Rom 6:23 that the "wages of sin is death." The word "death" in the Greek, θάνατος, does not mean to simply stop breathing; it is the death that sin brings, that which incurs the "punishment of God."[138]

Paul makes it abundantly clear that while God has given sinful humanity an opportunity for salvation through natural revelation, to reject that revelation is to incur the just punishment for sin. This does not eliminate the love of God, for it is the love of God that provides both the knowledge of Himself and the way of salvation: Jesus. Instead, the holiness of God will not allow sin to go unpunished in the same way that a good judge would not allow a murderer to go unpunished. You cannot simply elevate the love of God over and above His other attributes. He does not do that and we should not either, for at the moment that we do, we have broken the second commandment by creating a God in our own image, the God that we want Him to be.

Furthermore, to suggest that God as love means that He will accept everyone, is to not only have an incorrect view of God but also an incorrect view of love. One of the attributes of love is to protect. For example, if God didn't protect His children, and allowed the unrepentant to come into Heaven, then He wouldn't be a God of love. A father who defends his children from an intruder who is about to kill the father's children is not an unloving man. Instead it is His deep love for His son that causes him to protect him and become wrathful towards the murderer.

Romans 1:16-23 (and other passages like it) leave no room for the sinful to be left unpunished. Yet there is another teaching within Universalism that is somewhat less clear from this passage. Some argue that while Hell may exist, and God may indeed allow the unrepentant to go there, they will not remain there. They believe, as Origen said, that "Christ remains on the cross as long as one sinner remains in Hell,"[139] so as to say that there will be a day where all people, unrepentant sinners included, will find themselves in Heaven. This belief once again holds to the love of God in its defense, and while at first thought this does seem glamorous and loving, that is not the case. Instead, quite the opposite is true, for to bring all people to Heaven, including the unrepentant sinners, is to force God's love on those not wishing to receive it; and "forced love is a self-contradictory concept."[140] The love of God is an insufficient argument in favor of Universalism.

2. The Sovereignty and Omnipotence of God. Universalists argue that since God is sovereign and omnipotent that He can do anything He wants and will thus make sure that no one goes to Hell. They argue that if "God does not save all, then it is because He is not able to save all, but this is an untenable assumption. Why can the Lord not omnipotently exercise His sovereignty by sending some to Hell? By the same logic, but with a different premise, if God was not able to send some to perdition, then would that not also deny God's sovereignty and omnipotence?"[141]

God, out of His great love for humanity, has allowed humanity to make its own choice by granting free will. In so doing, God has allowed each person to make his own choice about salvation and eternity. Each person only has one life to live, for it is "appointed for man to die once, and after that the judgment" (Heb. 9:27). That judgment will only end in one of two ways: one will enter Heaven if he placed his faith in Christ, or one will enter Hell if he did not. Author C.S. Lewis says it this way: "There are only two kinds of people in the end: those who say to God, 'Thy will be done,' and those to whom God says, in the end, '*Thy* will be done.'"[142] Furthermore, for God to simply override His justice and holiness in favor of His love and mercy would not only be unfair but also un-God-like; it would be against His nature and would violate the standard by which He has chosen to live, thus making Him that which He is not—something other than the Ultimate Authority.

3. The Eternality of God. "Because God is eternal, He is not limited by time. If the destinies of people are fixed at death, then the capacity of God to work out His loving desires is limited by time. God is also infinitely patient. He has all eternity to woo people to

Himself."[143] This is the argument of many Universalists and a common Bible verse used to support this point is 2 Peter 3:9, which states, "The Lord is not slow in keeping his promise, as some understand slowness. Instead he is patient with you, not wanting anyone to perish, but everyone to come to repentance." God is indeed patient, far more than us, but while *He* lasts for forever, *His patience* does not. "Scripture abounds with examples where the Lord's patience, though incomparable to that of humans, does in fact run out. It is not infinite (Gen. 6:5-6; Exod. 32:7-10)."[144] Furthermore, the context of 2 Peter is such that anyone reading it must understand that judgment of the ungodly is common throughout the whole letter. "We must allow God to describe Himself as He is, not as we wish Him to be. The Lord is patient, far more so than any human, but the patience of the Lord does run out. It is not limitless. The biblical narratives back this up."[145]

One Universalist, Nels Ferre, actually wrote the following regarding the Universalist teachings in light of the theological arguments: "To preach to sinners that all will be saved will not reach them on their level of fear and hate of God. It will only secure them in their sin and self-sufficiency. Therefore, headed as they are away from God, they must be told, 'Repent or perish!'"[146] The argument by the Universalist is that, "If we tell people that everyone is already going to Heaven, then they won't change and live good, upright lives here on earth, so in order to help them do that, we lie to them and tell them that there is a Hell in order that they will live good lives on earth." It is almost impossible to believe that someone would say this, but it is to this measure that Universalists must go in order to prove their point. In addition to the theological arguments, Universalists make many appeals to Scripture to support their points. I want to tackle these biblical arguments next.

1. Colossians 1:19-20: "For God was pleased to have all his fullness dwell in him, and through him to reconcile to himself all things, whether things on earth or things in Heaven, by making peace through his blood, shed on the cross." The argument here is that God will one day reconcile all things to Himself, so eventually all people will be saved. The problem here is that "reconciling to Himself" is not the same as "everyone gets saved." As can be seen in the direct

context, Colossians 2:15 says, "And having disarmed the powers and authorities, he made a public spectacle of them, triumphing over them by the cross." Jesus has and will triumph over everything so that everything is reconciled. These "powers and authorities" are not joyfully submitting to the person of Christ, but they have been subjugated by a more dominant power.

2. Philippians 2:9-11: "Therefore God exalted him to the highest place and gave him the name that is above every name, that at the name of Jesus every knee should bow, in Heaven and on earth and under the earth, and every tongue acknowledge that Jesus Christ is Lord, to the glory of God the Father." Universalists argue that this verse shows that one day everyone will be saved, but the verse does not say that. This verse is similar to the one above as "the passage teaches that one day there will be cosmic subjection to Christ and recognition that Christ is Lord. The disrupted order of the universe will be set right. There is no reason that this could not be accomplished through the punishment of rebellion. Besides, in Philippians 3:19, Paul speaks of some whose "end is destruction."[147] Furthermore, James mentions that while the demons believe in God, they are not saved; they shudder (James 2:18). Simply believing in God or acknowledging his existence or Lordship is not enough for salvation. If it were, then the demons would already be saved.

3. 1 Corinthians 15:22: "For as in Adam all die, so in Christ all will be made alive." Universalists argue that the "scope of both instances of 'all' in 15:22 is the same. All humanity has died in Adam; likewise, all humanity will be made alive in Christ. This argument would be persuasive if Paul did not restrict the meaning of 'all' who are saved to those 'in Christ.' The benefits of Christ's death are granted to all who are in Christ, just as the penalty of Adam's sin is exercised on all who are in Adam."[148] Neither of these statement are all-inclusive categories, for if they were, then Jesus, the Word became flesh, would fall under the first category, making Him sinful. But if the first category doesn't apply to everyone, then the second sure doesn't have to either! One must be in Christ if he is to be made alive. The Universalist cannot ignore the part of the sentence that defeats his argument.

4. Romans 5:17: "Since by the one man's trespass, death reigned through that one man, how much more will those who receive the overflow of grace and the gift of righteousness reign in life through the one man, Jesus Christ." This is the same answer as the verse above in 1 Corinthians 15. The two designations of people are not all-inclusive, for Paul makes it clear that those who "reign in life through Christ" are not the same as those to whom death came. It is only those who "receive the overflow of grace and the gift of righteousness" who are saved.

5. 1 Timothy 2:4: God "desires all people to be saved and to come to the knowledge of the truth." This argument is that if God, who is omnipotent and sovereign, wills or desires for something to happen, then it will. "Universalists suggest that the divine desires of an omnipotent God cannot be thwarted, and eventually all will be saved. However, a desire that all be saved does not entail that all will be saved, even when that desire comes from the sovereign Lord of human history."[149] For, if God's desire always happened then what is to be said of cancer, house fires, earthquakes, hurricanes, or even sin, for that matter? If you believe that God's desire always comes to pass, then you must also believe that God is the orchestrator of every evil and horrible thing that happens in the world. Every child that is sexually abused is God's doing. Every person that dies of cancer is God's doing. Every hurricane that destroys property and kills people is God's doing. Every person that is tortured and brutally murdered by a terrorist organization is God's doing. This is a slippery slope that quickly leads to a very undesirable God.

6. 1 Timothy 4:10: Jesus is the "Savior of everyone, especially of those who believe." He is the Savior of everyone in the sense that there is none other who is able to save you. But notice that He is only (or especially) the Savior of those who believe in Him as the Savior. "There is no other Savior. He is the Savior of all people in the sense that if 'all people' are to be saved, it will only be through Jesus."[150]

7. John 12:32: "If I am lifted up from the earth I will draw all people to Myself." This verse comes immediately after some gentiles requested to see Him while in Jerusalem (12:20-21). The coming of the gentiles indicated that the moment of Jesus' crucifixion was at

hand. "His own, the Jewish people, had rejected Him (though not all), and the way of salvation was now open for all who would believe, both Jews and Gentiles."[151] All are now drawn or made available to Christ. Furthermore, to believe that John taught universalism based on 12:32 is to ignore the rest of his Gospel that requires faith for salvation (3:16; 5:24; 8:24; 10:25-26; 11:26; 20:31).

8. 1 John 2:2: "He is the atoning sacrifice for our sins, and not only for ours but also for the sins of the whole world." Once again, take the rest of the letter, and the author's other writings into account. It is obvious in reading John that Universalism is quite far from what he believes. This verse is simply talking about the fact that the "cross has cosmic and universal implications, such as defeating the principalities and powers (Col 1:19-20; 2:14-15), enabling the restoration of creation in the new heavens and earth (Rom 8:20-23) and making possible the bona fide offer of the gospel to all people"[152] (Matt 28:18-20; Luke 24:46-47; 1 Tim 4:10). Christ's sacrifice is for the whole world, but that is contingent upon the world responding to and accepting that sacrifice.

9. Hebrews 2:9: "But we do see Jesus, who was made lower than the angels for a little while, now crowned with glory and honor because he suffered death, so that by the grace of God he might taste death for everyone." "Universalist theology would require that even fallen angels be saved, but in the immediate context, the author of Hebrews explicitly states that God's help in the work of Christ does not extend to angels (Heb. 2:16). It is true that Jesus tasted death for all people; that is, Christ died, and a bona fide gospel offer is open to all. But that does not mean that all will believe and be saved."[153] Suppose I purchase a gift for my wife during the Christmas season. I wrap the gift and place a large bow on it and place it under the Christmas tree. On Christmas morning I tell Michelle, "That gift under the tree with the big bow on top is your gift." I have made that gift available to her. But what if instead of grabbing the gift and opening it and enjoying the contents of the gift, she ignores the gift and instead leaves it under the tree? That gift is hers, it has been made available to her, but until she receives it and takes it as her own, she will not have that gift. Christ's work on the cross provided the gift of salvation for all people, but each of us must individually receive that gift if we are to reap the benefits of it.

10. John 1:29: "The next day John saw Jesus coming toward him and said, "Look, the Lamb of God, who takes away the sin of the world!" This is the same situation as the previous few examples. Jesus alone is able to take away sins for the whole world, and His sacrifice is made available to the whole world, but nowhere in Scripture will you see a verse that says everyone shall be saved, or everyone's sins will be forgiven, or that everyone will be in Heaven. This is a statement about the availability of the work of Christ, not the appropriation of the work of Christ.

Ultimately, to bring all people to Heaven, including the unrepentant sinners, is to force God's love on those not wishing to receive it, and it is forcing the Bible to say something that it does not. If we are going to be honest and objective about what the Bible teaches, then we cannot support Universalism. Not only that, but we must fight against Universalism because of the danger it provides. If Universalism is true, it completely devalues the role of missions within Christianity. If everyone is going to Heaven anyway, then why bother with evangelizing the world? The logical end to Universalism is complete disinterest and disengagement with the Great Commission. For the sake of the world, we must expose and fight against the heresy of Universalism.

## HELL IS FOR REAL

In March of 2011, a book was published that sent shockwaves throughout the Christian world. Rob Bell, at the time a current mega-church pastor, published his book *Love Wins*, which, among other things questioned the existence of Hell and eternal punishment. After years of holding to an orthodox position that there was both a Heaven and a Hell, Bell argued that there would come a day when Hell was empty and all of humanity would find its way to Heaven. The reactions were varied and passionate. There were many who were comforted by his position and it wasn't long until the likes of *Time* Magazine, *Good Morning America* and Oprah were endorsing this spiritual trailblazer. However, there were many in the Christian world who called him a heretic for questioning the existence of Hell and redefining it from what it has been known to be for two millennia.

When it comes to a discussion of Hell, we must be consciously aware that the person in Scripture most responsible for our knowledge of Hell is Jesus. Jesus spoke about Hell extensively, far more than any other biblical character or author. You cannot separate Jesus from a discussion on Hell, for He is the foremost voice. If you choose to reject the doctrine of Hell or change from what the Bible says, you will also have to cut out a lot of red-letter words found in your Bible.

People similar to Rob Bell have a very difficult time coming to terms with the idea that billions of people will be sent to Hell. And in all honesty, all of us should have a very difficult time coming to grips with that. The problem is that his feelings informed his theology instead of allowing his theology to inform his feelings. In *Love Wins* he writes, "At the center of the Christian tradition since the first church, there have been a number who insist that history is not tragic, Hell is not forever, and love, in the end, wins and all will be reconciled to God."[154] The problem is that Jesus made things quite clear in Matthew 7:13-14 when He said, "Enter through the narrow gate. For wide is the gate and broad is the road that leads to destruction, and many enter through it. But small is the gate and narrow the road that leads to life, and only a few find it." Jesus was quite aware that not everyone was going to Heaven, in fact, He said that the majority of people would not.

I can argue all day long that Hell exists but as I've said time and again, my opinion does not matter. What does the Bible say? Scripture has much to say about Hell. In the many passages referencing Hell, it is very clear that Hell is a real place that provides an actual existence for the unrepentant, and a place that no one should ever wish to visit. Here are just a few facts about Hell:

- There will be weeping and gnashing of teeth (Matt 25:30).
- It is an eternal fire (Matt. 18:8)
- It is eternal punishment (Matt. 25:46)
- It is eternal destruction (2 Thess. 1:8-9)
- It is described in terms of fire (Matt. 5:22; Rev 20:15)
- It is described in terms of darkness (2 Pet. 2:17; Jude 6)
- It is unquenchable fire (Matt. 3:12)
- There the worm does not die and the fire is not quenched (Mark 9:48)

• Inhabitants will drink the wine of God's wrath, mixed in the cup of His anger (Rev. 14:9)
• Inhabitants will be tormented with fire and sulfur (Rev. 14:10)
• There will be no rest day or night (Rev. 14:11)
• There is a lake of fire and sulfur (Rev. 20:10)

"Universalism believes that death is not the final determiner; after death there is still opportunity for moral progress and repentance...that all would eventually come to God after a period of purgation."[155] Those who hold to this belief basically defend it in one of two ways. Either they try to defend it biblically, which quickly becomes far too difficult, or they see the biblical accounts describing eternal punishment as being threats more than predictions. Even further, many Universalists choose to ignore the Bible's position on the matter and appeal to the love of God instead. One famous Universalist, John A.T. Robinson, bishop of the Church of England, says, "It is futile to attempt to prove that Christ taught no belief in Hell or eternal punishment."[156] Even the staunch Universalist must admit that it is foolhardy to think that Universalism is biblically supported, because the Bible makes it quite clear in Hebrews 9:27 that "each of us are destined to die once, and after that to face judgment."

Hell is a real place and it is the destination for those who have not put their faith in Jesus. It is a horrifying and eternal place of punishment, the just penalty for all who have sinned; but for those who put their faith in Jesus, we need not fear this place, thanks to the work of Christ on the cross. Yet, the reality of Hell should motivate us to live godly lives and do everything we can to rescue people from ever reaching there.

## CONDITIONAL IMMORTALITY

Conditional immortality (also known as conditionalism or annihilationism) is the belief that only those who believe in Christ will last forever (in Heaven), while those who do not will cease to exist after a finite time of punishment. In other words, if you go to Heaven you will live forever, but if you go to Hell, you will only endure punishment until you have paid for your sins; then you will simply cease to exist.

A strong argument for conditional immortality is emotional. The thought of humans suffering eternal torment in Hell is horrifying, as one theologian writes, "Well emotionally I find the concept intolerable and do not understand how people can live with it without either cauterizing their feelings or cracking under the strain."[157] We should all find the thought of Hell as emotionally tough to swallow; indeed, it is the single worst thought in creation. But to base our theology on emotion is a grave error.

Universalism would prefer to do away with Hell altogether, but because that is so difficult to do biblically, it tries to at least lessen the blow by making it less severe. "In universalist understanding, if Hell exists at all, it will be remedial and purifying, not punitive, and temporal in duration, not eternal."[158] First of all, you won't find a place in Scripture to support that Hell is a purifying place or purgatorial existence. It is only described (as seen in the previous section) as a horrible place of torture and punishment for sins, not remedial, teaching discipline. Secondly, to suggest that it is temporal and not eternal also flies in the face of the biblical descriptions. For starters, as has also been demonstrated earlier, it is described as "eternal" time and time again. Additionally, Jesus quite clearly does away with this argument in the story of the Sheep and the Goats that Matthew records in his 25th chapter. In this chapter Matthew contrasts the sheep and the goats by contrasting "eternal punishment with eternal life. The same adjective of duration, *aionion* [translated as "eternal"], describes both the punishment of the wicked and the life of the righteous. Whatever the length of eternal life, eternal punishment lasts just as long."[159] "Either *aionion* carries the meaning of eternal, in which case the punishment described is eternal, or *aionion* means an age of limited duration, in which case the reward of Heaven is not eternal."[160] You see, the annihilationist wants Heaven to last for eternity but for Hell to be temporary. The problem is that you cannot have it both ways. Jesus uses the same word to describe the length of time in both Heaven and Hell. However long a person is in Heaven is just as long as a person is in Hell.

Another aspect to consider when evaluating conditional immortality is what it says about the penalty for sin and about the torture and death of Christ. When we consider what was necessary to save us, namely the crucifixion of Christ, should it be any wonder that sin carries with it a horrible penalty? To do away with Hell is to make the work of Christ far less significant than what it is. Jesus paid the ultimate price to rescue us. He did not rescue us from some make-believe place. He did not rescue us from some dystopian fairytale. He did not rescue us from some temporary time-out. He rescued us from the most horrible of all places. When you do away with Hell, or you diminish Hell, you diminish the work of Jesus.

The question is not, "How could a loving God send people to Hell for eternity?" The question is rather, "How could a just God allow sinners into Heaven for eternity?" You see, in order for God, the Heavenly Father, to protect Him and His children, there must be a standard by which Heaven is kept pure. Furthermore, God does not send people to Hell. We send ourselves to Hell when we condemn ourselves with our sin.

When I was in high school a tragedy struck my hometown. A major highway runs through the center of our town where the speed limit is 65 mph. One night as cars were driving on the highway a teenage boy attempted to cross the highway. He thought he could beat the oncoming traffic and tried to run across the highway. Devastatingly, one of those cars did not see the boy quickly enough in the night and hit the boy traveling 65 mph. The boy was killed instantly. Now, if I were to ask you who killed that boy, what would you say? Technically the man driving the car killed that boy, but it was not his fault. In actuality, it was the boy's mistake that killed him that night.

On the road of the afterlife drives God's vehicle of righteousness and holiness. He has made it clear that we should not sin and that if we sin we put ourselves in a vulnerable situation. In fact, the penalty for our sin is death. If we sin and willingly step into eternity with sin in our life, and God's vehicle of justice crashes into us, it is not God who has damned us to Hell; it is we who have put ourselves there. God desires for no one to go to Hell but for all to put their faith in Christ.

189

"Is it possible to preach the biblical gospel while simultaneously rejecting the future reality of Hell? The biblical writers were convinced that it is not. We would do well to hear them speak and model our praise, eschatological hope, and understanding of the gospel on their words."[161] Ultimately, preaching Hell, just as Christ did, is necessary for the Gospel, for with no Hell (and thus, only Heaven), then there is no need for salvation.

## PLURALISM

This book is not a book about religions or cults. I will not attempt to explain the proper way to evangelize people from different faiths or to explain the theology of certain major religions. There are many books that do a wonderful job of doing that,[162] but that is not the purpose of this book. Instead what I am doing in this chapter is exposing belief systems that have actually infiltrated the Church. I don't know of many Christians who see continuity and unity between Christianity and Buddhism. However, there are many Christians and many churches who hold to some of these incredibly destructive belief systems that will be addressed here. Functionally, and sometimes even consciously, they believe in and live with these heresies, heresies that have significantly diminished missions, the Gospel message and their own faith. Universalism isn't as obviously opposed to Christianity as Hinduism is, but it is just as destructive. Another such heresy is Pluralism.

Pluralism, as the name suggests, is the belief that there are many paths to God. Pluralists argue that there are as many paths to God as there are people, and we should not argue or fight about which way is right. Within this belief there are essentially two strains of belief: 1. There are many paths to many different gods, each of them legitimate in their own way or 2. There are many paths to the one true God and that essentially the Muslim, the Hindu and the Christian are all worshiping the same God. The most common position is the second. There are four primary arguments that "Christian" Pluralists use to defend their position, all of which do not stand up to the scrutiny of Scripture and logic.

Argument 1: *The Bible mentions the worship of other gods.* One of the pluralistic arguments is that the Bible specifically talks about many different religions and many different gods, and even the Israelites, at different points throughout history, worshiped many different gods. However, just because the Bible records those events does not mean that it condones those events. "A common pluralist mistake is to confuse description of real events with prescription of what ought to be. Simply put, 'is' is not equivalent to 'ought.' Pagan worship practices, though described, are unequivocally condemned throughout Scripture. Worship of the Lord is to be done on His terms as specifically prescribed by the Lord, without exception."[163]

One example of where pluralism is condemned is in John 4 and the story of Jesus and the Samaritan woman. The Samaritan argues that she is righteous as she is despite the fact that the Jews question her worship. Pluralists would argue that Jesus should affirm her spirituality since she does worship, just not as the Jews do. Jesus instead makes it quite clear that she must worship the One True God. If Pluralism was good with God, then why did Jesus witness to this woman?

Pluralists do not often realize, also, that to suggest that there are many ways to one God is not as easy as it sounds. They want the Christian to capitulate and simply allow for that belief system. They do not understand why Christians are so intent on conversion and why they can't just let people be. But for the Christian to say that there are many ways to get to the God of the Bible is to throw out the Bible and the person of Christ, who made it quite clear that He was the only way. If we are to be faithful Christians, then we must evangelize and convince the world of their need for Christ, not just whatever religion suits them the best.

Argument 2: *God is unknowable.* Another one of the Pluralist arguments is that since God is ineffable (too great to be described in words) and unknowable, then how can any religion or individual claim to know that they have found the true God and the true path to get to Him? This argument is based on the premise that God is unknowable and it is thus impossible for any religion or belief system (Christianity included) to say that they know the true God and that their way is the only way. "Such a claim is ultimately self-refuting because if God is truly unknowable and truth claims about Him cannot be made, we cannot know that He is unknowable. If we know that God is unknowable, then He really is not unknowable anymore (we know at least one fact about Him), which is impossible if He is unknowable."[164]

The problem with this from a Christian perspective, though, is that we do not agree that God is unknowable. God has made Himself known through Jesus Christ. Jesus came for a variety of reasons, but one of those reasons is so that humanity could see what God looks like. As John the Beloved wrote, "The Word became flesh and made his dwelling among us. We have seen his glory, the glory of the one and only Son, who came from the Father, full of grace and truth" (John 1:14). The incarnation put a face on God. What we celebrate at Christmas is the moment when God took on humanity. If you grew up singing Christmas carols then you will remember this line from *O Come All Ye Faithful*, which says, "God in flesh appearing."[165] In Christ, we see the face of God. We do know God, not completely, for that will not come until Heaven, but we know a great deal about Him, and most importantly, we know enough to know that He is the only God, Triune in nature and seen visibly in the second member of the Trinity, Jesus Christ, through whom alone salvation is attained.

Argument 3: *Leave people alone.* Pluralists argue that Christians should leave those in other religions alone. "Who knows," they argue, "they may be right? Perhaps more right than you, but at least as right as you. And if so, we should definitely not steer them in the wrong direction." But that is not the example of the Bible. The God of the Old Testament was constantly trying to keep His people separate from other religions, condemning the other gods and their acts. Let me be clear, the Bible does mention other gods. I am not denying the fact that there are other spiritual powers. But what is made incredibly clear in the Bible is that whatever gods there may be in this world, they pale in comparison to the matchlessness of Christ. They are nothing more than stones and wood. They have no power or authority over God Almighty. They are demons impersonating God. Jesus was very unique and particular. When Paul encountered people from other faiths (such as the Stoics and Epicureans in Acts

17), he did not let them be; he was determined to preach the only Gospel that he knew to be true. To simply leave other religions alone is to go against the command of the Scriptures and the example of our leaders, including our greatest Leader, Christ.

Pluralists would like for the Christian to simply succumb and say, "Ok fine, we believe our way and will follow our path, but we will let the other religions be. We won't argue whether all roads lead to Heaven. Just have it your way." The problem is that our God, our Lord, our Leader, will not allow that. We are compelled to speak the truth.

Argument 4: *Jesus never claimed to be the only way.* As we evaluated earlier, in John 14:6 Jesus very clearly states the He is the only way. But if that wasn't convincing enough, here are some other things He said, accounts that were recorded by eyewitnesses and substantiated by eyewitnesses:

- He claimed to be the King of an eternal kingdom (Luke 22:29)
- He claimed sovereignty over life and death (John 5:21-24)
- He accepted worship that could only be directed toward God (Matthew 28:17; Luke 24:52)
- He claimed sovereignty over eternal judgment and eternal reward (John 5:27)
- He said such things as "The one who has seen Me has seen the Father" (John 14:9)
- He said He was the only way to the Father (John 14:6)

That all sounds pretty blatant and particular to me. Jesus didn't leave His divinity up in the air. Pluralism does not have a foot to stand on when it tries to align itself with Christianity. Anyone who will try to argue that Pluralism and Christianity are just two branches of the same tree have never seen Christ's tree. The tree that Jesus died on provided salvation to all who would believe in Him alone, but it does not extend to any and every other belief system.

I love to read. I don't do it as often as I would like or prefer, but I love to read. One of the problems I have, though, is that there are so many incredible books out there. My list of desired books to read is always much longer than I have the time to actually read. Because of this, I never reread books. I figure that there are so many good books already out there that I haven't read that I don't want to take the time to reread books that I have already read. However, every once in a while an exceptionally good book comes along and a few years after reading it I have the desire to reread it. I haven't felt that way about many books, but I've felt it about a few (*Mere Christianity* by C.S. Lewis, *Interview with the Devil* by Clay Jacobsen, to name a couple). One of those books is *A God of Many Understandings?* by Todd L. Miles. I read this book during my sophomore year at Oral Roberts University and it immediately vaulted to one of my all-time favorite books. If you take the time to examine the endnotes in this book, then you will see that in this section of my book I have referenced that book a lot. I have marked up that book perhaps more than any other and it has proven to be incredibly helpful, both practically and theologically. Miles discusses many of these topics and as I close the discussion on Pluralism I want to let his voice be heard as he says it better than I ever could:

"Proclamation of the Lord Jesus Christ—His life, teaching, death and resurrection—is the biblical response to pluralism. Such a course takes wisdom and boldness, for the more biblically faithful the gospel message is proclaimed, the more offensive it will be to those who have drunk deeply from the poisoned waters of religious pluralism. There is no way around this reality. Jesus made exclusive claims that are utterly incompatible with all other religious systems. For if Jesus is correct, then Muhammad and Buddha were wrong. If Jesus is incorrect, then Christians are wrong. People in our current cultural milieu might wish that this were not the case, but wishing does not make it so. To dismiss the truth claims of Jesus as self-evidently wrong because His statements offend cultural sensibilities is not an argument against those truth claims; it is only a complaint that His claims are offensive. Though postmodern sensibilities try to argue otherwise, palatability does not reflect on the validity of a truth claim. Christians, of all people, ought to realize this because they are told in Scripture that their message will be rejected precisely because it is offensive to blinded human sensibilities (John 3:19; 1 Cor. 1:23; 2 Cor. 4:1-5)."[166]

## CHRISTIAN INCLUSIVISM

Recently there has been an influx of high-profile ministers and leaders who are switching from traditional orthodox positions within Christianity and following some new theology, one that is more appealing in the 21$^{st}$ century. People like Carlton Pearson and Rob Bell have started preaching a Gospel of Inclusion. Rob Bell's position on Heaven, Hell and salvation is most closely connected to a belief called Christian Inclusivism, a belief that is rapidly gaining in popularity among Christians today. If someone like Rob Bell could gain international attention and notoriety by championing Christian Inclusivism, it is a position that must be studied, and as you will see, one that has great implications for the evangelistic efforts of the Church.

Christian Inclusivism, simply defined, is the belief that there is salvation outside of Christianity and the Church, but still by means of Christ's salvific work. Inclusivism teaches that all people will be saved by the means of Christ, some even anonymously, as salvation is attained apart from a knowledge of Christ. This belief differs from Universalism in that Jesus is necessary for salvation. Jesus' death is the only way by which salvation can be attained, but it is not necessary to actually know of Jesus in order for that salvation to come about. In this belief system, Christianity is still seen as the "continuing vehicle of God's direct self-revelation... [and] the only religious movement to have been founded on earth by God in person."[167] Thus, Christianity is still seen as the only true religion and Christ is still seen as the only way to salvation, but the parameters for salvation have been expanded so as to include a whole host of people, namely those who have never heard the Gospel.

For the vast majority of church history, this position has been opposed by almost every major church denomination and leadership, but in the last couple centuries intolerance has become the sin of all sins and both the world and some branches of the Church have become critical of the exclusive nature of Christianity.

This position gained a lot of traction when the Catholic Church essentially declared this as its position with the publication of Vatican II in 1963-1965. For centuries the Catholic Church held to a position called *extra Ecclesiam nulla salus*, which when translated from Latin means, "outside the Church there is no salvation."[168] Another example of this would be Pope Innocent III in 1215 stating, "There is one Universal Church of the faithful, outside of which there is absolutely no salvation."[169] This, of course, was seen by much of the world as being both obnoxious and offensive. Obnoxiousness and offense, though, should not be grounds for theological waffling. The problem with this position, though, is that the Bible does not teach that one must be part of the Catholic Church in order to be saved. That is taking an ecclesiological (Church-like) approach to salvation rather than a Christological (Christ-like) one. Of course, I would disagree with the Catholics on this, for I believe that you may be part of any number of denominations (Catholicism included) yet still be a Christian. Salvation is not given to us by the Church but rather by Christ.

This position came under heavy scrutiny, particularly during the 20th century, as Christianity was viewed as too intolerant. In light of this, the Catholic Church convened to reassess their position on a variety of issues, one of which was its position on salvation apart from Christ, especially as it related to the unreached—those outside of the scope of the Church's reach. The conclusion of the Vatican II Council was essentially that in the sovereignty and mystery of God's will, salvation through Christ is afforded to even those who are unaware of it. Thus, in speaking of Christ's redemptive work, Vatican II states:

"All this holds true not only for Christians, but for all men of good will in whose hearts grace works in an unseen way. For, since Christ died for all men, and since the ultimate vocation of man is in fact one, and divine, we ought to believe that the Holy Spirit, in a manner known only to God, offers to every man the possibility of being associated with this paschal mystery."[170]

The position of the Catholic Church set the stage for a large part of Christianity, as this way was seen as more charitable and less hostile. This position was, for many, much easier to come to terms with concerning their view of a loving and inclusive God. Jesus was still the Savior; that position remained unchanged so as to differentiate it from Universalism. Now, though, "man—every man without exception whatever—has been redeemed by Christ...because with man—with each man without any exception whatever—Christ is in a way united, even when man is unaware of it."[171]

In case there was any confusion on what the points outlined in Vatican II mean for the unreached, the *Dogmatic Constitution on the Church* openly stated that this provision was made for "those who through no fault of their own do not know the gospel of Christ and those who, without blame on their part, have not yet arrived at an explicit knowledge of God."[172] In other words, the ignorant are excused from condemnation on the basis of their very ignorance. Not only are they excused, but they could also be saved while in ignorance, for as Pope Paul VI said, "God, in ways known to Himself, can lead those inculpably ignorant of the gospel to that faith."[173]

Now, while it has already been established that it is God's expressed desire that all people be saved, the Christian Inclusivist equates God's desire with His actions, and that is simply not the case. A differentiation must be made: God's will for salvation is not identical with salvation. "Should an individual shut his heart to the divine invitation, he would have only himself to blame for his damnation."[174] Once again, this goes back to the Romans 1 passage where God can be known through the natural world but that knowledge is not enough to save. Now, if *that* knowledge is not enough to save, then how could *no* knowledge be enough to save? The short answer is that it cannot. A lack of knowledge of Christ is insufficient for salvation, and in fact, far less sufficient than any knowledge of God, even through natural revelation.

The Romans 2 passage examined earlier is oftentimes used by Christians Inclusivists as a defense for their argument. They argue that "the law to themselves" is a way for the ignorant to be saved, even though they may not be aware of it. They continue to believe that Jesus is the Savior, but that knowledge of Him is unnecessary for salvation, or at least that salvation is possible (and in many cases, guaranteed) without knowledge of Him. Inclusivists hold to this passage as support that Christ could save all by virtue of the law that is followed. Knowledge of Jesus is unnecessary for salvation. They are anonymous Christians, included in salvation based on their good works, on their adherence to "the law to themselves," not on their knowledge and subsequent devotion to Christ, or of any act of repentance. The problem with all of this is that Romans 2:14 does not provide the ignorant or anonymous or unreached with a viable opportunity for salvation by virtue of the law, for this law, just like the Mosaic Law, is unable to be kept. No matter how hard one might strive, perfection will never be attained, and perfection is the requirement for salvation, only made possible through the atoning death and resurrection of the perfect Christ.

Christian Inclusivism has become the de facto position of the Catholic Church, and has opened wide the floodgates for evangelicals to do the same, which is why Christian Inclusivism is increasingly becoming a more popular position in Christianity. This position begs a great deal of questions, perhaps at the top of the list is, "Well, how does this salvation happen?" The answers vary. Some argue that because Christ died for all, then all are saved, whether they know it or not. Some argue that this is a work of the Holy Spirit. Though everyone may not know Christ, the Holy Spirit is present in all religions and leads men to salvation. Some simply say that they do not know how this mystery happens, but it does, nevertheless, happen.

What is commonly seen as an answer to how this happens, though, is that this is a product of good works. Inclusivism says, "Those in any religion who have not heard the Gospel 'through no fault of their own' may 'seek God with a sincere heart, and, moved by grace, try in their actions to do his will as they know it through the dictates of their conscience—those too may achieve eternal salvation.'"[175] In other words, whether one is a Muslim, a Hindu, a Christian or an atheist, if he seeks to do good, then that is a demonstration of regeneration of the Holy Spirit and that person is a Christian. As one Inclusivist put it, "every human being is a Christian, and he is not one always expressly but very often anonymously."[176] Salvation is not only provided to the knowledgeable or those within the Church, but there will be those who are saved by Christ but do not know it. They are described here as being unaware, and described elsewhere as ignorant Christians. What exactly, though, does this say for free will? Christ now saves people even if they don't know it? So Christ has now imposed His will on the Hindu or the Buddhist or the Atheist simply because that person has engaged in good works? Free will is thrown out in this perspective. Furthermore, what about those religions or religious beliefs that are staunchly opposed to Christianity and Christ? The Orthodox Jew knows Christ, yet knowingly and strongly rejects Him as the Messiah. If the Jew does good, though, he is then saved by Christ? Or what of the religions whose religious systems call for sins. There are some religions whose practices incorporate human sacrifice or orgies. These are not the type of behaviors reflected in Scripture as being Christian, but they are the laws for certain religions. They are now, unwillingly, yet anonymously saved through Christ? Listen to what Clark Pinnock, one of the main proponents of Inclusivism, says, "God will save even the atheist who, though rejecting God (as he understands God), responds positively to him implicitly by acts of love shown to the neighbor."[177]

Another argument is the fulfillment theory, namely that people all over the world worship things or objects or beings and this is their response to an innate desire to worship Christ. Humans naturally have an innate desire to worship, and that is evidence of regeneration, the Inclusivist will say. But desire is not equivalent to reality. Just because there is a desire to do good does not mean that one does it. An argument for this is Paul's encounter in Athens in Acts 17 where he references "An Unknown God." Inclusivists argue that "the Athenian worship of the unknown god demonstrated that they knew the true God although they did not recognize Him as the Creator. Such authentic worship is evidence that the Athenians were Christians, though unconsciously."[178] This is a complete disregard for context and hermeneutics! Paul never said that the worship of their unknown God was good. He rather used their unknown god to segue into a discussion about Jesus. In the Greek, Paul references the unknown god in neuter, nondescript Greek, but then transitions to Jesus in specific, masculine Greek. He makes a distinction between the two. Furthermore, the Athenians were polytheists. This was simply one of many gods that they were worshiping. Are we to assume, then, that since they included Christ (if that were the unknown god, which it is not) in the worship of all of their other gods, that they are saved? That is no different than Hinduism.

All of this is foolhardy and stands in contrast to the tenets of Scripture, which outline clearly what is (and is not) necessary for salvation. Good works is not good enough (Eph. 2:8-9). Salvation is a work of Christ alone, yet requires the decision of the individual (Rom 10:9-10). It requires confession that Christ is Lord and a belief that He has been raised from the dead. Salvation requires repentance (Acts 2:36; 16:30). When these things are absent, so too is salvation.

Prior to closing this discussion on Christian Inclusivism, there are two quite obvious points that must be addressed, two points that serve practically in evaluating the validity of this argument. The first has to do with those who believe that Christ will save all. If all are saved by Christ anyway, then why is there a need for missionary work? The unreached are already saved regardless of the Gospel being preached to them. Could not the time and money spent on missionary and evangelistic efforts be better spent on orphanages or churches or feeding the hungry? Of course! If the totality of humanity were already assured of salvation, then the missionary work of the Church should be immediately halted. This belief has massive implications for the Church.

The second point concerns those who would argue that while Christ will not save everyone, there are many who will be saved who do not know it. Those who hold to this position often say that the saving grace of God is given to those who by nature are obeying the laws and order which is known to them, not those who are aware of Christ but have made a conscious decision to reject Him. In other words, if people don't know about Jesus, they have a much better chance of being saved because they would not have had a chance to reject Him. If that were the case, then logically, would not the Christian do well to leave the unevangelized alone? For, if one is already anonymously saved by following the "law to themselves," then to present Christ would make the individual aware of Christ and thus give that person an opportunity to reject Him. Logically, it would actually be better to never evangelize the unreached, for if they are already saved apart from knowledge of Christ, then knowledge of Him has now provided a means by which to reject Him and not be saved. In fact, Vatican II says as much, "They could not be saved who, knowing that the Catholic Church was founded as necessary by God through Christ, would refuse either to enter it, or to remain in it...Only those who know the necessity of the Catholic Church and consciously reject it cannot be saved. Those who have not heard of the necessity of the church do not share such condemnation."[179]

If we are to believe what Vatican II concluded, then Jesus really made a mistake! Before ascending to Heaven, Jesus' final command was to "Go into all the world and proclaim the good news to the whole creation. The one who believes and is baptized will be saved; but the one who does not believe will be condemned" (Mark 16:15b-16). If those who had never heard were already saved, then Jesus' last words should have been something more like this, "Beloved, our time together has been wonderful, and I know that many of you will want to tell others about me and our experiences together, but whatever you do, do not tell anyone about me. My greatest desire is for all to be saved, and the best chance for the largest number of people to be saved is if they do not have a chance to reject me. So, please do not tell anyone about me." This, of course, is quite contrary to the Great Commission that Jesus gave us.

Charles Spurgeon, an evangelist himself with a desire to see the lost saved, once asked this question: "It is not a question of whether a heathen can be saved without hearing the gospel but rather, can the Church be saved if it does not obey Christ's commission?"[180] Spurgeon was well meaning, but on this particular point he was mistaken. Spurgeon was arguing that the Church has a responsibility to obey the Great Commission. I wholeheartedly agree with him on this point. But in trying to prove his point, he argued that it is irrelevant for us to wonder whether the unreached can be saved apart from the Gospel, and it is with this that I disagree, for if the heathen can be saved without hearing the Gospel, then obeying Christ's commission becomes rather pointless. Christ made His final words to His disciples a call to action because of the urgency that there is to save the lost. Christ made a call to engage in missionary work where those who had not heard about Him would hear about

Him; where those who were anonymous of Him would be so no longer; where those who were ignorant would be informed. He did this because He knew quite well that in this context, there is nothing blissful about ignorance.

Ultimately, this position is much more palatable because it allows for many, billions, in fact, to be saved all over the world who would otherwise be sent to Hell. Clark Pinnock shares the real motivation behind his theology: "How can it be that a God of perfect love could condemn people who never had an opportunity to respond to the Gospel? What kind of God would send large numbers of men, women and children to Hell without the remotest chance of responding to his truth?"[181] I get it. This is a horrible reality, but our emotions must not dictate our beliefs. Our motivation must not fuel our theology; our theology must fuel our motivation. Pinnock continues, "There is no way around it—we must hope that God's gift of salvation is being applied to people everywhere."[182] Hope must not trump truth, though. Honestly, if Pinnock and others like him put the same amount of effort and time into telling others about Jesus in unreached areas as they did in arguing why they shouldn't have to, the world would be a lot closer to being reached for Jesus! Ultimately, the Christian Inclusivist would have us believe that many (if not all) people are saved by means of Christ, a step in the right direction from Universalism, but just as wrong and misled as the Universalist! What Christ did is enough to save everyone, but only if each individual responds to that reality. I may have enough food to feed every person at the homeless shelter, but until the people come and eat, they will not be fed. "Salvation is found in no one else, for there is no other name under heaven given to men by which we must be saved" (Acts 4:12).

# PRACTICAL IMPLICATIONS

# CHAPTER 13

# WHAT DO I BELIEVE?

*TELL ME THE TRUTH*

Do you remember your first job? I'm not talking about cleaning the dishes or washing the bathroom, I'm talking about the first job you had where you actually made money. Maybe you sold lemonade. Perhaps you mowed your neighbor's lawn. Or, if you were like me, you babysat. I was probably ten years old when I got my first babysitting job. I took piano lessons and my teacher had her studio in her basement. I would take lessons from her for an hour but after my lesson ended she had another group of students that she had to teach and she had no one to watch her kids. So she hired me to watch her two kids upstairs while she taught downstairs.

The oldest was her daughter, probably around seven years old. The youngest was her son, probably five years old. The girl was a perfect angel. She was so kind and so sweet and incredibly obedient. There were never any problems with her. The boy, on the other hand, was the complete opposite. His goal in life was to wreak havoc. He destroyed anything his sister created. If he didn't get his way, he would let out these bloodcurdling screams. And he was anything but obedient.

One day, while babysitting them I decided it would be a good idea to watch a movie. This was before Netflix. This was before DVD's. This was the age of the VCR. If you were born in the 21ˢᵗ century or later, my guess is that you may not even know what these are. VCR's were larger, rectangular-shaped tapes with a reel, and it was how we all watched movies before DVDs. Well, as I went to put the VCR into the VCR player I noticed some resistance. I tried pushing it in and it wouldn't go in. I pulled out the VCR to look inside and I found out exactly why the tape wouldn't go in—the VCR was jammed with pancakes! I couldn't believe it! I called the two kids into the living room, showed them the pancake VCR machine and calmly asked them, "Which of you did this?" My question was met with silence. Now, if I'm being honest, there is absolutely no doubt in my mind which of the two had done this. I had an angel and a fiend standing in front of me. I knew that one was incapable of doing this and the other was probably proud of his work. However, I asked the question anyway, "Who did this? Tell me the truth." I had my suspicions but I could not simply go on my assumptions. I needed to know the truth. The boy looked at me and sheepishly confessed to the pancake crime.

As I think back on that story, I laugh, but I am also reminded of the many times in my life that I've heard or said the same phrase that I said that day: "Tell me the truth." As humans, we strive for truth. We live in a world where we are constantly trying to gain truth. We go to school for over a decade to learn truth. We ask questions to understand truth. We read books to increase our knowledge of the truth. Knowingly or unknowingly, we search for and desire truth. I have spent a lot of time and effort in the past few chapters discussing many different aspects of what is not true. I didn't want you to just hear my side of the argument. If I actually believe my perspective, then I am not concerned with the contrarian arguments. In fact, I believe that a truly strong argument for anything is only made if that position has also examined the opposing arguments. This is why I spent so much time examining Universalism, Conditional Immortality, Christian Inclusivism and others. But if I believe that all of those positions are wrong, then the question becomes, "What is right? Tell me the truth." So, what is the truth?

## THE MACEDONIAN MAN

I have had the privilege of teaching many times on the subject of evangelism and the necessity of preaching to the unreached. It is always an honor to preach and teach, and especially so on a subject as important as this. When the venue and time allow for it, I always try to have a time of questions and answers, because the subjects that I've discussed in this book deserve dialogue. One of the things that I have heard from people as an argument against my position is something that sounds like this: "I have a hard time believing that God would create humans and send Jesus and yet someone would live and die and never even have a chance to hear about Jesus. I believe that everyone will hear about Jesus at some point, even if it is just an angel appearing to them or Jesus appearing to them in a vision."

I completely understand the position that these people are taking. I realize that it is a difficult thing to accept that there are people in this world who will live and die having never heard about Jesus; but just because it is difficult or hard to believe something doesn't make it any less true. Take the words of Jesus, for example. When speaking of the end of the world, He said that one of the qualifications for His second coming was that people from all the nations of the world must hear the Gospel: "And the Gospel must first be preached to all the nations" (Mark 13:10). John writes in Revelation that in Heaven there will be "persons from every tribe and language and people and nation" (Revelation 5:9). What is evident from Scripture is that Christ will not return until there is at least a representative in the body of Christ from every tribe, nation and tongue, which necessitates that every tribe, nation and tongue must be exposed to the Gospel. Now, if every person had heard about Jesus through a vision of Jesus or an angel's appearance, then it would be hard to believe that there wouldn't be at least one person from each ethnic group who had already accepted Christ. Yet, based on the fact that the Lord has not returned, that does not seem to be the case. I travel to places all over the world where they have never heard the name of Jesus. For generations these people's ancestors have lived and died without knowledge of Christ, until we come and tell them.

Yet, there are many who want to justify their inactivity with the belief that if they don't do evangelistic work then the angels will do it for them. They argue that even though people need to know Jesus, humans do not need to tell them. God, in His sovereignty, could have set up the proclamation of the Gospel and salvation of humanity to happen any number of ways. For example, a widely held belief is that people can be saved through the appearance of angels. I ask you, though, is there even one Bible verse to support this viewpoint? Can you show me one verse where an angel leads someone to Christ? I am not in the business of questioning God's ways, for He knows far better than I do, and He has chosen to do things a certain way. He could have set it up so that angels are the preachers of the Gospel, but He did not. Instead He left that all-important command to you and to me. In Scripture, angels are not the ones preaching the Gospel. God determined that to be the job of humanity. The story of Cornelius, which will be examined more closely later on, is a great example of that. The angel appeared to Cornelius, who knew nothing of Jesus, but instead of telling Cornelius about Jesus, he instructed Cornelius to send for Peter so that Peter could share the Gospel. Another great example of this is found in the life of Paul:

*Paul and his companions traveled throughout the region of Phrygia and Galatia, having been kept by the Holy Spirit from preaching the word in the province of Asia. When they came to the border of Mysia, they tried to enter Bithynia, but the Spirit of Jesus would not allow them to. So they passed by Mysia and went down to Troas. During the night Paul had a vision of a man of Macedonia standing and begging him, "Come over to Macedonia and help us." After Paul had seen the vision, we got ready at once to leave for Macedonia, concluding that God had called us to preach the gospel to them. – Acts 16:6-10*

In Macedonia was a man, perhaps many people, who were desperate for the Gospel. At a time where very few in the world had heard the Gospel, there were people in Macedonia who were desperate for the message of Christ. They cried out to the God of the heavens to reveal Himself. God didn't send an angel to tell them about Christ, instead He reached out to Paul. Paul, being attentive and obedient to the leading of the Holy Spirit, made his way to Macedonia. There are people all over the world who are crying out for the message of the Gospel and God's response to them is not to send angels but rather to send humans, people like you and like me. People often ask us why we go to the places that we go. How do we decide where to go? There are a number of factors that go into the decision of where to minister, but one of the primary reasons is because of the prayers of the people to whom we are ministering. I truly believe that when we go to minister, we become an answered prayer to the people in that place. God says, "You will seek me and find me when you seek me with all your heart" (Jer. 29:13). There are people all over the world who are seeking for the one true God, and when we listen to and obey the leading of the Holy Spirit, we go to specific places in response to the prayers of those in that place who are seeking for the one true God, just like the Macedonian man.

## *THE ROAD TO DAMASCUS*

Another common argument is that if angels will not show up to the unevangelized, then Jesus Himself will do it through visions and dreams. There are many who believe that the unreached can be saved through a vision of Jesus. Now, it is important to point out that there are many modern-day testimonies, particularly by those in the Muslim world, who claim that Jesus has appeared to them. The Christian Inclusivist uses this argument to say things like, "See, God will make sure that the right people get saved anyway, even if He has to show up to them Himself." The problem with an example like a Muslim, though, is that Muslims already have knowledge of Jesus. The Muslim has surely already heard the Gospel and even the Islamic Holy Scriptures speak about Jesus. It is not as though there is no knowledge of Jesus, so this is not a good example for those who have not heard. Additionally, while Jesus is appearing to Muslims and other religious peoples through dreams and visions, those who do not know Jesus are not typically coming to faith in Him simply through that vision.

Longtime Southern Baptist missionary David Garrison, a missionary to the Islamic world, mostly in Libya, says, "The tragic thing is that unless someone is there to tell them [Muslims] what the dream or vision means or to present to them a Scripture in their own language so they can read it and hear it and understand it and then find the Jesus of the Bible, they're left with this haunting sense of, who was this? What does this mean?"[183] Even when those who do not know Jesus receive a vision of Jesus, they are still in need of someone to tell them about Jesus.

GO

Acts 8 tells the story of Philip and the Ethiopian eunuch. Though the Ethiopian had the Scriptures and was reading them, he was still confused without the presence of Philip, for when Philip asked if the Ethiopian understood the Scriptures the man responded, "'How can I unless someone explains it to me?'...Then Philip began with that very passage of Scripture and told him the good news about Jesus" (Acts 8:31, 35). Even with the Bible, the man was still in need of Philip's witness in order to be saved.

The example of Paul, though, is probably the one most common for those who argue that the Lord will save those who have never heard, even through a vision. Paul's story is one of the greatest redemption stories in Scripture. Here is a man who hated Jesus and Christians. His job was to travel around the region arresting Christians. If he were alive today, he would likely approve of the acts of ISIS or Hamas or some other terrorist organization in their treatment of Christians. His testimony is an incredible one where, while on the road to Damascus to arrest Christians, Jesus appeared to him in a vision, which led to his salvation (Acts 9). Here is an example of someone being saved through a vision of Jesus. Yet, there are a few things to remember when examining this story:

1. In 1 Corinthians 15:8 Paul says, "and last of all he [Jesus] appeared to me also, as to one abnormally born." Paul himself acknowledges that his experience was an abnormal one. This should not be the expectation; it should be the exception.

2. Paul was already aware of Jesus. Paul is not a representative of somebody who has never heard the Gospel because he was certainly familiar with the Gospel and Jesus. In fact, he was specifically going to Damascus to arrest Christians. Thus, those trying to argue for Paul's conversion as an example of how someone could be saved apart from hearing the Gospel do not have a representative in Paul.

3. Even though Jesus appears to Saul on the road to Damascus, He responds that Saul is to head to the city and there he will be told what to do. At the same time, in a vision the Lord instructs a godly man, Ananias, to go to Paul to tell him the truth of the Gospel and pray with him. Notice that the Lord sent Ananias to Saul after the vision. In other words, Jesus' appearance was enough to begin the process for Saul, but Jesus knew that Saul needed more than just a

vision, so He sent Ananias, who told Saul, "Get up, be baptized and wash your sins away, calling on his name" (Acts 22:16b). God sent Ananias to lead Saul in salvation. He didn't send an angel. He didn't stop at a vision of Himself. He directed Ananias to go to Saul.

Paul's example does not support the possibility of someone with no knowledge of God being saved; it actually does quite the opposite. The simple fact of the matter is that those who do not have the Gospel are desperately in need of us to tell them. We cannot expect a vision or a dream of Jesus to save them. We have no biblical basis for an angel to lead anyone to Christ. Instead, what is incredibly obvious from Scripture is the clear imperative to go and preach the Gospel to those who have never heard, for without the proclamation of the Gospel, there is no biblical reason to believe that anyone without the knowledge of Christ will come to faith in Him.

## THE BUFFET LINE

I'm not sure how you feel about food, but I love it. For me, eating is not a chore or just some sort of an occurrence. Meals are an event. I look forward to dinner. I have never understood those people who forget to eat. I remember when I was at University and I'd hear a girl say, "You know I just realized that I forgot to eat lunch today." What? How does that happen? How could you forget something as wonderful and exciting as a meal?

Along with my love for food is a love for buffets. I love quality food, but I also like a good deal and getting my money's worth, so I love buffets. Now, for obvious reasons, I do not go to buffets often. If I care about my body whatsoever then staying away from buffets is important. Furthermore, the Bible does say that gluttony is a sin and I try to avoid sin. But every once in a while I enjoy going to a buffet.

Now, imagine if you were at a restaurant with a buffet line full of incredible food and you were starving. You saw a number of people at their tables with full plates and you grabbed your own plate to head to the buffet line. But as you arrived at the buffet, you were stopped by the manager who told you that you were not allowed to eat until others had went through the line. You looked around and noticed that everyone else in the restaurant already had food on their plates. You asked, "Sir, I think everyone has already been through the line once, do you mind if I go through it now?" The manager responded, "No, we would like everyone to go through the line a few times and have their fill before you start." "But sir," you reply, "that seems a little unfair. I am starving and all of these people have already eaten." Indeed, this mentality does seem unfair, and yet this is oftentimes how we treat the message of the Gospel.

*It has always been my ambition to preach the gospel where Christ was not known, so that I would not be building on someone else's foundation. Rather, as it is written: "Those who were not told about him will see, and those who have not heard will understand."* – Romans 15:20-21

As you read this Scripture it is easy to see Paul's perspective on evangelism. He was intent on preaching the Gospel where it had not yet been preached. There is certainly value and importance in preaching the Gospel where people have already heard it, as there are many who surround us every day who have heard the Gospel, but need to hear it again. I am not encouraging us to stop preaching in places that have heard, but I think that a stronger emphasis must be placed on preaching the Gospel where it has not been preached. It is unfair and unethical to force a hungry patron to wait to go through the buffet line once until someone has gone through the buffet line multiple times.

I come from the mindset that everyone should have a chance to go through the buffet line once before someone goes through it twice. And when it comes to evangelism, there are so many people in the world who have yet to hear the Gospel even once, while others hear it on a daily basis. I think it's about time that we refocused our efforts to reach those who have not yet heard, because apart from hearing the proclaimed Gospel of Jesus Christ, no one will come to faith in Him.

## CHRISTIAN EXCLUSIVISM

I have referenced Christian Exclusivism a lot throughout this book, and if only by comparison to the other worldviews, you probably have a good handle on what it is. I have argued that Universalism, Pluralism, Christian Inclusivism and so much else is wrong and runs contrary to Scripture. While many of the viewpoints of Christian Exclusivism have been communicated, I need to highlight some, for this is the worldview of Scripture.

1. First of all, by virtue of the name itself, those who hold to Christian Exclusivism are oftentimes seen as arrogant and unloving. Critics of Christian Exclusivism argue that this position puts a limit on the love of God and the ability that He has to bring all men unto salvation or to provide salvation to those who have not heard the Gospel. To this I pose this situation: Suppose a judge has a son whom he loves very much. The judge's son commits murder and is brought before that same judge, now as a convicted criminal. The judge, while unwavering in his love for his son, is still forced to act rightly and justly by giving his son the sentence worthy of murder. The father's love for his son has not diminished in any way. In fact, the hardest thing he will ever have to do is condemn his son, but to do otherwise would not only be unloving but unjust; and God is neither. It is not the Christian Exclusivist who lessens the love of God; it is rather the Christian Inclusivist and Universalist who lessen the justice of God.

To presume that Christian Exclusivism somehow limits or belittles the love and grace of God is simply closed-minded. God is continually beckoning the world unto Himself. "God's self-offer should not be thought of as a single event, or as something which happens occasionally or even intermittently in one's life."[184] It should rather be understood as "an abiding possibility of human freedom."[185] As has been adequately explained previously, God "desires for everyone to be saved and to come to the knowledge of the truth" (1 Tim 2:4). Christian Exclusivism does not waver on this issue. Rather, it simply balances the love of God with the holiness and justice of God.

2. Another standard belief in Christian Exclusivism is that of free will. "Were grace to be an imposition, then it would simply not be grace, but a consumption of human nature by the divine."[186] God is not a bully who forces salvation upon those who do not want it. He is a gentleman who only comes in when invited. "Despite our

hoping that all are saved, if salvation is to have any meaning at all, we must admit the possibility that one can refuse salvation." [187]Of course all Christians would wish for the salvation of humanity, but salvation becomes worthless if applied to all people anyway. In that case it is not unlike a boy receiving a trophy from his soccer coach for his excellent performance, only to notice that every other player on his team also received the same trophy. Sure, the trophy is nice, but it is meaningless if every other person also receives the same trophy, regardless of performance.

Christian Exclusivism maintains the belief that each person chooses which God he shall serve. If the path to Christ is chosen, then the trophy of salvation will be the reward, but if another path is chosen, then God will allow it and so allow the judgment that accompanies that decision. We can hope that all will be saved, but that does not change the reality that all will not be saved, and the reason for this is because God, in His omnipotence and sovereignty, has determined that we should have the right to choose. Exclusivism allows for that right.

3. Yet another aspect that is often misunderstood or misconstrued when discussing Christian Exclusivism is the idea that salvation is somehow not available to all people. Nothing could be further from the truth. "The fact that righteousness is to come by faith, rather than by birth, as it came during the period that the Jews alone were the chosen race, is therefore the way that salvation is opened to all humanity,"[188] not just to the Church or to a certain ethnicity, but to everyone. Christian Exclusivism does not exclude anyone from salvation based on race, gender or any other area of distinction. The only stipulation for salvation is exactly what Scripture says, "Believe on the Lord Jesus, and you will be saved" (Acts 16:34).

4. Exclusivists believe that "There is salvation in no one else, for there is no other name under heaven given among mortals by which we must be saved" (Acts 4:12) and "Everyone who calls on the name of the Lord shall be saved" (Rom 10:13). Salvation is not an anonymous or ignorant event. Salvation is not something upon which one stumbles. Salvation is not something about which one is surprised. Salvation is an intentional, conscious act that

requires repentance (Acts 2:38) and acknowledgement of Christ's death and resurrection for the forgiveness of sins (Romans 10:9-10). If salvation is found in no one else besides Jesus, then Universalism is not possible, for the majority of the world does not believe in Christ as Savior. And if it is only those who call upon the name of the Lord and believe in their heart that He has been raised from the dead, then there are no anonymous or ignorant Christians. Christian Inclusivism, while philosophically appealing, is simply untrue.

5. Christian Exclusivism champions the evangelist because salvation is only made possible through the proclamation of the Gospel. Based on Scripture, salvation is an act that can only be attained by those to whom the Gospel has been preached, whereby a conscious surrender to the lordship of Jesus—not any good man or false god or moral way of life—is possible. That is precisely why Paul, not only one of Christianity's greatest theologians but also greatest missionaries, states the following:

*Everyone who calls on the name of the Lord shall be saved. But how are they to call on one in whom they have not believed? And how are they to believe in one of whom they have never heard? And how are they to hear without someone to proclaim him? And how are they to proclaim him unless they are sent? As it is written, 'How beautiful are the feet of those who bring good news!'* – Romans 10:13-15

Here Paul asks a series of rhetorical questions and the point that he is making is that in order for someone to be saved, he must call upon the name of the Lord. Following a moral code or worshiping some "unknown god" (Acts 17:23) is insufficient for salvation. Salvation requires belief in order to call. It requires knowledge in order to believe. It requires hearing in order to know. It requires proclamation in order to be heard. And it requires someone sent in order for it to be proclaimed.

If that is indeed the case, then the relevance and significance of missions and the Great Commission takes on a whole new intensity, for much of the world is not only apart from Christ, but they are also unaware of Christ, and hopelessly lost. The unreached and unrepentant sinner knows of God, as demonstrated in Romans 1:18, but natural revelation alone is not enough to save; that only comes through Jesus. But, if a "human being of whatever race or background can stand before God on the basis of having trusted his purposes in Christ, then such salvation is now open to any who will so trust God,"[189] begging the question, why has the evangelization of the lost not become the Church's greatest priority? Is not the lost coming to Christ, Heaven's greatest joy, Hell's greatest tragedy and the Church's greatest responsibility? There are many reasons for why this is the case, and my goal was not to examine every possible reason why missionary work is neglected, but surely one of those reasons is because of the many devastatingly fatal beliefs that so many people have, namely that those who have not heard of Christ are not necessarily damned. Harold Netland says it well when he writes:

"One simply cannot understand the remarkable Protestant missionary effort of the nineteenth century, including the work of missionary pioneers such as William Carey, Adoniram Judson, David Livingstone and Hudson Taylor, without appreciating the premise underlying their efforts: salvation is to be found only in the person and work of Jesus Christ, and those who die without the saving gospel of Christ face an eternity apart from God."[190]

The motivation behind the work of missionaries and evangelists is directly tied to the fact that they believe that without their ministry, people will not be saved. Scripture makes it quite clear that those who have not heard are sinful and without excuse before God and desperately in need of the knowledge of Christ to be saved. My prayer is that this reality will provide motivation for the Church to make sure that Christ's Great Commission is no longer the Church's Great Omission.

## CORNELIUS

There is perhaps no better story in Scripture to deal with the position of those who have not heard the Gospel than the story of Cornelius found in Acts 10:1-11:18. The story of Cornelius begins by describing Cornelius, saying, "In Caesarea there was a man named Cornelius, a centurion of the Italian Cohort, as it was called. He was a devout man who feared God with all his household; he gave alms generously to the people and prayed constantly to God" (Acts 10:1-2). Reading this verse in light of the recent discussion, would it not seem to many that Cornelius was in many ways righteous and probably saved? Here was a man who devoutly feared and prayed to God and who also cared for the poor. Initially, it would seem that this is precisely the criterion for a Christian. The story goes on to explain, though, that an angel appeared to Cornelius and instructed him to call for Peter to come to his house and share the truth of the Gospel. Peter, after at first denying to go because the man was a gentile, went to Cornelius' house and preached "all that the Lord [had] commanded [him] to say" (Acts 10:33). Upon hearing the Gospel, all of Cornelius's household believed in Jesus and were filled with the Holy Spirit.

Obviously there are more details to this story than have been recounted, but that is the gist of the story and the necessary parts in light of this subject. The first thing to notice is that despite the fact that the opening verses seem to describe a righteous man, Cornelius was unaware of Christ. Thus, Cornelius becomes for many an example of an anonymous or ignorant Christian, worshiping God and following the law written on his heart. If that were the case, though, and if Cornelius were already saved, then why would the angel bother him and instruct him to go disturb Peter to come to his house to tell him the Gospel message? Certainly that would be pointless.

There are some who would argue that this was simply done so that Cornelius and his family would be filled with the Holy Spirit. They were already saved but they needed the infilling of the Holy Spirit and that is why Peter came. And indeed, if chapter 10 were the only chapter, then perhaps that assumption could be made, but in Peter's retelling of the experience in chapter 11 there is no question as to the reason why Peter visited Cornelius, for the angel instructed Cornelius, "Send to Joppa and bring Simon, who is called Peter; he will give you a message by which you and your entire household will be saved" (Acts 11:13b-14). "Even though Cornelius was a God fearer, he had to hear the Gospel for salvation."[191] Cornelius himself recognized that despite his good deeds and his devotion to a higher power, he was not saved. It was only when Peter arrived and told him of Jesus that he came into relationship with God.

This story is incredibly relevant to the topic of this book as Cornelius' example demonstrates quite beautifully the necessity for preaching the Gospel. Obviously Cornelius was doing good things, but good deeds done by a sinful human are insufficient to save. Furthermore, God did not see Cornelius as saved, for if he had, then he would not have sent an angel to instruct him to send for Peter to hear the Gospel message. That would have been simply unnecessary. Lastly, God did not simply show up to Cornelius in a vision for him to be made aware of and believe in Christ. Nor did God send an angel to share the Gospel message with Cornelius. Instead, God sent an angel to instruct Cornelius to send for a human to share the Gospel. This is how God has ordained the work of the Great Commission. The message of salvation is the most wonderful message in the world as it is the only message that brings eternal life, and yet God has chosen to entrust humanity, and specifically the Church, with this message. The content of the universe's most important message has been given to each Christian, and it is for this reason that Christ's final command before ascending to Heaven was to proclaim this message to the entire world.

## PILATE'S QUESTION

Clothed in a torn robe, wearing a painful crown and so beaten and bloody that he was barely distinguishable as a human, there stood Jesus before Pilate. One considered himself to be the most powerful man in the room. The other was the most powerful man in the universe. As Pilate sat on his throne and examined Jesus, he was perplexed as to why this Jewish carpenter had caused so much trouble. Jesus did not look the part of a rebel or a zealot or an insurrectionist, yet this man had turned the world upside down. As he listened to Jesus he did not find His words to be confusing or altogether dangerous. Then, in response to Pilate's question of whether Jesus was a king, He says, "You say that I am a king. In fact, the reason I was born and came into the world is to testify to the truth. Everyone on the side of truth listens to me" (John 18:37). Pilate then asks the question so many of us have asked ourselves, "What is truth?" What he didn't realize that day is that he was staring Truth right in the face.

# WHAT DO I BELIEVE?

There are so many people today who are asking the same question that Pilate asked all those years ago. This question has given way to many countless religions, cults and belief systems. This question has divided homes, disrupted cultures and caused wars. The answer to this question is the most important thing any of us will ever know. There are many things in this life that are true—the sky is blue, marble is hard, and women love shoes—but there is one truth that stands above the rest. Jesus is the truth. To know the truth is liberating, but to truly know Truth means knowing Jesus. The question is not as much about "What is truth?" as much as it is about "Who is truth?" As religions and worldviews vary and become more numerous all the time, the significance of knowing the answer to this question becomes all the more critical. Regardless of the arguments and questions that may arise, may you always look unto Jesus for your answer. He is the perfect picture of truth that this world has ever known, and in Him is found the answer to Pilate's question and any others that we may have. Jesus is Truth.

# CHAPTER 14

# WHAT CAN I DO?

*STARFISH*

As you come to the end of this book I realize that it could easily feel a little overwhelming. When you look at the world around you there are so many needs. Any time you watch the news or receive news notifications, it seems as though the world is getting worse and worse. In this book I've outlined many of the things in the Church that must be reevaluated and the many areas that need reform, and it can feel incredibly burdensome. Even as I have spent time researching and writing and editing, I have at times been overwhelmed with how much needs to be done. Yet the answer to the mounting number of people who need Jesus is not to sit by and watch the world waste away. We must take action and make a difference.

There are many who would argue that there is far too much to be done, that no individual could make a difference, yet the history of humanity has displayed the incredible difference that one person can have. It only took one man (Moses) to deliver the Israelites out of the hand of the most powerful empire in the world. It only took one woman (Esther) to save an entire people group from extinction. It only took one Man (Jesus) to split time in half and make salvation available to the entire human race. Do not become so overwhelmed with how much there is to be done that it causes you to do nothing. No life is insignificant. Whenever I think of mounting odds and the feeling of insignificance, I am reminded of one of my favorite stories: The Starfish Story.

"Once upon a time, there was a wise man who used to go to the ocean to do his writing. He had a habit of walking on the beach before he began his work.

One day, as he was walking along the shore, he looked down the beach and saw a human figure moving like a dancer. He smiled to himself…and walked faster to catch up.

As he got closer, he noticed that the figure was that of a young man, and that what he was doing was not dancing at all. The young man was reaching down to the shore, picking up small objects, and throwing them into the ocean.

He came closer still and called out "Good morning! May I ask what it is that you are doing?"

The young man paused, looked up, and replied "Throwing starfish into the ocean."

"I must ask, then, why are you throwing starfish into the ocean?" asked the somewhat startled wise man.

To this, the young man replied, "The sun is up and the tide is going out. If I don't throw them in, they'll die."

Upon hearing this, the wise man commented, "But, young man, do you not realize that there are miles and miles of beach and there are starfish all along every mile? You can't possibly make a difference!"

At this, the young man bent down, picked up yet another starfish, and threw it into the ocean. As it met the water, he said, "It made a difference for that one."[192]

The reality is that there are so many people in this world who need Jesus, and attempting to reach every single person and meet every single need is a futile endeavor, but none of us are called to do everything. Instead, we are each called to do something. My hope is that many of you have come to the end of this book asking yourself the question, "What can I do?" I'm so glad you asked.

### *PRAY*

Prayer is such an underrated weapon in the arsenal of the Christian. Most Christians believe in prayer. Most Christians understand that it's important, and they try to pray on a regular basis, but I don't believe that most of us realize the supernatural power of prayer. It was Hannah's prayer that healed her womb so that she brought forth Samuel. It was Elijah's prayer that controlled the weather in Israel. It was Jesus' prayer that gave Him the strength to go to the cross.

When it comes to the Great Commission, prayer is of utmost importance. When speaking of the harvest fields of people, Jesus told His disciples, "The harvest is plentiful but the workers are few. Ask the Lord of the harvest, therefore, to send out workers into his harvest field" (Matthew 9:37-38). Part of the Great Commission work is prayer. Not only must we actively participate in evangelism but we must also pray that others would join forces with us. There are many people I know who, for any number of reasons, are unable to travel with us to Asia or Africa, but they have committed to pray for us and our ministry, and their involvement is no less important.

One of my favorite verses concerning evangelism is in Psalm 2:8 where the Lord tells us, "Ask me, and I will make the nations your inheritance, the ends of the earth your possession." God instructs us to pray faith-filled prayers for issues of great importance. Is there any greater prayer that we could pray than for the salvation of the nations? James, the half-brother of Jesus, wrote that we do not have because we do not ask (James 4:2). Instead of praying for green lights on our way to work or instead of praying that our favorite sports team will win, what if we started praying for the Lord to give us the nations as our inheritance? Instead of living a life hoping for money or land or stock options, what if you started living a life where your inheritance was people?

When we get to Heaven one day, we will not be able to bring our home or our car or our electronics. There is only one thing we can bring with us to Heaven—people. So many of us live our lives trying to climb the corporate ladder or move into a nicer neighborhood. We are looking for a temporal inheritance. But Christ is far more interested in giving us an inheritance of eternal worth. May we begin to pray for an inheritance of people.

*GIVE*

Money. This subject is one of the most uncomfortable subjects to discuss, and yet it consumes so much of our world and what we do. There are many who view money as evil, yet they work 40 hours a week to get more of it. There are many who love money, and commit horrible crimes in order to obtain it. When it comes to the Church, there are many on the outside who think the Church is one big con to try to cheat people out of their money. While there are certainly those who do peddle the Word of God and look for ways to deceive people into giving, that is not the heart of God.

God is a God of abundance and plenty (John 10:10). He desires to meet the needs of His people (Philippians 4:19) and for them to prosper (3 John 2). Some people think that Christianity and money are polar opposites, but the Bible has much to say about money. In fact, Jesus spoke about money more than any other topic apart from the Kingdom of God. "The Bible offers 500 verses on prayer, fewer than 500 verses on faith, and more than 2,000 verses on money."[193] And when it comes to the Great Commission, money plays a very important role.

It takes money to reach people. It takes money to rent stadiums to preach the Gospel. It takes money to produce Bibles to deliver to new believers. It takes money to purchase plane tickets. It takes money to plant churches. It takes money for a minister to live. It is for this reason that Paul had no problem asking churches for money, as he did over and over again (1 Corinthians 9:11; 1 Corinthians 16:1-3; Philippians 4:15-16). It was only through the generous giving of individuals and churches that any of Paul's ministry was made possible.

Not only that, but Jesus was dependent upon the gifts of others. He was responsible for 12 employees. The disciples had jobs of their own that they left to follow Jesus. He was responsible for their health and wellbeing. The 13 of them had no job other than the ministry, yet you will not find them begging for food or sleeping on the side of the road. Why? Because they had individuals who supported them in their ministry. Jewish leaders like Joseph of Arimathea, Nicodemus and others would likely have supported His ministry. In fact, Luke writes the following in Luke 8:1-3, "After this, Jesus traveled about from one town and village to another, proclaiming the good news of the kingdom of God. The Twelve were with him, and also some women who had been cured of evil spirits and diseases: Mary (called Magdalene) from whom seven demons had come out; Joanna the wife of Chuza, the manager of Herod's household; Susanna; and many others. These women were helping to support them out of their own means." Individuals who believed in the ministry of Jesus were financially supporting the work that He was doing.

In order for the Great Commission to be accomplished, it will demand the sacrificial giving of Christians. Obviously not every person is called to be a full-time minister, and that is a good thing, for if everyone was a missionary, then how would the missionary have the funds to do his job? Most Christians are not called to full-time vocational ministry, but that does not diminish their partnership or responsibility in the evangelistic efforts of the Body of Christ; it just takes on a different role.

In 1 Samuel 30:1-25 there is an incredibly important story that describes the relationship between the one who goes and the one who stays behind. David and a detachment of 600 soldiers arrived home after a long and tiresome journey throughout Philistia, having conquered the Philistines. While they were gone, however, the Amalekites had captured their wives and children and all of their belongings, and David and his men were devastated. David sought the Lord on what to do and the Lord told him to pursue the Amalekites with the assurance that the Lord would give David the victory. David informed his mourning men of the plan and it seemed good to all of them. The only problem was that 200 of the 600 men were so exhausted from the war with the Philistines that they could not go with David and the other 400 men. Instead they stayed back at the camp and guarded the remaining supplies. David and his 400 men conquered the Amalekites and recovered all of the people and possessions that had been stolen from them.

When David and the 400 men returned to the other 200 men who had stayed behind, some of the 400 men became proud and selfish saying, "Because they did not go out with us, we will not share with them the plunder we recovered" (22). The ones who left saw themselves as more important and valuable than those who had stayed behind to guard the supplies. Yet David responded, "No, my brothers, you must not do that with what the Lord has given us… The share of the man who stayed with the supplies is to be the same as that of him who went down to the battle. All will share alike" (23-24).

This story demonstrates the relationship between the goers and the givers. Not everyone is called to be a full-time evangelist, and yet that does not mean that those who stay back with the supplies are any less vital or important to the Great Commission. The principal that David instituted is just as true today as it was then: both the one who stays and the one who goes share in the same harvest and reap the same rewards. If you are not called to be a full-time evangelist or missionary or pastor, that doesn't make you any less a part of the ministry; but it also doesn't excuse you from the ministry. Some of the most influential men and women in mission work are those who help to fund and finance the work of the Lord. This same thought is carried into the New Testament.

*"Everyone who calls on the name of the Lord will be saved." How, then, can they call on the one they have not believed in? And how can they believe in the one of whom they have not heard? And how can they hear without someone preaching to them? And how can anyone preach unless they are sent? As it is written: "How beautiful are the feet of those who bring good news!"* – Romans 10:13-15

When Paul wrote this passage to the Church in Rome it was most likely following his third missionary journey. For years Paul had been preaching the Gospel in places that had never heard it. He traveled hundreds of miles from his home to preach the Gospel to unreached people. Then he interrupted his missionary evangelism to write to far-away Rome. This congregation wasn't made up of missionaries and evangelists. These were fishermen, masons, homemakers, carpenters, politicians, bakers, silversmiths, teachers and many other things. These people may have felt like they were somehow inferior to Paul because he was a full-time minister. They may have felt like their work wasn't as significant as that of an evangelist. And so Paul wrote this passage.

Paul begins with the end result, explaining that when the lost call upon the Lord they are saved. That moment, though, does not just simply happen. Paul explains that there is a series of steps that lead to that all-important decision. Paul backtracks the steps like this:

# WHAT CAN I DO?

1. Call on the Lord.
2. Believe in the Lord.
3. Hear the Gospel.
4. Preach the Gospel.
5. Send the Preacher.

Here Paul shows the process of how the unreached come to know Christ. The lost cannot be saved until they call on the Lord. And they cannot call on the Lord until they have believed in the Lord. And they cannot believe in the Lord until they have heard the Gospel. And they cannot hear the Gospel unless someone preaches it to them. And the preacher cannot preach the Gospel unless someone sends him to do so. You can almost hear the gratitude in Paul's words. Paul is saying, "Thank you, Romans. Thank you for your finances. Thank you for your prayers. It is because of you that the lame man was healed in Lystra. It is because of you that Lydia was saved in Philippi. And it is because of you that Crispus' entire household was saved in Corinth. You faithfully worked as a silversmith to send a portion of your money to help me. You consistently prayed with your family for me. You are the reason I was able to do what I did. Thank you."

Paul explains that there is a process of salvation. Someone does not stumble into salvation. Rather, salvation happens when someone calls on the Lord after having believed. But that only happens after they have first heard the Gospel preached to them. Yet Paul takes things one step further. The beginning of this process does not begin with the preacher; it begins with the sender. The person who sends and the person who goes play an equal part in the salvation process. One of the things that you can do to help fulfill Christ's Great Commission is to give financially to ministers and ministries who are actively involved in the Great Commission. And as much as there is a need for laborers, there is also a need for givers.

In preparation for this book I did a lot of research and one of the most disappointing and devastating things I learned had to do with Christian giving in general, but specifically to Great Commission efforts. As connected as our world may seem, and in many ways it is, there are still so many people who have no access to the Gospel. The Joshua Project, an organization with a focus on evangelizing unreached people groups, defines "unreached people groups" in this way: "There is no indigenous community of believing Christians with adequate numbers and resources to evangelize their own people,"[194] and in many cases it is even worse than that. Of the 16,324 people groups on the earth, 6,573 of them are classified as "unreached." These 6,573 people groups make up a total of over 3 billion people worldwide.[195] What this means is that over 40% of earth's population is unreached. A number far larger than that makes up the amount of people who do not know Jesus, since just because someone has access to the Gospel does not mean that he has accepted it. I have come to know that all too well.

What these statistics show us is that despite the advancements in technology and travel, much of our world is still shut out from the Gospel. And as I'm sure you can imagine, these unreached people groups do not reside in North America. Those who have never heard, those who are unreached are unreached because they live in areas where it is not convenient or even safe to preach the Gospel. Yet, it is to these places that the Gospel must go.

As desperate as the unreached world is for Jesus, there is very little giving that is going towards evangelistic efforts reaching those areas. According to a study done in 2015, the annual income of all church members worldwide is $42 trillion.[196] Yet despite that, only $700 billion of that $42 trillion was given to Christian causes,[197] which is a ridiculous .017%. It should be noted that $700 billion is also the same amount of money that Americans spend on Christmas each year. In other words, the entire (global) Christian Church gives the same amount of money to Christian causes annually as Americans spend on Christmas. Unfortunately, it gets much worse than that.

Of the $700 billion that is given to Christian causes worldwide, only $45 billion is given to missions. Only 6.4% of all the money that is given to Christian causes actually goes toward mission work.[198] Now, how is that $45 billion allocated to mission causes? Where does the small percentage of money that is actually given to Christian causes end up? Nearly 97% goes to pastoral ministries of local churches, mostly in Christian nations. Another 2.9% goes to "home missions" in those same Christian nations.

Finally, $450 million (0.01%) is distributed to ministries working in the "unreached" world (as described earlier).[199] To give you a grasp on how little $450 million is in this context, that is the same amount of money that, in 2011, Americans spent on Halloween costumes. Oh, but not just on any costumes. That is the amount that Americans spent on Halloween costumes for their pets![200] To represent it another way, "the $450 million going toward unreached people groups is only .001% of the $42 trillion income of Christians (i.e. for every $100,000 that Christians make, they give $1 to the unreached)."[201]

I want to be clear: I am not at all encouraging people to stop giving to their local Church. I am not petitioning to have less money go towards mission and outreach efforts in reached nations and areas. Those things must persist. There is a great need for outreach in even the most Christian of places. I am not advocating for a smaller amount of giving to Christian causes. Instead I am imploring the worldwide Church to step up its giving all around, but particularly as it pertains to reaching those who do not know Jesus. I get sick to my stomach thinking that Christians are giving only $1 out of every $100,000 to reach those who have never heard the Gospel. As believers we will be held accountable for our lives, and that includes our finances. How can we justify to God that we really care about the Great Commission when we spend as much money on Halloween costumes for our pets as we do to bring the Gospel where it is not known?

From 2001 to 2005, "American agencies focused on evangelism/discipleship saw combined income grow by 2.7 percent...those focused on relief/development saw theirs grow by a whopping 74.3 percent."[202] In other words, even where giving increases, it does not increase in areas that specialize in reaching the lost. There are so many wonderful things that we can do with our money, even many wonderful Christian things that we can do. We can build churches and orphanages. We can rescue children out of sex trafficking. We can build homes for the needy. We can feed the hungry. We can produce music and movies and books. All of these are incredibly important things, but they are not the most important thing. When Jesus left this earth His command was to preach the Gospel and make disciples. It was about as simple a command as He could have communicated, yet we have almost completely dropped the ball on making it come to pass.

In the 21st century, social justice has become the cry among so many millennials. And social justice is incredibly important, "but social justice issues, as significant as they are, do not replace the Great Commission. Hunger, poverty, oppression, sickness, death are evidences of a fallen world. Christ came to redeem the world and inaugurate His kingdom, where such evils will have no place... Healing and relief of poverty are effects of the Gospel; they are not the Gospel themselves. Concern for the poor should never replace the biblical mandate to witness to the crucified and risen King."[203]

If we really want to call ourselves Christians, then it will demand that we care about the Great Commission. And if we really care about the Great Commission, then it's about time that we started putting our money where our mouth is. There is a world that is desperately in need of Jesus, and one of the ways that all of us can help bring Jesus to the world is through our giving. What can you do? Find ministers and missionaries and evangelists and ministries who are traveling to the uttermost bounds of the earth and partner with them to reach this world for Jesus. David needed the 200 men. Paul needed the Romans. The Great Commission work today needs you.

## GO

I have talked to many people who have been hesitant to give all that they are to the Lord. From a young age they had a perspective of God that somehow His desires for them were very different than what they would ever want. They were concerned that if they fully devoted their lives to the Lord that they wouldn't like their lives. They believed that serving God might mean never getting married. Or they believed that God would force them to live in rural Africa for the rest of their lives as a missionary, despite the fact that they had no desire to do so.

This view of God is an unfortunate one. It makes God out to be a dictator, who is concerned only with His own desires rather than our own. The reality is that God is the opposite. God isn't interested in forcing you to do His will. He wants to work with you to help your desires come to pass. As David says, "Delight yourself in the Lord and He will give you the desires of your heart" (Psalm 37:4). Notice what that verse says. God's desire is that *your* desires be fulfilled. And in actuality, those desires become the same as His desires, because as you delight yourself in the Lord, His desires become your own.

So, for those of you who have no desire to live in another country, I am not interested in forcing you to do so any more than God is. In fact, if you have to be pushed to live in another country, then you'd probably make a miserable missionary anyway. That being said, just because you are not called to live in another country does not exclude your active participation in the Great Commission, even as it pertains to the "going" part of "Go into all the world."

Throughout the years I have had so many laypeople (doctors, business owners, athletes, stay-at-home moms, etc.) come on trips with me to other countries. They are not wanting/planning on doing this full-time, but they want to go, just as Jesus commanded us to do. I encourage Christians, regardless of vocation, to make it a habit to go on mission trips. It is one thing to hear the stories; it is another to experience them. It is one thing see the pictures; it's another thing to live the pictures. There is so much value and joy in being able to be on the frontlines of evangelism. Mission trips have always helped me to reset my perspective and remember what is truly important in life.

*"But you will receive power when the Holy Spirit comes on you; and you will be my witnesses in Jerusalem, and in all Judea and Samaria, and to the ends of the earth." –* Acts 1:8

For some of you reading this, the thought of traveling internationally can seem daunting, and that is why Jesus said what He did in Acts 1:8. The example that Jesus gave us is quite clear. He commands the disciples to go into the entire world and preach the Gospel, and yet He doesn't do so blindly or without any direction. He instructs the disciples in a very organized way. Paul says in 1 Corinthians 14:33 that, "Our God is not a God of disorder, but of peace." So when God gives us instructions, He will do so in an orderly way, with step-by-step instructions. This is exactly what He does in Acts 1:8. He tells the disciples to begin in Jerusalem. This was their city. This was where they were from and where they lived.

This was the city with which they were familiar. Jesus didn't want them to travel to some remote area and begin a brand new ministry without having first learned right where they were. He specifically told them to start in their own city and community. This is important for you to recognize, because it means that you can start mission work today. You do not have to move somewhere else in order to begin the Great Commission.

Not only does Jesus tell the disciples to start in Jerusalem, but He also tells them to continue to take manageable steps. Yes, the goal one day is to reach the entire world, but Jesus does not expect (or even want) the disciples to simply move from point "A" to point "Z". Jesus wants people to continue to follow Him and go one step at a time. After Jerusalem He instructs the disciples to go to Judea (their state), Samaria (their larger region) and only then, after having done that, should they go to the ends of the earth. Start in your city, but don't take a giant leap from your city to the ends of the earth. Psalm 119:5 says, "Your word is a lamp to my feet and a light to my path." It does not say that the Word is a huge spotlight to your highway. God is going to lead you one step at a time, but you must keep in step with His order.

After having been faithful with Jerusalem, though, God desires for you to eventually extend to the ends of the earth. I know that there are so many people in North America that need Jesus. I am not belittling the efforts to reach people for Jesus in America, because certainly it needs to be done, but to say that America is unreached would be very far from the truth. As many non-Christians as there are in America, there is so much accessibility to the Gospel. There is a Church in every town. There are numerous Christian TV and radio stations. There are Christian books and Bibles sold at every Wal-Mart and Target. There is no shortage of opportunities for salvation in North America. In fact, a study done a few years ago discovered there while there are 4.19 million full-time Christian workers worldwide, 95% of them are working within the Christian world.[204]

When Jesus gave the Great Commission to the disciples, the world was as unreached as possible. Only a very few people in the Middle East had ever even heard of Jesus. The task of reaching the world for Jesus was far more overwhelming then that it is now, but that didn't stop the disciples. They took Jesus' call seriously and started spreading the Gospel to the uttermost bounds of the earth. In 100 AD there were "360 people for every believer. Now there are 7.3 people for every believer,"[205] and yet there are still so many people who have never heard about Jesus. "In 100 AD there were 12 unreached people groups for every congregation of believers. Now there is 1 unreached people group for every 1,000 congregations."[206]

Could you imagine if the Christian Church began to take the Great Commission seriously? If we stopped just talking about the Great Commission and started doing it, could you imagine what would happen? Yes, the task is great, but there was a time when it was far greater, and that didn't stop the early Church from spreading the Gospel across the earth. It is time for us to do the same today, starting in Jerusalem (our hometown), but not stopping there. The world needs us. Will you go?

For those who have not heard the Gospel, the "going" aspect of the Great Commission is of utmost importance. So, what about those who have never heard the Gospel? "The biblical response is a clear and decisive command: Go tell them! The Spirit-inspired biblical authors did not spend time philosophizing or theologizing over the state of the unevangelized."[207] Gathering support for a "shared optimism concerning the fate of those who have never heard does not help anybody, least of all the unevangelized."[208] How did Paul deal with the unevangelized? He told them about Jesus. How did the disciples deal with the unevangelized? They told them about Jesus. In a world where so many people do not know Jesus, what is our response? We must go and tell them about Jesus.

Author and Pastor Francis Chan has some incredibly good things to say on a variety of issues, the Great Commission included. In a sermon he preached recently he demonstrated the Church's response to the Great Commission by comparing it to his daughter. He said, "You know, if I tell my daughter, 'Go clean your room,' she doesn't come back to me two hours later saying, 'I memorized what you said. I can say it in Greek. My friends are going to come over and we're going to have a study about what it would be like if I cleaned my room.' She knows better than that."[209] It is foolish for us to think that we are obeying Christ's command by simply memorizing or studying or discussing the Great Commission. We will one day stand before the Judge and be asked how we fulfilled the Great Commission. I pray that we have a good answer for Him.

# CONCLUSION

When the Holy Spirit came at Pentecost almost 2,000 years ago, He came at a strategic time. During Pentecost, as is evidenced in Acts 2, there were Jews who had come from hundreds, and even thousands of miles away to celebrate the feast. Thus, when Peter preached and 3,000 accepted Christ, the message of the Gospel was able to spread to areas of the world much sooner than it would have been able to do otherwise. Those converted Jews returned home as evangelists and missionaries to their own communities, cities and countries, and thankfully so, as the ability to spread the Gospel to far-away places was no easy task. To preach the Gospel in Crete and Arabia and Rome required a lot of time and effort. During this time period, certainly the Gospel spread, but it did so with great difficulty.

*"Very truly I tell you, whoever believes in me will do the works I have been doing, and they will do even greater things than these, because I am going to the Father." – John 14:12*

Have you ever thought about this verse? At first glance, this statement seems ridiculous. How could any of us possibly exceed the works of Christ? Yet, as I survey the landscape of our world today, I can see how this can be. Jesus began His ministry at the age of 30 and only ministered for three years. There are some who will do twenty times that many years of ministry. Not only that, but at the time of Christ, it is suggested that only 300 million people inhabited the earth[210]—more than that amount today inhabit the USA alone. There are so many more people to reach today than there were then. In addition to that, the accessibility of travel is vastly different today than it was for Jesus. What would have taken Jesus weeks or months to get to a certain location, may take us only a few hours.

As I examine the global ministry opportunities that we have today, we are certainly privileged to live at this point in history. We can travel to almost anywhere in the world in a day. At our fingertips is the accessibility to reach the entire world, and yet, so much of our time and resources is spent on the reached world. It is challenging to get ministers or ministries to look beyond their four walls, and yet the Great Commission was never designed to be for Jerusalem alone.

The internet age has given us many opportunities for global ministry. I am constantly communicating with people from all over the world. The Gospel is being dispersed to people who would have never had access to it before. Those in need can seek Christ through the Internet. And yet, there are still billions of people who have not heard the Gospel and are in need of personal contact. Just because we have access does not mean the rest of the world does, and it does not negate our commission to go. In the 21$^{st}$ century we have so many luxuries, and I feel privileged to live in the time that we do, but let us not take that for granted. With great opportunity comes great responsibility and the greatest responsibility that we have is to reach this world for Jesus.

### MICHELLE

I love my wife. As you've read this book I'm sure you've noticed that. I feel so blessed to be her husband. There are many reasons why I love her. She does 99% of our cooking. She's a bargain shopper. She packs my lunch every day. I've never heard her use vulgar language. She makes her family and my family a priority. She loves people and she loves Jesus. If you ever have the privilege of meeting Michelle, you won't be able to help but fall in love with her.

There have been so many times when Michelle has amazed me and made me so proud. But I'm not sure if I've ever been as proud of her or as amazed at her as I was during the hardest time of her life. Earlier I shared the story of Michelle's mother's death. This is still a recent event. It is still fresh. It still hurts. Honestly, I don't like thinking back to those moments, but this story is an exception to that.

My mother-in-law was one of six siblings. She was a strong woman of God who loved her family. Her siblings know the truth about Christ, and some of them even attend church every once in a while, but whether they or their spouses truly know Christ is another matter. Every day my mother-in-law would pray for the salvation of her siblings and their spouses and she would speak with her family often about Jesus. Her greatest desire was that her family would come to know Jesus.

The day of my mother-in-law's death the doctors instructed us to call all of the family to say their goodbyes. The prognosis was not good and they knew that her death was imminent. My mother-in-law was unconscious and unresponsive, but she was alive. That afternoon her hospital room filled with her siblings, Michelle's aunts and uncles. They would grab my mother-in-law's hand and say their goodbyes. Eventually the whole family was in the hospital room. There was a lot of crying. The whole family was hurting.

We stood in the room in silence, no one entirely sure of what else to say. Michelle sat next to her mom, grabbed her mom's hand and broke the silence. "You know, if mom could speak right now I know what she would say. She would tell you that her greatest desire is for all of you to be in Heaven. I still believe for her healing, but I know that even if she dies, I will see my mom again because I have a relationship with Jesus. I will see her again in Heaven. But unless you know Jesus then you will not get a chance to see her again. Salvation is the hardest thing to gain, in fact, on our own it is impossible, but the good news is that Jesus has already done the hard part. All we have to do is receive. The Bible says, 'Everyone who calls on the name of the Lord shall be saved.' There is nothing my mom wants more than to see each of you again one day in Heaven with Jesus."

I watched with wonder as my wife shared the Gospel with her aunts and uncles. She was hurting more than at any other time in her life. It would have been very easy to simply shrug off the opportunity for witnessing because of her hurt. When it comes to sharing the Gospel, it is usually more difficult to witness to family members than to complete strangers, but that did not stop her from witnessing. With tears running down her face she shared the Gospel because she recognized that above her pain, the most important thing in this life is for those who do not know Christ to come into relationship with Him.

I didn't know that I could fall more in love with Michelle, but as I watched my wife's strength and love shine through to her family, my love grew more than ever before. I have never been more proud of anyone than I was of Michelle in that moment. Since then Michelle has continued to amaze me, as I know she will do for the rest of our lives, but for as long as I live I will remember that moment. Michelle reminded me of what matters most in life: people. It would have been easy for her to focus on her own hurt and her own pain, but instead she looked outwardly. She chose to deny her own preferences and interests, and focus on people who needed Jesus. That is what this book is all about. My prayer is that we would see the world's need for the message of the Gospel and respond appropriately. Jesus has entrusted the most important message this world has ever known to you and to me. The Great Commission isn't just for missionaries or evangelists or pastors. It is for you and for me and for all who confess Christ. May Christ's last words become our first priority. "God, help us to fulfill your Great Commission and go."

# ENDNOTES

1. The Bible. Print. New International Version. All Scriptures are quoted from
the NIV unless otherwise noted.
2. In Matthew 17:24-27 Jesus pays the temple tax for Peter and Himself but not for any of the other disciples. The temple tax was only required for men 20 years and older. Since Jesus was responsible for the affairs of his disciples, one could argue that all of the disciples aside from Peter were under the age of 20.
3. Mark L. Strauss, *Four Portraits, One Jesus: A Survey of Jesus and the Gospels* (Grand Rapids: Zondervan Publishing, 2007).
4. Martin Luther King Jr., "I Have a Dream" (speech, The Lincoln Memorial, Washington, D.C., August 28, 1963).
5. *The Harvest*, directed by Chuck Klein (Venture Media, 1996), DVD.
6. "Human Numbers through Time," NOVA, accessed September 2, 2015, http://www.pbs.org/wgbh/nova/worldbalance/numb-nf.html.
7. "Global Statistics," Joshua Project, accessed September 2, 2015, http://joshuaproject.net/global_statistics.
8. Ibid.
9. Craig Blomberg, *Matthew. Vol. 22. The New American Commentary* (Nashville: Broadman & Holman Publishers, 1992).
10. F. D. Bruner, *The Christbook* (Waco: Word, 1987), 366.
11. Walter Bauer, *A Greek-English Lexicon of the New Testament and Other Early Christian Literature* (Chicago: The University of Chicago Press, 1979), s.v. "phileo."
12. "Four Kinds of Love," Truth or Tradition?, accessed September 4, 2015, http://www.truthortradition.com/articles/four-kinds-of-love.

13. Albert Mehrabian, *Nonverbal Communication* (Piscataway: Transaction Publishers, 1972), 182.

14. Gary Chapman, *The Five Love Languages* (Chicago: Northfield Publishing, 1995).

15. J.I. Packer, *131 Christians Everyone Should Know* (Nashville: Holman Bible Publishers, 2000).

16. Os Hillman, *Change Agent* (Lake Mary: Charisma House Publishing, 2011).

17. "1% It Appears to Be Such an Insignificant Percentage," One1Fluence, accessed September 28, 2015, http://www.growingleaders.com/onefluence/Manifesto.pdf.

18. Seyoon Kim, *Christ and Caesar: The Gospel and the Roman Empire in the Writings of Paul and Luke* (Grand Rapids: William B. Eerdmans Publishing, 2008).

19. James Swanson, *Dictionary of Biblical Languages with Semantic Domains: Greek (New Testament)* (Oak Harbor: Logos Research Systems, Inc., 1997), "παρακαλέω."

20. "Our Founders," CRU, accessed September 29, 2015, http://www.cru.org/about/our-leadership/our-founders.html.

21. "The Rules of the Pharisees," Pursue God, accessed September 29, 2015, http://www.pursuegod.org/rules-pharisees/.

22. Ibid.

23. Dr. Jeffrey Lamp, "Hermeneutics" (Lecture, Oral Roberts University, Tulsa, OK, September, 2010).

24. Heidi Kinner, "The Samaritan Woman," St. Peter's Cathedral, accessed September 30, 2015, http://static1.squarespace.com/static/54cc87b9e4b04aed407b7971/t/54dec432 e4b0406 fb3d2b935/1423885362287/3.23.14+-+Samaritan+Woman++Heidi+Kinner.pdf.

25. Ibid.

26. Brian Williams, "Notes and Reflections On Jesus and the Samaritan Woman at the Well," Academia.edu, accessed September 30, 2015, http://www.academia.edu/1747111/ Notes_and_Reflections_on_Jesus_and_the_Samaritan_Woman_at_the_ Well.

27. Walter A. Elwell, ed., *Baker Encyclopedia of the Bible*, (Grand Rapids: Baker Publishing Group, 1997), s.v. "Disciple."

28. Todd L. Miles, *A God Of Many Understandings?* (Nashville: B&H Publishing Group, 2010), 350.

29. Reinhard Bonnke, *Living a Life of Fire* (Orlando: E-R Productions, LLC, 2009).

30. Ibid.

31. Timothy Keller, "The Call to Discipleship: Luke 9: 20-25, 51-62," C.S. Lewis Institute, accessed October 2, 2015, http://www.cslewisinstitute.org/The_Call_To_Discipleship_ page1.

32. Miles, *A God Of Many Understandings?*, 350.

33. Michael Jaffarian, "The Statistical State of the North American Protestant Missions Movement, from the Mission Handbook, 20th Edition," *International Bulletin of Missionary Research,* 32, no. 1 (January, 2008): 35.

34. Ibid., 36.

35. Miles, *A God Of Many Understandings?*, 351.

36. Ibid., 343.

37. Tom Rath, *Strengths Finder 2.0* (New York: Gallup Press, 2007).

38. "Achiever," Gallup, accessed October 15, 2015,http://www.gallup.com/business journal/622/achiever.aspx.

39. Trevor Quinn, "That's the Stupidest Thing I've Ever Heard: American Workers Fail to Use 429 Million Days of Accrued Holiday," Daily Mail, accessed October 15, 2015, http://www.dailymail.co.uk/travel/travel_news/article-2782028/MasterCard-ad-encourages-American-workers-book-holiday.html.

40. Ibid.

41. "Too Busy Not to Pray," Christianity Today, accessed October 15, 2015, http://www.christianitytoday.com/moi/2011/006/december/too-busy-not-to-pray.html.

42. Paul Daugherty, "Tempo" (Sermon, Victory Christian Center, Tulsa, OK, September 6, 2015).

43. Swanson, *Dictionary of Biblical Languages*, "χρεστος."

44. Robert Jamieson, A. R. Fausset, and David Brown, *Commentary Critical and Explanatory on the Whole Bible* (Oak Harbor: Logos Research Systems, Inc., 1997), "χρεστος."

45. By this I mean the place of Hell and the place of Heaven. Therefore, I am not including Jesus' statements about the Kingdom of Heaven or eternal life, unless they specifically apply to the place of Heaven.

46. Ray Comfort, *Way of the Master* (Alachua: Bridge-Logos Publishers, 2006), 105.

47. Dr. Donald R. Hayes, *The Pentagon of Faith: Sacred Theism vs. Secular Humanism* (Dillon: Hawkstone Publishers, LLC, 2012), 6.

48. *The Way of the Master*, directed by Ray Comfort and Kirk Cameron (Genesis Publishing Group, 2005), DVD.

49. Ibid.

50. Ray Comfort, "Hell's Best Kept Secret: True and False Conversion" (MP4 of lecture), accessed March 28, 2015, https://www.youtube.com/watch?v=cJvottOv-7Q.

51. George Whitefield, *Eighteen Sermons Preached by the Late Rev. George Whitefield* (Bedford: Applewood Books, 1771).

52. Ray Comfort, *Luther Gold* (Alachua: Bridge Logos Foundation, 2009), 47.

53. Ibid., 48.

54. Philip Yancey, *The Jesus I Never Knew*, (Grand Rapids: Zondervan Publishing, 1995), 78.

55. Ibid., 80.

56. Fredrick J. Long, *Kairos: a Beginning Greek Grammar* (Mishawaka: Logos Research Systems, 2005), 37. Logos Bible Software.

57. Ibid.

58. Gerald L. Borchert, *John 12-21*, Vol. 25B (The New American Commentary; Nashville: Broadman and Holman Publishers, 2002), 46. Logos Bible Software.

59. C.S. Lewis, *Mere Christianity* (London: Geoffrey Bles, 1952), 55.

60. Frank J. Matera, *Romans*: *Paideia Commentary on the New Testament* (Grand Rapids: Baker Academic, 2010), 5.

61. I I. Howard Marshall et al., eds., *New Bible Dictionary* (Downers Grove: InterVarsity Press, 1996), s.v. "Epistle to the Romans."

62. Philip A. Bence, *Acts: A Bible Commentary in the Wesleyan Tradition* (Indianapolis: Wesleyan Publishing House, 1998), 72.

63. Joseph A. Fitzmyer, *Romans: The Anchor Bible Commentary* (New York: Doubleday and Company, Inc., 1993), 95.

64. Ibid., 96.

65. William Greathouse and George Lyons, *Romans 1-8: New Beacon Bible Commentary* (Kansas City: Beacon Hill Press, 2008), 69.

66. Matthew Black, *Romans: New Century Bible Commentary* (London: Marshall, Morgan & Scott, 1989), 38.

67. John A. Witmer, *Romans*: The Bible Knowledge Commentary: An Exposition of the Scriptures (Wheaton: Victor Books, 1985), 443. Logos Bible Software.

68. Greathouse, *Romans 1-8*, 69.

69. Karl Barth, *The Epistle to the Romans* translated by Edwyn C. Hoskyns (London: Oxford University Press, 1933), 43.

70. N. T. Wright, *Paul for Everyone: Romans, Part One* (Louisville: Westminster John Knox Press, 2005), 16.

71. Witmer, *Romans*, 445.

72. Kenneth Boa and William Kruidenier, *Romans*: Holman New Testament Commentary (Nashville: Broadman and Holman Publishers, 2000), 50. Logos Bible Software.

73. Kenneth Boa and William Kruidenier, *Romans*: Holman New Testament Commentary (Nashville: Broadman and Holman Publishers, 2000), 52. Logos Bible Software.

74. Swanson, *Dictionary of Biblical Languages*, "ἐπιγινώσκω."

75. W.W. Sanday, *Romans: International Critical Commentary* (Edinburgh: T & T Clark, 1901), 43.

76. Fitzmyer, *Romans*, 279.

77. Ibid.

78. Swanson, *Dictionary of Biblical Languages*, "γνωστός."

79. Everett F. Harrison, *Romans: Expositor's Bible Commentary* (Grand Rapids: Zondervan, 1977), 23.

80. Soren Kierkegaard, *Sickness Unto Death* (Princeton: Princeton University Press, 1980), 126.

81. Ambrosiaster, *Romans: Ancient Christian Commentary* (Downers Grove: InterVarsity Press, 2005), 35.

82. Richard Alan Young, "The Knowledge of God in Romans 1 Exegetical and Theological Reflections: 18-23," *Journal of the Evangelical Theological Society* 43 (2000): 697, accessed January 28, 2014, http://ehis.ebscohost.com/ehost/pdfviewer/pdfviewer?sid=c4b973d2-dbcd-477e-8a3b86bed92664a2%40sessionmgr112&vid =14&hid=116.

83. Van A. Harvey, *A Handbook of Theological Terms: Their Meaning and Background Exposed in Over 300 Articles* (New York: The Macmillan Company, 1964), 158.

84. Richard H. Bell, *No One Seeks for God: An Exegetical and Theological Study of Romans 1:18-3:20* (Tubingen: Mohr-Siebeck, 1998), 93.

85. Karl Barth, *Theologian of Freedom* (Minneapolis: Fortress Press, 1991), 154.

86. N. T. Wright, *The Letter to the Romans: Introduction, Commentary, and Reflections: The New Interpreter's Bible* (Nashville: Abingdon Press, 2002), 432.

87. Augustine, *Romans: Ancient Christian Commentary* (Downers Grove: InterVarsity Press, 2005), 35.

88. James Comper Gray and George M. Adams, *Romans-Revelation: Gray & Adams Bible Commentary* (Grand Rapids: Zondervan, 1958), 11.

89. Kenneth Boa and William Kruidenier, *Romans*: Holman New Testament Commentary (Nashville: Broadman and Holman Publishers, 2000), 59. Logos Bible Software.

90. John Murray, *The Epistle to the Romans: The New International Commentary on the New Testament* (Grand Rapids: William B. Eerdmans Publishing, 1997), 40.

91. Ibid.

92. Ibid., 41.

93. Sanday, *Romans*, 44.

94. Ibid.

95. John Chrysostom, *Homilies on the Acts of the Apostles and the Epistle to the Romans: Nicene and Post-Nicene Fathers* (Grand Rapids: William B. Eerdmans, 1980), 352.

96. Murray, *The Epistle to the Romans*, 41.

97. Greathouse, *Romans 1-8*, 74.

98. Wright, *Paul for Everyone*, 16.

99. Ambrosiaster, Romans, 40.

100. Chrysostom, *Homilies on the Acts of the* Apostles, 352.

101. N.T. Wright, *Evil and the Justice of God* (Downers Grove: InterVarsity Press, 2006), 52.

102. G. Bertram, *Theological Dictionary of the New Testament Vol. IV* (Grand Rapids: William B. Eerdmans Publishing Co., 1984) "μωρος." Logos Bible Software.

103. Brendan Byrne, *Romans: Sacra Pagina* (Collegeville: Liturgical Press, 1996), 69.

104. Murray, *The Epistle to the Romans*, 42-43.

105. Boa, *Romans*, 79.

106. Murray, *The Epistle to the Romans*, 41.

107. Grant Osborne, *Romans: The IPV New Testament Commentary Series* (Downers Grove: InterVarsity Press, 2010), 67.

108. C.H. Dodd, *The Epistle to the Romans: The Moffatt New Testament Commentary* (New York: Harper and Brothers, 1932), 34.

109. F.F. Bruce, *Romans*: Tyndale New Testament Commentaries (Downers Grove: InterVarsity Press, 1985), 84.

110. Witmer, *Romans* 445.

111. Osborne, *Romans*, 67.

112. Bruce, *Romans*, 84.

113. Witmer, *Romans*, 445.

114. Bruce, *Romans*, 84.

115. Witmer, *Romans*, 445.

116. Fitzmyer, *Romans*, 305.

117. Swanson, *Dictionary of Biblical Languages*, "ποιητής."

118. Ibid.

119. Fitzmyer, *Romans*, 309.

120. Ibid.

121. Klyne R. Snodgrass, "Justification by Grace—to the Doers: An Analysis of the Place of Romans 2 in the Theology of Paul," *New Testament Studies* 42 (1986): 73.

122. K. E. Kirk, *The Epistle to the Romans*: The Clarendon Bible (Oxford: Clarendon Press, 1955), 180.

123. Michel, Otto. *Der Brief an Die Romer* (Gottingen: Vandenhoeck & Ruprecht, 1963), 118.

124. Bertram, *Theological Dictionary of the New Testament*, "φύσι ς ."

125. C. K. Barrett, *A Commentary on the Epistle to the Romans: Harper's New Testament Commentaries* (Peabody: Hendrickson Publishers, 1987), 51.

126. Jeffrey S. Lamp, "Paul, the Law, Jews, and Gentiles: A Contextual and Exegetical Reading of Romans 2:12-16," *Journal of the Evangelical Theological Society* 42 (1999): 46.

127. Swanson, *Dictionary of Biblical Languages*, "συμμαρτυρέω."

128. Chrysostom, *Homilies on the Acts of the* Apostles, 365.

129. Bruce, *Romans*, 84.

130. Bertram, *Theological Dictionary of the New Testament*, "π ο ι έ ω."

131. Lamp, "Paul, the Law, Jews, and Gentiles," 49.

132. Murray, *The Epistle to the Romans*, 77.

133. Edwin A. Blum, "Shall You Not Surely Die?," *Themelios: An International Journal for Pastors and Students of Theological and Religious Studies* 4, no. 2 (1978): 4.

134. J. Peter Schineller, "Christ and Church: A Spectrum of Views," *Theological Studies* 37 (1976): 560, accessed January 29, 2014, http://ehis.ebscohost.com/ehost/pdfviewer/pdfviewer?sid=c4b973d2-dbcd-477e-8a3b-86bed92664a2%40sessionmgr 112&vid=19&hid=4113.

135. Arnold Toynbee, "What Should Be the Christian Approach to the Contemporary Non-Christian Faiths?" in *Attitudes Toward Other Religions* (ed. Owen Thomas; London: University Press of America, 1969), 160.

136. John Hick, "The non-absoluteness of Christianity," in *The Myth of Christian Uniqueness: Toward a Pluralistic Theology of Religions* (eds. John Hick and Paul Knitter; Eugene: Wipf & Stock Publishers, 1987), 16.

137. Wilbert R. Shenk, "Is Jesus the Only Way to God?" *Vision* 7 (2007): 83, accessed January 29, 2014, http://ehis.ebscohost.com/ehost/pdfviewer/ pdfviewer?sid=c4b973d2-dbcd-477e-8a3b86bed9 2664a2%40sessionmgr112&vid=19&hid=115

138. Swanson, *Dictionary of Biblical*, "θάνατος."

139. Blum, "Shall You Not Surely Die?," 6.

140. Norman L. Geisler, *Baker Encyclopedia of Christian Apologetics*: Baker Reference Library (Grand Rapids: Baker Academic, 1999) 282.

141. Harold Lindsell, "Universalism Today: Part Two," *BSac* 122 (January, 1965): 39.

142. C.S. Lewis, *The Great Divorce* (London: Geoffrey Bles Publishers, 1945), 69.

143. Miles, *A God Of Many Understandings?*, 103.

144. Ibid., 110.

145. Ibid., 118-119.

146. Nels Ferrè, "Universalism: Pro and Con," *Christianity Today*7 (March, 1963): 24.

147. Miles, *A God Of Many Understandings?*, 118.

148. Ibid., 109.

149. Ibid.

150. Ibid., 114.

151. Ibid., 111.

152. Ibid., 112.

153. Ibid.

154. Rob Bell, *Love Wins* (Grand Rapids: William B. Eerdmans Publishing, 2011), 109.

155. Miles, *A God Of Many Understandings?*, 100.

156. J. A. T. Robinson, "Universalism—Is it Heretical?" *SJT 2* (1949): 154.

157. John Stott, "John Stott's Response to Chapter 6," in Edwards and Stott, *Evangelical Essentials*, 314.

158. Miles, *A God Of Many Understandings?*, 121.

159. Ibid., 124.

160. Ibid., 130.

161. Ibid., 136.

162. See *The Kingdom of the Cults* by Walter Martin and *Jesus Among Other Gods* by Ravi Zacharias.

163. Miles, *A God Of Many Understandings?*, 164.

164. Ibid., 172.

165. John F. Wade, *O Come, All Ye Faithful*, 1751.

166. Miles, *A God Of Many Understandings?*, 181-182.

167. John Hick, *Disputed Questions in Theology and the Philosophy of Religion* (Basingstoke: Palgrave Macmillan, 1993), 23.

168. Orlando O. Espín, *An Introductory Dictionary of Theology and Religious Studies* (Collegeville: Liturgical Press, 2007), s.v. "Vatican Council."

169. Miles, *A God Of Many Understandings?*, 185.

170. Pope Paul VI, *Gaudium et Spes* (Pastoral Constitution on the Church in the Modern World), December 7, 1965, pt. 22.

171. Pope John Paul II, *Redemptor Homimis* (The Redeemer of Man) 1979, chapter 2, pt. 14.

172. Pope Paul VI, *Lumen Gentium* (Dogmatic Constitution on the Church), November 21, 1964, chap. 2, pt. 16.

173. Pope Paul VI, *Ad Gentes* (On the Mission Activity of the Church) December 7, 1965, chap. 1, pt. 7.

174. Anita Roper, *The Anonymous Christian* translated by Joseph Donceel (New York: Sheed and Ward, Inc., 1966), 5.

175. Miles, *A God Of Many Understandings?*, 189.

176. Roper, *The Anonymous Christian*, 127.

177. Clark Pinnock, *A Wideness in God's Mercy: The Finality of Jesus Christ in a World of Religions* (Grand Rapids: Zondervan, 1992), 98.

178. G. Khodr, "Christianity in a Pluralistic World—the Economy of the Holy Spirit," *ER* 23 (1971): 118.

179. Pope Paul VI, *Dogmatic Constitution on the Church: Lumen Gentium* (1964), 14.

180. Greathouse, *Romans 1-8*, 43.

181. Pinnock, *A Wideness in God's*, 154.

182. Clark Pinnock, *Flame of Love: A Theology of the Holy Spirit* (Downers Grove: InterVarsity, 1996), 188.

183. Bob Paulson, "How God is Moving with Dreams and Visions in the Muslim World," Charisma News, accessed on December 20, 2015, http://www.charismanews.com/world/ 45206-how-god-is-moving-with-dreams-and-visions-in-the-muslim-world

184. Roper, *The Anonymous*, 26.

185. Karl Rahner, *Experience of the Spirit: Source of Theology: Theological Investigations, Vol. 16* (London: Dalton, Longman and Todd, 1979), 56.

186. Eamonn Conway, *The Anonymous Christian—A Relativised Christianity?* (Frankfurt: Peter Lang, 1993), 17.

187. Ibid.

188. Paul J. Achtemeier, *Romans: Interpretation: A Bible Commentary for Teaching & Preaching* (Louisville: John Knox Press, 1986), 37.

189. Ibid.

190. Harold Netland, *Encountering Religious Pluralism: The Challenge to Christian Faith & Mission* (Downers Grove: InterVarsity, 2001): 27.

191. Miles, *A God Of Many Understandings?*, 322.

192. Loren Eisely, *The Star Thrower* (New York: Mariner Books, 1979).

193. Greg Laurie, "Money and Motives," OnePlace.com, accessed December 23, 2015, http://www.oneplace.com/ministries/a-new-beginning/read/articles/money-and-motives-9220.html.

194. "Global Statistics," Joshua Project, accessed December 23, 2015, http://joshuaproject.net/global_statistics.

195. Ibid.

196. Todd M. Johnson, "Christianity 2015: Religious Diversity and Personal Contact," *International Bulletin of Missionary Research* 39, no. 1 (2015): 1, accessed December 23, 2015, https://static1.squarespace.com/static/4f661fde24ac1097e013deea/t/550f7d77e4b0907feba099b0/1427078519637/StatusGlobalChristianity2015_CSGC_IBMR.pdf.

197. Ibid.

198. David B. Barrett and Todd M. Johnson, *World Christian Trends* (Pasadena: William Carey Library Publishers, 2013), 656.

199. Mark R. Baxter, *The Coming Revolution: Because Status Quo Missions Won't Finish the Job* (Mustang: Tate Publishing & Enterprises),12.

200. "Missions Statistics," The Traveling Team, accessed December 23, 2015, http://www.thetravelingteam.org/stats/.

201. Ibid.

202. Jaffarian, "The Statistical State," 35.

203. Miles, *A God Of Many Understandings?*, 351.

204. "Missions Statistics," The Traveling Team.

205. Ralph D. Winter, *Perspectives on the World Christian Movement: A Reader* (Pasadena: William Carey Library Publishers, 2009) s.v. "Finishing the Task: The Unreached Peoples Challenge."

206. Ibid.

207. C.W. Morgan and R.A. Peterson, *Faith Comes by Hearing* (Downers Grove: IVP Academic, 2008), 253.

208. Ibid.

209. Francis Chan, "Simon Says" (MP4 of lecture), accessed December 28, 2015, https://www.youtube.com/watch?v=BibuOmp-dhY.

210. "Growth of the World's Population," English Online, accessed December 23, 2015, http://www.english-online.at/geography/world-population/world-population-growth.htm